The Story of
Prophets and Kings

Spot Illustrations by James L. Converse

THE STORY OF

PROPHETS

AND

KINGS

As Illustrated in the Captivity and Restoration of Israel

by E. G. WHITE

Author of *Patriarchs and Prophets*
Desire of Ages
The Acts of the Apostles
The Triumph of God's Love

Volume 1

Published jointly by

REVIEW AND HERALD® PUBLISHING ASSOCIATION
Washington, DC 20039-0555
Hagerstown, MD 21740

PACIFIC PRESS PUBLISHING ASSOCIATION
Boise, ID 83707
Oshawa, Ontario, Canada

Foreword

The Story of Prophets and Kings is the second in a series of five outstanding volumes spanning sacred history. It was, however, the last book of the series to be written, and the last of many rich works to come from the gifted pen of Ellen G. White. Through her seventy years of speaking and writing in America and abroad, Mrs. White ever kept before the public the larger significance of the events of history, revealing that in the affairs of men are to be detected the unseen influences of righteousness and evil—the *hand* of God and the *work* of the great adversary.

The author with deep insight in providential workings draws the curtain aside and reveals a philosophy of history by which the events of the past take on eternal significance. She expressed this philosophy in this way:

"The strength of nations and of individuals is not found in the opportunities and facilities that appear to make them invincible; it is not found in their boasted greatness. That which alone can make them great or strong is the power and purpose of God. They themselves by their attitude toward His purpose, decide their own destiny.

"Human histories relate man's achievements, his victories in battle, his success in climbing to worldly greatness. God's history describes man as heaven views him."

This volume, *Prophets and Kings,* opens with the account of Solomon's glorious reign over Israel, a united kingdom, with the temple of Jehovah—the center of true worship. Here are traced the vicissitudes of a favored and chosen people, torn between allegiance to God and serving the gods of the nations about them. And here are seen vividly, through a crucial period of this world's history, the dramatic evidences of the raging conflict between Christ and Satan for the hearts and allegiance of men.

The book abounds in fascinating character studies—the wise Solomon, whose wisdom did not keep him from transgression; Jeroboam, the self-serving man of policy, and the evil results which followed his reign; the mighty and fearless Elijah; Elisha, the prophet of peace and healing; Ahaz, the fearful and wicked; Hezekiah, the loyal and good-hearted; Daniel, the beloved of God; Jeremiah, the prophet of sorrow; Haggai, Zechariah, and Malachi, prophets of the restoration. Beyond them all rises in glory the coming King, the Lamb of God, the only-begotten Son, in whom the typical sacrifices find fulfillment.

Patriarchs and Prophets, the first book of the series, spans world history from creation to the close of David's reign; *The Desire of Ages,* the third book, treats of the life and ministry of Christ; this volume, *Prophets and Kings* fits between these two. *The Acts of the Apostles,* the fourth, portrays the history of the early Christian church, and *The Triumph of God's Love,* the last in the series, traces the conflict story to our day and then on in a prophetic vein to the earth made new.

The Story of Prophets and Kings, having enjoyed a circulation which has demanded many printings since its first appearance, is now presented to the public in attractive form with type reset, but with no change of text or pagination. This new edition is embellished with attractive illustrations, many of them original paintings designed especially for this work.

That this volume with its rich lessons of faith in God and His Son, the Saviour of the world, and the stories of His providence in the lives of great men and women of Old Testament times may deepen the religious experience and enlighten the minds of all who read its pages is the sincere wish of the publishers and

THE BOARD OF TRUSTEES OF THE
ELLEN G. WHITE PUBLICATIONS.

Page numbers in brackets in this book indicate the pages in the standard edition used for compiling the *Comprehensive Index to the Writings of Ellen G. White.*

Contents

The Vineyard of the Lord

IT WAS for the purpose of bringing the best gifts of Heaven to all the peoples of earth that God called Abraham out from his idolatrous kindred and bade him dwell in the land of Canaan. "I will make of thee a great nation," He said, "and I will bless thee, and make thy name great; and thou shalt be a blessing." Genesis 12:2. It was a high honor to which Abraham was called—that of being the father of the people who for centuries were to be the guardians and preservers of the truth of God to the world, the people through whom all the nations of the earth should be blessed in the advent of the promised Messiah.

Men had well-nigh lost the knowledge of the true God. Their minds were darkened by idolatry. For the divine statutes, which are "holy, and just, and good" (Romans 7:12), men were endeavoring to substitute laws in harmony with the purposes of their own cruel, selfish hearts. Yet God in His mercy did not blot them out of existence. He purposed to give them opportunity for becoming acquainted with Him through His church. He designed that the principles revealed through His people should be the means of restoring the moral image of God in man.

God's law must be exalted, His authority maintained; and to the house of Israel was given this great and noble work. God separated them from the world, that He might commit to them a sacred trust. He made them the depositaries of His law, and He purposed through them to preserve among men the knowledge of Himself. Thus the light of heaven was to shine out to a world enshrouded in darkness, and a voice was to be heard appealing to all peoples to turn from idolatry to serve the living God.

"With great power, and with a mighty hand," God brought His chosen people out of the land of Egypt. Exodus 32:11. "He sent Moses His servant; and Aaron whom He had chosen. They showed His signs among them, and wonders in the land of Ham." "He rebuked the Red Sea also, and it was dried up: so He led them through the depths." Psalms 105:26, 27; 106:9. He rescued them from their servile state, that He might bring them to a good land, a land which in His providence He had prepared for them as a refuge from their enemies. He would bring them to Himself and encircle them in His everlasting arms; and in return for His goodness and mercy they were to exalt His name and make it glorious in the earth.

"The Lord's portion is His people; Jacob is the lot of His inheritance. He found him in a desert land, and in the waste howling wilderness; He led him about, He instructed him, He kept him as the apple of His eye. As an eagle stirreth up her nest, fluttereth over her young, spreadeth abroad her wings, taketh them, beareth them on her wings: so the Lord alone did lead him, and there was no strange god with him." Deuteronomy 32:9-12. Thus He brought the Israelites unto Himself, that they might dwell as under the shadow of the Most High. Miraculously preserved from the perils of the wilderness wandering, they were finally established in the Land of Promise as a favored nation.

By means of a parable, Isaiah has told with touching pathos the story of Israel's call and training to stand in the world as Jehovah's representatives, fruitful in every good work:

"Now will I sing to my well-beloved a song of my beloved touching His vineyard. My well-beloved hath a vineyard in a very fruitful hill: and He fenced it, and gathered out the stones thereof, and planted it with the choicest vine, and built a tower in the midst of it, and also made a wine press therein: and He looked that it should bring forth grapes." Isaiah 5:1, 2.

Through the chosen nation, God had purposed to bring blessing to all mankind. "The vineyard of the Lord of hosts," the prophet declared, "is the house of Israel, and the men of Judah His pleasant plant." Isaiah 5:7.

To this people were committed the oracles of God. They were hedged about by the precepts of His law, the everlasting principles of truth, justice, and purity. Obedience to these principles was to be their protection, for it would save them from destroying themselves by sinful practices. And as the tower in the vineyard, God placed in the midst of the land His holy temple.

Christ was their instructor. As He had been with them in the wilderness, so He was still to be their teacher and guide. In the tabernacle and the temple His glory dwelt in the holy Shekinah above the mercy seat. In their behalf He constantly manifested the riches of His love and patience.

Through Moses the purpose of God was set before them and the terms of their prosperity made plain. "Thou art an holy people unto the Lord thy God," he said; "the Lord thy God hath chosen thee to be a special people unto Himself, above all people that are upon the face of the earth."

"Thou hast avouched the Lord this day to be thy God, and to walk in His ways, and to keep His statutes, and His commandments, and His judgments, and to hearken unto His voice: and the Lord hath avouched thee this day to be His peculiar people, as He hath promised thee, and that thou shouldest keep all His commandments; and to make thee high above all nations which He hath made, in praise, and in name, and in honor; and that thou mayest be an holy people unto the Lord thy God, as He hath spoken." Deuteronomy 7:6; 26:17-19.

The children of Israel were to occupy all the territory which God appointed them. Those nations that rejected the worship and service of the true God were to be dispossessed. But it was God's purpose that by the revelation of His character through Israel men should be drawn unto Him. To all the world the gospel invitation was to be given. Through the teaching of the sacrificial service, Christ was to be uplifted before the nations, and all who would look unto Him should live. All who, like Rahab the Canaanite and Ruth the Moabitess, turned from idolatry to the worship of the true God were to unite themselves with His chosen people. As the numbers of Israel increased, they were to enlarge their borders until their kingdom should embrace the world.

But ancient Israel did not fulfill God's purpose. The Lord declared, "I had planted thee a noble vine, wholly a right seed: how then art thou turned into the degenerate plant of a strange vine unto Me?" "Israel is an empty vine, he bringeth forth fruit unto himself." "And now, O inhabitants of Jerusalem, and men of Judah, judge, I pray you, betwixt Me and My vineyard. What could have been done more to My vineyard, that I have not done in it? Wherefore, when I looked that it should bring forth grapes, brought it forth wild grapes? And now go to; I will tell you what I will do to My vineyard: I will take away the hedge thereof, and it shall be eaten up; and break down the wall thereof, and it shall be trodden down: and I will lay it waste: it shall not be pruned, nor digged; but there shall come up briers and thorns: I will also command the clouds that they rain no rain upon it. For . . . He looked for judgment, but behold oppression; for righteousness, but behold a cry." Jeremiah 2:21; Hosea 10:1; Isaiah 5:3-7.

The Lord had through Moses set before His people the result of unfaithfulness. By refusing to keep His covenant, they would cut themselves off from the life of God, and His blessing could not come upon them. At times these warnings were heeded, and rich blessings were bestowed upon the Jewish nation and through them upon surrounding peoples. But more often in their history they forgot God and lost sight of their high privilege as His representatives. They robbed Him of the service He required of them, and they robbed their fellow men of religious guidance and a holy example. They desired to appropriate to themselves the fruits of the vineyard over which they had been made stewards. Their covetousness and greed caused them to be despised even by the heathen. Thus the Gentile world was given occasion to misinterpret the character of God and the laws of His kingdom.

With a father's heart, God bore with His people. He pleaded with them by mercies given and mercies withdrawn. Patiently He set their sins before them and in forbearance waited for their acknowledgment. Prophets and messengers were sent to urge His claim upon the husbandmen; but, instead of being welcomed, these men of discernment and spiritual power were treated as enemies. The husbandmen persecuted and killed them. God sent still other messengers, but they received the same treatment as the first, only that the husbandmen showed still more determined hatred.

The withdrawal of divine favor during the period of the Exile led many to repentance, yet after their return to the Land of Promise the Jewish people repeated the mistakes of former generations and brought themselves into political conflict with surrounding nations. The prophets whom God sent to correct the prevailing evils were received with the same suspicion and scorn that had been accorded the messengers of earlier times; and thus, from century to century, the keepers of the vineyard added to their guilt.

The goodly vine planted by the divine Husbandman upon the hills of Palestine was despised by the men of Israel and was finally cast over the vineyard wall; they bruised it and trampled it under their feet and hoped that they had destroyed it forever. The Husbandman removed the vine and concealed it from their sight. Again He planted it, but on the other side of the wall and in such a manner that the stock was no longer visible. The branches hung over the wall, and grafts might be joined to it; but the stem itself was placed beyond the power of men to reach or harm.

Of special value to God's church on earth today—the keepers of His vineyard—are the messages of counsel and admonition given through the prophets who have made plain His eternal purpose in behalf of mankind. In the teachings of the prophets, His love for the lost race and His plan for their salvation are clearly revealed. The story of Israel's call, of their successes and failures, of their restoration to divine favor, of their rejection of the Master of the vineyard, and of the carrying out of the plan of the ages by a goodly remnant to whom are to be fulfilled all the covenant promises —this has been the theme of God's messengers to His church throughout the centuries that have passed. And today God's message to His church—to those who are occupying His vineyard as faithful husbandmen—is none other than that spoken through the prophet of old:

"Sing ye unto her, A vineyard of red wine. I the Lord do keep it; I will water it every moment: lest any hurt it, I will keep it night and day." Isaiah 27:2, 3.

Let Israel hope in God. The Master of the vineyard is even now gathering from among men of all nations and peoples the precious fruits for which He has long been waiting. Soon He will come unto His own; and in that glad day His eternal purpose for the house of Israel will finally be fulfilled. "He shall cause them that come of Jacob to take root: Israel shall blossom and bud, and fill the face of the world with fruit." Verse 6.

chapter 1

Solomon

IN THE reign of David and Solomon, Israel became strong among the nations and had many opportunities to wield a mighty influence in behalf of truth and the right. The name of Jehovah was exalted and held in honor, and the purpose for which the Israelites had been established in the Land of Promise bade fair of meeting with fulfillment. Barriers were broken down, and seekers after truth from the lands of the heathen were not turned away unsatisfied. Conversions took place, and the church of God on earth was enlarged and prospered.

Solomon was anointed and proclaimed king in the closing years of his father David, who abdicated in his favor. His early life was bright with promise, and it was God's purpose that he should go on from strength to strength, from glory to glory, ever approaching nearer the similitude of the character of God, and thus inspiring His people to fulfill their sacred trust as the depositaries of divine truth.

During his closing years of life King David sought to pass on to his son Solomon the lessons God had taught him.

David knew that God's high purpose for Israel could be met only as rulers and people should seek with unceasing vigilance to attain to the standard placed before them. He knew that in order for his son Solomon to fulfill the trust with which God was pleased to honor him, the youthful ruler must be not merely a warrior, a statesman, and a sovereign, but a strong, good man, a teacher of righteousness, an example of fidelity.

With tender earnestness David entreated Solomon to be manly and noble, to show mercy and loving-kindness to his subjects, and in all his dealings with the nations of earth to honor and glorify the name of God and to make manifest the beauty of holiness. The many trying and remarkable experiences through which David had passed during his lifetime had taught him the value of the nobler virtues and led him to declare in his dying charge to Solomon: "He that ruleth over men must be just, ruling in the fear of God. And he shall be as the light of the morning, when the sun riseth, even a morning without clouds; as the tender grass springing out of the earth by clear shining after rain." 2 Samuel 23:3, 4.

Oh, what an opportunity was Solomon's! Should he follow the divinely inspired instruction of his father, his reign would be a reign of righteousness, like that described in the seventy-second psalm:

"Give the king Thy judgments, O God,
And Thy righteousness unto the king's son.
He shall judge Thy people with righteousness,
And Thy poor with judgment. . . .
He shall come down like rain upon the mown grass:
As showers that water the earth.

In his days shall the righteous flourish;
And abundance of peace so long as the moon endureth.
He shall have dominion also from sea to sea,
And from the river unto the ends of the earth. . . .
The kings of Tarshish and of the isles shall bring presents:
The kings of Sheba and Seba shall offer gifts.
Yea, all kings shall fall down before him:
All nations shall serve him.
For he shall deliver the needy when he crieth;
The poor also, and him that hath no helper. . . .
Prayer also shall be made for him continually;
And daily shall he be praised. . . .
His name shall endure forever:
His name shall be continued as long as the sun:
And men shall be blessed in him:
All nations shall call him blessed.

"Blessed be the Lord God, the God of Israel,
Who only doeth wondrous things.
And blessed be His glorious name forever:
And let the whole earth be filled with His glory;
    Amen, and Amen."

In his youth Solomon made David's choice his own, and for many years he walked uprightly, his life marked with strict obedience to God's commands. Early in his reign he went with his counselors of state to Gibeon, where the tabernacle that had been built in the wilderness still was, and there he united with his chosen advisers, "the captains of thousands and of hundreds," "the judges," and "every governor in all Israel, the chief of the fathers," in offering sacrifices to God and in consecrating themselves fully to the Lord's service. 2 Chronicles 1:2. Comprehending something of the magnitude of the duties connected with the kingly office, Solomon knew that those bearing heavy burdens must seek the Source of Wisdom for guidance, if they would fulfill their responsibilities acceptably. This led him to encourage his counselors to unite with him heartily in making sure of their acceptance with God.

Above every earthly good, the king desired wisdom and understanding for the accomplishment of the work God had given him to do. He longed for quickness of mind, for largeness of heart, for tenderness of spirit. That night the Lord appeared to Solomon in a dream and said, "Ask what I shall give thee." In his answer the young and inexperienced ruler gave utterance to his feeling of helplessness and his desire for aid. "Thou hast showed unto Thy servant David my father great mercy," he said, "according as he walked before Thee in truth, and in righteousness, and in uprightness of heart with Thee; and Thou hast kept for him this great kindness, that Thou hast given him a son to sit on his throne, as it is this day.

"And now, O Lord my God, Thou hast made Thy servant king instead of David my father: and I am but a little child: I know not how to go out or come in. And Thy servant is in the midst of Thy people which Thou hast chosen, a great people, that cannot be numbered nor counted for multitude. Give therefore Thy servant an understanding heart to judge Thy people, that I may discern between good and bad: for who is able to judge this Thy so great a people?

"And the speech pleased the Lord, that Solomon had asked this thing."

"Because this was in thine heart," God said to Solomon, "and thou hast not asked riches, wealth, or honor, nor the life of thine enemies, neither yet hast asked long life; but hast asked wisdom and knowledge for thyself, that thou mayest judge My people," "behold, I have done according to thy words: lo, I have given thee a wise and an understanding heart; so that there was none like thee before thee, neither after thee shall any arise like unto thee. And I have also given thee that which thou hast not asked, both riches, and honor," "such as none of the kings have had that have been before thee, neither shall there any after thee have the like."

"And if thou wilt walk in My ways, to keep My statutes and My commandments, as thy father David did walk, then I will lengthen thy days." 1 Kings 3:5-14; 2 Chronicles 1:7-12.

God promised that as He had been with David, so He would be with Solomon. If the king would walk before the Lord in uprightness, if he would do what God had commanded him, his throne would be established and his reign would be the means of exalting Israel as "a wise and understanding people," the light of the surrounding nations. Deuteronomy 4:6.

The language used by Solomon while praying to God before the ancient altar at Gibeon reveals his humility and his strong desire to honor God. He realized that without divine aid he was as helpless as a little child to fulfill the responsibilities resting on him. He knew that he lacked discernment, and it was a sense of his great need that led him to seek God for wisdom. In his heart there was no selfish aspiration for a knowledge that would exalt him above others. He desired to discharge faithfully the duties devolving upon him, and he chose the gift that would be the means of causing his reign to bring glory to God. Solomon was never so rich or so wise or truly great as when he confessed, "I am but a little child: I know not how to go out or come in."

Those who today occupy positions of trust should seek to learn the lesson taught by Solomon's prayer. The higher the position a man occupies, the greater the responsibility that he has to bear, the wider will be the influence that he exerts and the greater his need of dependence on God. Ever should he remember that with the call to work comes the call to walk circumspectly before his fellow men. He is to stand before God in the attitude of a learner. Position does not give holiness of character. It is by honoring God and obeying His commands that a man is made truly great.

The God whom we serve is no respecter of persons. He who gave to Solomon the spirit of wise discernment is willing to impart the same blessing to His children today. "If any of you lack wisdom," His word declares, "let him ask of God, that giveth to all men liberally, and upbraideth not; and it shall be given him." James 1:5. When a burden bearer desires wisdom more than he desires wealth, power, or fame, he will not be disappointed. Such a one will learn from the Great Teacher not only what to do, but how to do it in a way that will meet with the divine approval.

So long as he remains consecrated, the man whom God has endowed with discernment and ability will not manifest an eagerness for high position, neither will he seek to rule or control. Of necessity men must bear responsibilities; but instead of striving for the supremacy, he who is a true leader will pray for an understanding heart, to discern between good and evil.

The path of men who are placed as leaders is not an easy

one. But they are to see in every difficulty a call to prayer. Never are they to fail of consulting the great Source of all wisdom. Strengthened and enlightened by the Master Worker, they will be enabled to stand firm against unholy influences and to discern right from wrong, good from evil. They will approve that which God approves, and will strive earnestly against the introduction of wrong principles into His cause.

The wisdom that Solomon desired above riches, honor, or long life, God gave him. His petition for a quick mind, a large heart, and a tender spirit was granted. "God gave Solomon wisdom and understanding exceeding much, and largeness of heart, even as the sand that is on the seashore. And Solomon's wisdom excelled the wisdom of all the children of the east country, and all the wisdom of Egypt. For he was wiser than all men; . . . and his fame was in all nations round about." 1 Kings 4:29-31.

"And all Israel . . . feared the king: for they saw that the wisdom of God was in him, to do judgment." 1 Kings 3:28. The hearts of the people were turned toward Solomon, as they had been toward David, and they obeyed him in all things. "Solomon . . . was strengthened in his kingdom, and the Lord his God was with him, and magnified him exceedingly." 2 Chronicles 1:1.

For many years Solomon's life was marked with devotion to God, with uprightness and firm principle, and with strict obedience to God's commands. He directed in every important enterprise and managed wisely the business matters connected with the kingdom. His wealth and wisdom, the magnificent buildings and public works that he constructed during the early years of his reign, the energy, piety, justice, and magnanimity that he revealed in word and deed, won the loyalty of his subjects and the admiration and homage of the rulers of many lands.

The name of Jehovah was greatly honored during the first part of Solomon's reign. The wisdom and righteousness revealed by the king bore witness to all nations of the excellency of the attributes of the God whom he served. For a time Israel was as the light of the world, showing forth the greatness of Jehovah. Not in the surpassing wisdom, the fabulous riches, the far-reaching power and fame that were his, lay the real glory of Solomon's early reign; but in the honor that he brought to the name of the God of Israel through a wise use of the gifts of Heaven.

As the years went by and Solomon's fame increased, he sought to honor God by adding to his mental and spiritual strength, and by continuing to impart to others the blessings he received. None understood better than he that it was through the favor of Jehovah that he had come into possession of power and wisdom and understanding, and that these gifts were bestowed that he might give to the world a knowledge of the King of kings.

Solomon took an especial interest in natural history, but his researches were not confined to any one branch of learning. Through a diligent study of all created things, both animate and inanimate, he gained a clear conception of the Creator. In the forces of nature, in the mineral and the animal world, and in every tree and shrub and flower, he saw a revelation of God's wisdom; and as he sought to learn more and more, his knowledge of God and his love for Him constantly increased.

Solomon's divinely inspired wisdom found expression in songs of praise and in many proverbs. "He spake three thousand proverbs: and his songs were a thousand and five. And he spake of trees, from the cedar tree that is in Lebanon even unto the hyssop that springeth out of the wall: he spake also of beasts, and of fowl, and of creeping things, and of fishes." 1 Kings 4:32, 33.

In the proverbs of Solomon are outlined principles of holy living and high endeavor, principles that are heaven-born and that lead to godliness, principles that should govern every act of life. It was the wide dissemination of these principles, and the recognition of God as the One to whom all praise and honor belong, that made Solomon's early reign a time of moral uplift as well as of material prosperity.

"Happy is the man that findeth wisdom," he wrote, "and the man that getteth understanding. For the merchandise of it is better than the merchandise of silver, and the gain thereof than fine gold. She is more precious than rubies: and all the things thou canst desire are not to be compared unto her. Length of days is in her right hand; and in her left hand riches and honor. Her ways are ways of pleasantness, and all her paths are peace. She is a tree of life to them that lay hold upon her: and happy is every one that retaineth her." Proverbs 3:13-18.

"Wisdom is the principal thing; therefore get wisdom: and with all thy getting get understanding." Proverbs 4:7. "The fear of the Lord is the beginning of wisdom." Psalm 111:10. "The fear of the Lord is to hate evil: pride, and arrogancy, and the evil way, and the froward mouth, do I hate." Proverbs 8:13.

O that in later years Solomon had heeded these wonderful words of wisdom! O that he who had declared, "The lips of the wise disperse knowledge" (Proverbs 15:7), and who had himself taught the kings of the earth to render to the King of kings the praise they desired to give to an earthly ruler, had never with a "froward mouth," in "pride and arrogancy," taken to himself the glory due to God alone!

chapter 2

The Temple and Its Dedication

THE long-cherished plan of David to erect a temple to the Lord, Solomon wisely carried out. For seven years Jerusalem was filled with busy workers engaged in leveling the chosen site, in building vast retaining walls, in laying broad foundations,—"great stones, costly stones, and hewed stones,"—in shaping the heavy timbers brought from the Lebanon forests, and in erecting the magnificent sanctuary. 1 Kings 5:17.

Simultaneously with the preparation of wood and stone, to which task many thousands were bending their energies, the manufacture of the furnishings for the temple was steadily progressing under the leadership of Hiram of Tyre, "a cunning man, endued with understanding, . . . skillful to work in gold, and in silver, in brass, in iron, in stone, and in timber, in purple, in blue, and in fine linen, and in crimson." 2 Chronicles 2:13, 14.

Thus as the building on Mount Moriah was noiselessly

upreared with "stone made ready before it was brought thither: so that there was neither hammer nor ax nor any tool of iron heard in the house, while it was in building," the beautiful fittings were perfected according to the patterns committed by David to his son, "all the vessels that were for the house of God." 1 Kings 6:7; 2 Chronicles 4:19. These included the altar of incense, the table of shewbread, the candlestick and lamps, with the vessels and instruments connected with the ministrations of the priests in the holy place, all "of gold, and that perfect gold." 2 Chronicles 4:21. The brazen furniture,—the altar of burnt offering, the great laver supported by twelve oxen, the lavers of smaller size, with many other vessels,—"in the plain of Jordan did the king cast them, in the clay ground between Succoth and Zeredathah." 2 Chronicles 4:17. These furnishings were provided in abundance, that there should be no lack.

Of surpassing beauty and unrivaled splendor was the palatial building which Solomon and his associates erected for God and His worship. Garnished with precious stones, surrounded by spacious courts with magnificent approaches, and lined with carved cedar and burnished gold, the temple structure, with its broidered hangings and rich furnishings, was a fit emblem of the living church of God on earth, which through the ages has been building in accordance with the divine pattern, with materials that have been likened to "gold, silver, precious stones," "polished after the similitude of a palace." 1 Corinthians 3:12; Psalm 144:12. Of this spiritual temple Christ is "the chief Cornerstone; in whom all the building fitly framed together groweth unto an holy temple in the Lord." Ephesians 2:20, 21.

Stones for the temple, hewed and squared
at the quarry, were brought to the site
and put into place by dedicated workers.
© P.P.P.A.   JOHN STEEL, ARTIST

[36] 13

At last the temple planned by King David, and built by Solomon his son, was completed. "All that came into Solomon's heart to make in the house of the Lord," he had "prosperously effected." 2 Chronicles 7:11. And now, in order that the palace crowning the heights of Mount Moriah might indeed be, as David had so much desired, a dwelling place "not for man, but for the Lord God" (1 Chronicles 29:1), there remained the solemn ceremony of formally dedicating it to Jehovah and His worship.

The spot on which the temple was built had long been regarded as a consecrated place. It was here that Abraham, the father of the faithful, had revealed his willingness to sacrifice his only son in obedience to the command of Jehovah. Here God had renewed with Abraham the covenant of blessing, which included the glorious Messianic promise to the human race of deliverance through the sacrifice of the Son of the Most High. See Genesis 22:9, 16-18. Here it was that when David offered burnt offerings and peace offerings to stay the avenging sword of the destroying angel, God had answered him by fire from heaven. See 1 Chronicles 21. And now once more the worshipers of Jehovah were here to meet their God and renew their vows of allegiance to Him.

The time chosen for the dedication was a most favorable one—the seventh month, when the people from every part of the kingdom were accustomed to assemble at Jerusalem to celebrate the Feast of Tabernacles. This feast was preeminently an occasion of rejoicing. The labors of the harvest being ended and the toils of the new year not yet begun, the people were free from care and could give themselves up to the sacred, joyous influences of the hour.

At the appointed time the hosts of Israel, with richly clad representatives from many foreign nations, assembled in the temple courts. The scene was one of unusual splendor. Solomon, with the elders of Israel and the most influential men among the people, had returned from another part of the city, whence they had brought the ark of the testament. From the sanctuary on the heights of Gibeon had been transferred the ancient "tabernacle of the congregation, and all the holy vessels that were in the tabernacle" (2 Chronicles 5:5); and these cherished reminders of the earlier experiences of the children of Israel during their wanderings in the wilderness and their conquest of Canaan, now found a permanent home in the splendid building that had been erected to take the place of the portable structure.

In bringing to the temple the sacred ark containing the two tables of stone on which were written by the finger of God the precepts of the Decalogue, Solomon had followed the example of his father David. Every six paces he sacrificed. With singing and with music and with great ceremony, "the priests brought in the ark of the covenant of the Lord unto his place, to the oracle of the house, into the most holy place." Verse 7. As they came out of the inner sanctuary, they took the positions assigned them. The singers—Levites arrayed in white linen, having cymbals and psalteries and harps—stood at the east end of the altar, and with them a hundred and twenty priests sounding with trumpets. See verse 12.

"It came even to pass, as the trumpeters and singers were as one, to make one sound to be heard in praising and thanking the Lord; and when they lifted up their voice with the trumpets and cymbals and instruments of music, and praised the Lord, saying, For He is good; for His mercy endureth forever: that then the house was filled with a cloud, even the house of the Lord; so that the priests could not stand to minister by reason of the cloud: for the glory of the Lord had filled the house of God." Verses 13, 14.

Realizing the significance of this cloud, Solomon declared: "The Lord hath said that He would dwell in the thick darkness. But I have built an house of habitation for Thee, and a place for Thy dwelling forever." 2 Chronicles 6:1, 2.

"The Lord reigneth;
  Let the people tremble:
  He sitteth between the cherubims;
  Let the earth be moved.

"The Lord is great in Zion;
  And He is high above all the people.
  Let them praise Thy great and terrible name;
  For it is holy. . . .

"Exalt ye the Lord our God,
  And worship at His footstool;
  For He is holy."
Psalm 99:1-5.

"In the midst of the court" of the temple had been erected "a brazen scaffold," or platform, "five cubits long, and five cubits broad, and three cubits high." Upon this Solomon stood and with uplifted hands blessed the vast multitude before him. "And all the congregation of Israel stood." 2 Chronicles 6:13, 3.

"Blessed be the Lord God of Israel," Solomon exclaimed,

"who hath with His hands fulfilled that which He spake with His mouth to my father David, saying, . . . I have chosen Jerusalem, that My name might be there." Verses 4-6.

Solomon then knelt upon the platform, and in the hearing of all the people offered the dedicatory prayer. Lifting his hands toward heaven, while the congregation were bowed with their faces to the ground, the king pleaded: "Lord God of Israel, there is no God like Thee in the heaven, nor in the earth; which keepest covenant, and showest mercy unto Thy servants, that walk before Thee with all their heart."

"Will God in very deed dwell with men on the earth? Behold, heaven and the heaven of heavens cannot contain Thee; how much less this house which I have built? Have respect therefore to the prayer of Thy servant, and to his supplication, O Lord my God, to hearken unto the cry and the prayer which Thy servant prayeth before Thee: that Thine eyes may be open upon this house day and night, upon the place whereof Thou hast said that Thou wouldest put Thy name there; to hearken unto the prayer which Thy servant prayeth toward this place. Hearken therefore unto the supplications of Thy servant, and of Thy people Israel, which they shall make toward this place: hear Thou from Thy dwelling place, even from heaven; and when Thou hearest, forgive. . . .

"If Thy people Israel be put to the worse before the enemy, because they have sinned against Thee; and shall return and confess Thy name, and pray and make supplication before Thee in this house; then hear Thou from the heavens, and forgive the sin of Thy people Israel, and bring them again unto the land which Thou gavest to them and to their fathers.

"When the heaven is shut up, and there is no rain, because they have sinned against Thee; yet if they pray toward this place, and confess Thy name, and turn from their sin, when Thou dost afflict them; then hear Thou from heaven, and forgive the sin of Thy servants, and of Thy people Israel, when Thou hast taught them the good way, wherein they should walk; and send rain upon Thy land, which Thou hast given unto Thy people for an inheritance.

"If there be dearth in the land, if there be pestilence, if there be blasting, or mildew, locusts, or caterpillars; if their enemies besiege them in the cities of their land; whatsoever sore or whatsoever sickness there be: then what prayer or what supplication soever shall be made of any man, or of all Thy people Israel, when everyone shall know his own sore and his own grief, and shall spread forth his hands in his house: then hear Thou from heaven Thy dwelling place, and forgive, and render unto every man according unto all his ways, whose heart Thou knowest; . . . that they may fear Thee, to walk in Thy ways, so long as they live in the land which Thou gavest unto our fathers.

"Moreover concerning the stranger, which is not of Thy people Israel, but is come from a far country for Thy great name's sake, and Thy mighty hand, and Thy stretched-out arm; if they come and pray in this house; then hear Thou from the heavens, even from Thy dwelling place, and do according to all that the stranger calleth to Thee for; that all people of the earth may know Thy name, and fear Thee, as doth Thy people Israel, and may know that this house which I have built is called by Thy name.

"If Thy people go out to war against their enemies by the

way that Thou shalt send them, and they pray unto Thee toward this city which Thou hast chosen, and the house which I have built for Thy name; then hear Thou from the heavens their prayer and their supplication, and maintain their cause.

"If they sin against Thee, (for there is no man which sinneth not,) and Thou be angry with them, and deliver them over before their enemies, and they carry them away captives unto a land far off or near; yet if they bethink themselves in the land whither they are carried captive, and turn and pray unto Thee in the land of their captivity, saying, We have sinned, we have done amiss, and have dealt wickedly; if they return to Thee with all their heart and with all their soul in the land of their captivity, whither they have carried them captives, and pray toward their land, which Thou gavest unto their fathers, and toward the city which Thou hast chosen, and toward the house which I have built for Thy name: then hear Thou from the heavens, even from Thy dwelling place, their prayer and their supplications, and maintain their cause, and forgive Thy people which have sinned against Thee.

"Now, my God, let, I beseech Thee, Thine eyes be open, and let Thine ears be attent unto the prayer that is made in this place. Now therefore arise, O Lord God, into Thy resting place, Thou, and the ark of Thy strength: let Thy priests, O Lord God, be clothed with salvation, and let Thy saints rejoice in goodness. O Lord God, turn not away the face of Thine anointed: remember the mercies of David Thy servant." Verses 14-42.

As Solomon ended his prayer, "fire came down from

heaven, and consumed the burnt offering and the sacrifices." The priests could not enter the temple because "the glory of the Lord had filled the Lord's house." "When all the children of Israel saw . . . the glory of the Lord upon the house, they bowed themselves with their faces to the ground upon the pavement, and worshiped, and praised the Lord, saying, For He is good; for His mercy endureth forever."

Then king and people offered sacrifices before the Lord. "So the king and all the people dedicated the house of God." 2 Chronicles 7:1-5. For seven days the multitudes from every part of the kingdom, from the borders "of Hamath unto the river of Egypt," "a very great congregation," kept a joyous feast. The week following was spent by the happy throng in observing the Feast of Tabernacles. At the close of the season of reconsecration and rejoicing the people returned to their homes, "glad and merry in heart for the goodness that the Lord had showed unto David, and to Solomon, and to Israel His people." Verses 8, 10.

The king had done everything within his power to encourage the people to give themselves wholly to God and His service, and to magnify His holy name. And now once more, as at Gibeon early in his reign, Israel's ruler was given evidence of divine acceptance and blessing. In a night vision the Lord appeared to him with the message: "I have heard thy prayer, and have chosen this place to Myself for an house of sacrifice. If I shut up heaven that there be no rain, or if I command the locusts to devour the land, or if I send pestilence among My people; if My people, which are called by My name, shall humble themselves, and pray, and seek My face, and turn from their wicked ways; then will I hear from

As Solomon ended his prayer dedicating the temple, "fire came down from heaven, and consumed the . . . sacrifices."

heaven, and will forgive their sin, and will heal their land. Now Mine eyes shall be open, and Mine ears attent unto the prayer that is made in this place. For now have I chosen and sanctified this house, that My name may be there forever: and Mine eyes and Mine heart shall be there perpetually." Verses 12-16.

Had Israel remained true to God, this glorious building would have stood forever, a perpetual sign of God's especial favor to His chosen people. "The sons of the stranger," God declared, "that join themselves to the Lord, to serve Him, and to love the name of the Lord, to be His servants, everyone that keepeth the Sabbath from polluting it, and taketh hold of My covenant; even them will I bring to My holy mountain, and make them joyful in My house of prayer: their burnt offerings and their sacrifices shall be accepted upon Mine altar; for Mine house shall be called an house of prayer for all people." Isaiah 56:6, 7.

In connection with these assurances of acceptance, the Lord made very plain the path of duty before the king. "As for thee," He declared, "if thou wilt walk before Me, as David thy father walked, and do according to all that I have commanded thee, and shalt observe My statutes and My judgments; then will I establish the throne of thy kingdom, according as I have covenanted with David thy father, saying, There shall not fail thee a man to be ruler in Israel." 2 Chronicles 7:17, 18.

Had Solomon continued to serve the Lord in humility, his entire reign would have exerted a powerful influence for good over the surrounding nations, nations that had been so favorably impressed by the reign of David his father and by the wise words and the magnificent works of the earlier years of his own reign. Foreseeing the terrible temptations that attend prosperity and worldly honor, God warned Solomon against the evil of apostasy and foretold the awful results of sin. Even the beautiful temple that had just been dedicated, He declared, would become "a proverb and a byword among all nations" should the Israelites forsake "the Lord God of their fathers" and persist in idolatry. Verses 20, 22.

Strengthened in heart and greatly cheered by the message from heaven that his prayer in behalf of Israel had been heard, Solomon now entered upon the most glorious period of his reign, when "all the kings of the earth" began to seek his presence, "to hear his wisdom, that God had put in his heart." 2 Chronicles 9:23. Many came to see the manner of his government and to receive instruction regarding the conduct of difficult affairs.

As these people visited Solomon, he taught them of God as the Creator of all things, and they returned to their homes with clearer conceptions of the God of Israel and of His love for the human race. In the works of nature they now beheld an expression of His love and a revelation of His character; and many were led to worship Him as their God.

The humility of Solomon at the time he began to bear the burdens of state, when he acknowledged before God, "I am but a little child" (1 Kings 3:7), his marked love of God, his profound reverence for things divine, his distrust of self, and his exaltation of the infinite Creator of all—all these traits of character, so worthy of emulation, were revealed during the services connected with the completion of the temple, when during his dedicatory prayer he knelt in the humble position of a petitioner. Christ's followers today should guard against the tendency to lose the spirit of reverence and godly fear. The Scriptures teach men how they should approach their Maker—with humility and awe, through faith in a divine Mediator. The psalmist has declared:

> "The Lord is a great God,
> And a great King above all gods. . . .
> O come, let us worship and bow down:
> Let us kneel before the Lord our Maker."
> Psalm 95:3-6

Both in public and in private worship it is our privilege to bow on our knees before God when we offer our petitions to Him. Jesus, our example, "kneeled down, and prayed." Luke 22:41. Of His disciples it is recorded that they, too, "kneeled down, and prayed." Acts 9:40. Paul declared, "I bow my knees unto the Father of our Lord Jesus Christ." Ephesians 3:14. In confessing before God the sins of Israel,

Ezra knelt. See Ezra 9:5. Daniel "kneeled upon his knees three times a day, and prayed, and gave thanks before his God." Daniel 6:10.

True reverence for God is inspired by a sense of His infinite greatness and a realization of His presence. With this sense of the Unseen, every heart should be deeply impressed. The hour and place of prayer are sacred, because God is there. And as reverence is manifested in attitude and demeanor, the feeling that inspires it will be deepened. "Holy and reverend is His name," the psalmist declares. Psalm 111:9. Angels, when they speak that name, veil their faces. With what reverence, then, should we, who are fallen and sinful, take it upon our lips!

Well would it be for old and young to ponder those words of Scripture that show how the place marked by God's special presence should be regarded. "Put off thy shoes from off thy feet," He commanded Moses at the burning bush, "for the place whereon thou standest is holy ground." Exodus 3:5. Jacob, after beholding the vision of the angel, exclaimed, "The Lord is in this place; and I knew it not. . . . This is none other but the house of God, and this is the gate of heaven." Genesis 28:16, 17.

In that which was said during the dedicatory services, Solomon had sought to remove from the minds of those present the superstitions in regard to the Creator, that had beclouded the minds of the heathen. The God of heaven is not, like the gods of the heathen, confined to temples made with hands; yet He would meet with His people by His Spirit when they should assemble at the house dedicated to His worship.

Centuries later Paul taught the same truth in the words: "God that made the world and all things therein, seeing that He is Lord of heaven and earth, dwelleth not in temples made with hands; neither is worshiped with men's hands, as though He needed anything, seeing He giveth to all life, and breath, and all things; . . . that they should seek the Lord, if haply they might feel after Him, and find Him, though He be not far from every one of us: for in Him we live, and move, and have our being." Acts 17:24-28.

> "Blessed is the nation whose God is the Lord;
> And the people whom He hath chosen for His own
>   inheritance.
> The Lord looketh from heaven;
> He beholdeth all the sons of men.
> From the place of His habitation
> He looketh upon all the inhabitants of the earth."

> "The Lord hath prepared His throne in the heavens;
> And His kingdom ruleth over all."

> "Thy way, O God, is in the sanctuary:
> Who is so great a God as our God?
> Thou art the God that doest wonders:
> Thou hast declared Thy strength among the people."
>   Psalms 33:12-14; 103:19; 77:13, 14.

Although God dwells not in temples made with hands, yet He honors with His presence the assemblies of His people. He has promised that when they come together to seek Him, to acknowledge their sins, and to pray for one another, He will meet with them by His Spirit. But those who assemble to worship Him should put away every evil thing. Unless they worship Him in spirit and truth and in the beauty of holiness, their coming together will be of no avail. Of such the Lord declares, "This people draweth nigh unto Me with their mouth, and honoreth Me with their lips; but their heart is far from Me." Matthew 15:8, 9. Those who worship God must worship Him "in spirit and in truth: for the Father seeketh such to worship Him." John 4:23.

"The Lord is in His holy temple: let all the earth keep silence before Him." Habakkuk 2:20.

chapter 3

Pride of Prosperity

WHILE Solomon exalted the law of heaven, God was with him, and wisdom was given him to rule over Israel with impartiality and mercy. At first, as wealth and worldly honor came to him, he remained humble, and great was the extent of his influence. "Solomon reigned over all kingdoms from the river [Euphrates] unto the land of the Philistines, and unto the border of Egypt." "He . . . had peace on all sides round about him. And Judah and Israel dwelt safely, every man under his vine and under his fig tree, . . . all the days of Solomon." 1 Kings 4:21, 24, 25.

But after a morning of great promise his life was darkened by apostasy. History records the melancholy fact that he who had been called Jedidiah,—"Beloved of the Lord" (2 Samuel 12:25, margin),—he who had been honored by God with tokens of divine favor so remarkable that his wisdom and uprightness gained for him world-wide fame, he who had led others to ascribe honor to the God of Israel, turned from the

Solomon's apostasy, at first gradual, eventually led him to unite in cruel and degrading rites of idol worship.

worship of Jehovah to bow before the idols of the heathen.

Hundreds of years before Solomon came to the throne, the Lord, foreseeing the perils that would beset those who might be chosen as rulers of Israel, gave Moses instruction for their guidance. Directions were given that he who should sit on the throne of Israel should "write him a copy" of the statutes of Jehovah "in a book out of that which is before the priests the Levites." "It shall be with him," the Lord said, "and he shall read therein all the days of his life: that he may learn to fear the Lord his God, to keep all the words of this law and these statutes, to do them: that his heart be not lifted up above his brethren, and that he turn not aside from the commandment, to the right hand, or to the left: to the end that he may prolong his days in his kingdom, he, and his children, in the midst of Israel." Deuteronomy 17:18-20.

In connection with this instruction the Lord particularly cautioned the one who might be anointed king not to "multiply wives to himself, that his heart turn not away: neither shall he greatly multiply to himself silver and gold." Verse 17.

With these warnings Solomon was familiar, and for a time he heeded them. His greatest desire was to live and rule in accordance with the statutes given at Sinai. His manner of conducting the affairs of the kingdom was in striking contrast with the customs of the nations of his time—nations who feared not God and whose rulers trampled underfoot His holy law.

In seeking to strengthen his relations with the powerful kingdom lying to the southward of Israel, Solomon ventured upon forbidden ground. Satan knew the results that would attend obedience; and during the earlier years of Solomon's reign—years glorious because of the wisdom, the beneficence, and the uprightness of the king—he sought to bring in influences that would insidiously undermine Solomon's loyalty to principle and cause him to separate from God. That the enemy was successful in this effort, we know from the record: "Solomon made affinity with Pharaoh king of Egypt, and took Pharaoh's daughter, and brought her into the City of David." 1 Kings 3:1.

From a human point of view, this marriage, though contrary to the teachings of God's law, seemed to prove a blessing; for Solomon's heathen wife was converted and united with him in the worship of the true God. Furthermore, Pharaoh rendered signal service to Israel by taking Gezer, slaying "the Canaanites that dwelt in the city," and giving it "for a present unto his daughter, Solomon's wife." 1 Kings 9:16. This city Solomon rebuilt and thus apparently greatly strengthened his kingdom along the Mediterranean seacoast. But in forming an alliance with a heathen nation, and sealing the compact by marriage with an idolatrous princess, Solomon rashly disregarded the wise provision that God had made for maintaining the purity of His people. The hope that his Egyptian wife might be converted was but a feeble excuse for the sin.

For a time God in His compassionate mercy overruled this terrible mistake; and the king, by a wise course, could have checked at least in a large measure the evil forces that his imprudence had set in operation. But Solomon had begun to lose sight of the Source of his power and glory. As inclination gained the ascendancy over reason, self-confidence increased, and he sought to carry out the Lord's purpose in his own way. He reasoned that political and commercial alliances with the surrounding nations would bring these nations to a knowledge of the true God; and he entered into unholy alliance with nation after nation. Often these alliances were sealed by marriages with heathen princesses. The commands of Jehovah were set aside for the customs of surrounding peoples.

Solomon flattered himself that his wisdom and the power of his example would lead his wives from idolatry to the worship of the true God, and also that the alliances thus formed would draw the nations round about into close touch with Israel. Vain hope! Solomon's mistake in regarding himself as strong enough to resist the influence of heathen associates was fatal. And fatal, too, the deception that led him to hope that notwithstanding a disregard of God's law on his part, others might be led to revere and obey its sacred precepts.

The king's alliances and commercial relations with heathen nations brought him renown, honor, and the riches of this world. He was enabled to bring gold from Ophir and silver from Tarshish in great abundance. "The king made silver and gold at Jerusalem as plenteous as stones, and cedar trees made he as the sycamore trees that are in the vale for abundance." 2 Chronicles 1:15. Wealth, with all its attendant temptations, came in Solomon's day to an increasingly large number of people; but the fine gold of character was dimmed and marred.

So gradual was Solomon's apostasy that before he was aware of it, he had wandered far from God. Almost imperceptibly he began to trust less and less in divine guidance and blessing, and to put confidence in his own strength. Little by little he withheld from God that unswerving obedience which was to make Israel a peculiar people, and he conformed more and more closely to the customs of the surrounding nations. Yielding to the temptations incident to his success and his honored position, he forgot the Source of his prosperity. An ambition to excel all other nations in power and grandeur led him to pervert for selfish purposes the heavenly gifts hitherto employed for the glory of God. The money which should have been held in sacred trust for the benefit of the worthy poor and for the extension of principles of holy living throughout the world, was selfishly absorbed in ambitious projects.

Engrossed in an overmastering desire to surpass other nations in outward display, the king overlooked the need of acquiring beauty and perfection of character. In seeking to glorify himself before the world, he sold his honor and integrity. The enormous revenues acquired through commerce with many lands were supplemented by heavy taxes. Thus pride, ambition, prodigality, and indulgence bore fruit in cruelty and exaction. The conscientious, considerate spirit that had marked his dealings with the people during the early part of his reign, was now changed. From the wisest and most merciful of rulers, he degenerated into a tyrant. Once the compassionate, God-fearing guardian of the people, he became oppressive and despotic. Tax after tax was levied upon the people, that means might be forthcoming to support the luxurious court.

The people began to complain. The respect and admiration they had once cherished for their king was changed into disaffection and abhorrence.

As a safeguard against dependence on the arm of flesh, the Lord had warned those who should rule over Israel not to multiply horses to themselves. But in utter disregard of this command, "Solomon had horses brought out of Egypt." "And they brought unto Solomon horses out of Egypt, and out of all lands." "Solomon gathered together chariots and horsemen: and he had a thousand and four hundred chariots, and twelve thousand horsemen, whom he bestowed in the cities for chariots, and with the king at Jerusalem." 2 Chronicles 1:16; 9:28; 1 Kings 10:26.

More and more the king came to regard luxury, self-indulgence, and the favor of the world as indications of greatness. Beautiful and attractive women were brought from Egypt, Phoenicia, Edom, Moab, and from many other places. These women were numbered by hundreds. Their religion was idol worship, and they had been taught to practice cruel and degrading rites. Infatuated with their beauty, the king neglected his duties to God and to his kingdom.

His wives exerted a strong influence over him and gradually prevailed on him to unite with them in their worship. Solomon had disregarded the instruction that God had given to serve as a barrier against apostasy, and now he gave himself up to the worship of false gods. "It came to pass, when Solomon was old, that his wives turned away his heart after other gods: and his heart was not perfect with the Lord his God, as was the heart of David his father. For Solomon went after Ashtoreth the goddess of the Zidonians, and after Milcom the abomination of the Ammonites." 1 Kings 11:4, 5.

On the southern eminence of the Mount of Olives, opposite Mount Moriah, where stood the beautiful temple of Jehovah, Solomon erected an imposing pile of buildings to be used as idolatrous shrines. To please his wives, he placed huge idols, unshapely images of wood and stone, amidst the groves of myrtle and olive. There, before the altars of heathen deities, "Chemosh, the abomination of Moab," and "Molech, the abomination of the children of Ammon," were practiced the most degrading rites of heathenism. Verse 7.

Solomon's course brought its sure penalty. His separation from God through communication with idolaters was his ruin. As he cast off his allegiance to God, he lost the mastery of himself. His moral efficiency was gone. His fine sensibilities became blunted, his conscience seared. He who in his early reign had displayed so much wisdom and sympathy in restoring a helpless babe to its unfortunate mother (see 1 Kings 3:16-28), fell so low as to consent to the erection of an idol to whom living children were offered as sacrifices. He who in his youth was endowed with discretion and understanding, and who in his strong manhood had been inspired to write, "There is a way which seemeth right unto a man, but the end thereof are the ways of death" (Proverbs 14:12), in later years departed so far from purity as to countenance licentious, revolting rites connected with the worship of Chemosh and Ashtoreth. He who at the dedication of the temple had said to his people, "Let your heart therefore be perfect with the Lord our God" (1 Kings 8:61), became himself an offender, in heart and life denying his own words. He mistook license for liberty. He tried—but at what cost!—to unite light with darkness, good with evil, purity with impurity, Christ with Belial.

From being one of the greatest kings that ever wielded a scepter, Solomon became a profligate, the tool and slave of others. His character, once noble and manly, became enervated and effeminate. His faith in the living God was supplanted by atheistic doubts. Unbelief marred his happiness, weakened his principles, and degraded his life. The justice and magnanimity of his early reign were changed to despotism and tyranny. Poor, frail human nature! God can do little for men who lose their sense of dependence upon Him.

During these years of apostasy, the spiritual decline of Israel progressed steadily. How could it be otherwise when their king had united his interests with satanic agencies? Through these agencies the enemy worked to confuse the minds of the Israelites in regard to true and false worship, and they became an easy prey. Commerce with other nations brought them into intimate contact with those who had no love for God, and their own love for Him was greatly lessened. Their keen sense of the high, holy character of God was deadened. Refusing to follow in the path of obedience, they transferred their allegiance to the enemy of righteousness. It came to be a common practice to intermarry with idolaters, and the Israelites rapidly lost their abhorrence of idol worship. Polygamy was countenanced. Idolatrous mothers brought their children up to observe heathen rites. In the lives of some, the pure religious service instituted by God was replaced by idolatry of the darkest hue.

Christians are to keep themselves distinct and separate from the world, its spirit, and its influences. God is fully able to keep us in the world, but we are not to be of the world. His love is not uncertain and fluctuating. Ever He watches over His children with a care that is measureless. But He requires undivided allegiance. "No man can serve two masters: for either he will hate the one, and love the other; or else he will hold to the one, and despise the other. Ye cannot serve God and mammon." Matthew 6:24.

Solomon was endued with wonderful wisdom, but the world drew him away from God. Men today are no stronger than he; they are as prone to yield to the influences that caused his downfall. As God warned Solomon of his danger, so today He warns His children not to imperil their souls by affinity with the world. "Come out from among them," He pleads, "and be ye separate, . . . and touch not the unclean thing, and I will receive you, and will be a Father unto you, and ye shall be My sons and daughters, saith the Lord Almighty." 2 Corinthians 6:17, 18.

In the midst of prosperity lurks danger. Throughout the ages, riches and honor have ever been attended with peril to humility and spirituality. It is not the empty cup that we have difficulty in carrying; it is the cup full to the brim that must be carefully balanced. Affliction and adversity may cause sorrow, but it is prosperity that is most dangerous to spiritual life. Unless the human subject is in constant submission to the will of God, unless he is sanctified by the truth, prosperity will surely arouse the natural inclination to presumption.

In the valley of humiliation, where men depend on God to teach them and to guide their every step, there is comparative safety. But the men who stand, as it were, on a lofty pinnacle, and who, because of their position, are supposed to possess great wisdom—these are in gravest peril. Unless such men make God their dependence, they will surely fall.

Whenever pride and ambition are indulged, the life is marred, for pride, feeling no need, closes the heart against the infinite blessings of Heaven. He who makes self-glorification his aim will find himself destitute of the grace of God, through whose efficiency the truest riches and the most satisfying joys are won. But he who gives all and does all for Christ will know the fulfillment of the promise, "The blessing of

the Lord, it maketh rich, and He addeth no sorrow with it."
Proverbs 10:22. With the gentle touch of grace the Saviour
banishes from the soul unrest and unholy ambition, changing
enmity to love and unbelief to confidence. When He speaks
to the soul, saying, "Follow Me," the spell of the world's en-
chantment is broken. At the sound of His voice the spirit of
greed and ambition flees from the heart, and men arise, eman-
cipated, to follow Him.

chapter 4

Results of Transgression

PROMINENT among the primary causes that led Solomon into extravagance and oppression was his failure to maintain and foster the spirit of self-sacrifice.

When, at the foot of Sinai, Moses told the people of the divine command, "Let them make Me a sanctuary; that I may dwell among them" (Exodus 25:8), the response of the Israelites was accompanied by the appropriate gifts. "They came, everyone whose heart stirred him up, and everyone whom his spirit made willing," and brought offerings. Exodus 35:21. For the building of the sanctuary, great and extensive preparations were necessary; a large amount of the most precious and costly material was required, but the Lord accepted only freewill offerings. "Of every man that giveth it willingly with his heart ye shall take My offering," was the command repeated by Moses to the congregation. Exodus

Riches and honor caused Solomon to lose sight of God's high purpose for him and to glory in the splendor of his kingdom.

25:2. Devotion to God and a spirit of sacrifice were the first requisites in preparing a dwelling place for the Most high.

A similar call to self-sacrifice was made when David turned over to Solomon the responsibility of building the temple. Of the assembled multitude David asked, "Who then is willing to consecrate his service this day unto the Lord?" 1 Chronicles 29:5. This call to consecration and willing service should ever have been kept in mind by those who had to do with the erection of the temple.

For the construction of the wilderness tabernacle, chosen men were endowed by God with special skill and wisdom. "Moses said unto the children of Israel, See, the Lord hath called by name Bezaleel, . . . of the tribe of Judah; and He hath filled him with the Spirit of God, in wisdom, in understanding, and in knowledge, and in all manner of workmanship. . . . And He hath put in his heart that he may teach, both he, and Aholiab, . . . of the tribe of Dan. Them hath He filled with wisdom of heart, to work all manner of work, of the engraver, and of the cunning workman, and of the embroiderer, . . . and of the weaver, even of them that do any work. . . . Then wrought Bezaleel and Aholiab, and every wisehearted man, in whom the Lord put wisdom and understanding." Exodus 35:30-35; 36:1. Heavenly intelligences cooperated with the workmen whom God Himself had chosen.

The descendants of these workmen inherited to a large degree the talents conferred on their forefathers. For a time these men of Judah and Dan remained humble and unselfish; but gradually, almost imperceptibly, they lost their hold upon God and their desire to serve Him unselfishly. They asked higher wages for their services, because of their superior skill as workmen in the finer arts. In some instances their request was granted, but more often they found employment in the surrounding nations. In place of the noble spirit of self-sacrifice that had filled the hearts of their illustrious ancestors, they indulged a spirit of covetousness, of grasping for more and more. That their selfish desires might be gratified, they used their God-given skill in the service of heathen kings, and lent their talent to the perfecting of works which were a dishonor to their Maker.

It was among these men that Solomon looked for a master workman to superintend the construction of the temple on Mount Moriah. Minute specifications, in writing, regarding every portion of the sacred structure, had been entrusted to the king; and he could have looked to God in faith for consecrated helpers, to whom would have been granted special skill for doing with exactness the work required. But Solomon lost sight of this opportunity to exercise faith in God. He sent to the king of Tyre for a man "cunning to work in gold, and in silver, and in brass, and in iron, and in purple, and crimson, and blue, and that can skill to grave with the cunning men . . . in Judah and in Jerusalem." 2 Chronicles 2:7.

The Phoenician king responded by sending Huram, "the son of a woman of the daughters of Dan, and his father was a man of Tyre." Verse 14. Huram was a descendant, on his mother's side, of Aholiab, to whom, hundreds of years before, God had given special wisdom for the construction of the tabernacle.

Thus at the head of Solomon's company of workmen there was placed a man whose efforts were not prompted by an unselfish desire to render service to God. He served the god of this world, mammon. The very fibers of his being were inwrought with the principles of selfishness.

Because of his unusual skill, Huram demanded large wages. Gradually the wrong principles that he cherished came to be accepted by his associates. As they labored with him day after day, they yielded to the inclination to compare his wages with their own, and they began to lose sight of the holy character of their work. The spirit of self-denial left them, and in its place came the spirit of covetousness. The result was a demand for higher wages, which was granted.

The baleful influences thus set in operation permeated all branches of the Lord's service, and extended throughout the kingdom. The high wages demanded and received gave to many an opportunity to indulge in luxury and extravagance. The poor were oppressed by the rich; the spirit of self-sacrifice was well-nigh lost. In the far-reaching effects of these influences may be traced one of the principal causes of the terrible apostasy of him who once was numbered among the wisest of mortals.

The sharp contrast between the spirit and motives of the people building the wilderness tabernacle, and of those engaged in erecting Solomon's temple, has a lesson of deep significance. The self-seeking that characterized the workers on the temple finds its counterpart today in the selfishness that rules in the world. The spirit of covetousness, of seeking for the highest position and the highest wage, is rife. The willing service and joyous self-denial of the tabernacle workers is seldom met with. But this is the only spirit that should actuate the followers of Jesus. Our divine Master has given an example of how His disciples are to work. To those whom He bade,

"Follow Me, and I will make you fishers of men" (Matthew 4:19), He offered no stated sum as a reward for their services. They were to share with Him in self-denial and sacrifice.

Not for the wages we receive are we to labor. The motive that prompts us to work for God should have in it nothing akin to self-serving. Unselfish devotion and a spirit of sacrifice have always been and always will be the first requisite of acceptable service. Our Lord and Master designs that not one thread of selfishness shall be woven into His work. Into our efforts we are to bring the tact and skill, the exactitude and wisdom, that the God of perfection requires of the builders of the earthly tabernacle; yet in all our labors we are to remember that the greatest talents or the most splendid services are acceptable only when self is laid upon the altar, a living, consuming sacrifice.

Another of the deviations from right principles that finally led to the downfall of Israel's king was his yielding to the temptation to take to himself the glory that belongs to God alone.

From the day that Solomon was entrusted with the work of building the temple, to the time of its completion, his avowed purpose was "to build an house for the name of the Lord God of Israel." 2 Chronicles 6:7. This purpose was fully recognized before the assembled hosts of Israel at the time of the dedication of the temple. In his prayer the king acknowledged that Jehovah had said, "My name shall be there." 1 Kings 8:29.

One of the most touching portions of Solomon's dedicatory prayer was his plea to God for the strangers that should come from countries afar to learn more of Him whose fame had been spread abroad among the nations. "They shall hear," the king pleaded, "of Thy great name, and of Thy strong hand, and of Thy stretched-out arm." In behalf of every one of these stranger worshipers Solomon had petitioned: "Hear Thou, . . . and do according to all that the stranger calleth to Thee for: that all people of the earth may know Thy name, to fear Thee, as do Thy people Israel; and that they may know that this house, which I have builded, is called by Thy name." Verses 42, 43.

At the close of the service, Solomon had exhorted Israel to be faithful and true to God, in order that "all the people of the earth may know," he said, "that the Lord is God, and that there is none else." Verse 60.

A Greater than Solomon was the designer of the temple; the wisdom and glory of God stood there revealed. Those who were unacquainted with this fact naturally admired and praised Solomon as the architect and builder; but the king disclaimed any honor for its conception or erection.

Thus it was when the Queen of Sheba came to visit Solomon. Hearing of his wisdom and of the magnificent temple he had built, she determined "to prove him with hard questions" and to see for herself his famous works. Attended by a retinue of servants, and with camels bearing "spices, and gold in abundance, and precious stones," she made the long journey to Jerusalem. "And when she was come to Solomon, she communed with him of all that was in her heart." She talked with him of the mysteries of nature; and Solomon taugh her of the God of nature, the great Creator, who dwells in the highest heaven and rules over all. "Solomon told her all her questions: there was not anything hid from the king, which he told her not." 1 Kings 10:1-3; 2 Chronicles 9:1, 2.

"When the Queen of Sheba had seen all Solomon's wisdom, and the house that he had built, . . . there was no more spirit in her." "It was a true report," she acknowledged, "which I heard in mine own land of thine acts, and of thy wisdom: howbeit I believed not their words, until I came, and mine eyes had seen it:" "and, behold, the half was not told me: thy wisdom and prosperity exceedeth the fame which I heard. Happy are thy men, happy are these thy servants, which stand continually before thee, and that hear thy wisdom." 1 Kings 10:4-8; 2 Chronicles 9:3-6.

By the time of the close of her visit the queen had been so fully taught by Solomon as to the source of his wisdom and prosperity that she was constrained, not to extol the human agent, but to exclaim, "Blessed be the Lord thy God, which delighted in thee, to set thee on the throne of Israel: because the Lord loved Israel forever, therefore made He thee king, to do judgment and justice." 1 Kings 10:9. This is the impres-

5—P.A.K.

sion that God designed should be made upon all peoples. And when "all the kings of the earth sought the presence of Solomon, to hear his wisdom, that God had put in his heart" (2 Chronicles 9:23), Solomon for a time honored God by reverently pointing them to the Creator of the heavens and the earth, the Ruler of the universe, the All-wise.

Had Solomon continued in humility of mind to turn the attention of men from himself to the One who had given him wisdom and riches and honor, what a history might have been his! But while the pen of inspiration records his virtues, it also bears faithful witness to his downfall. Raised to a pinnacle of greatness and surrounded with the gifts of fortune, Solomon became dizzy, lost his balance, and fell. Constantly extolled by men of the world, he was at length unable to withstand the flattery offered him. The wisdom entrusted to him that he might glorify the Giver, filled him with pride. He finally permitted men to speak of him as the one most worthy of praise for the matchless splendor of the building planned and erected for the honor of "the name of the Lord God of Israel."

Thus it was that the temple of Jehovah came to be known throughout the nations as "Solomon's temple." The human agent had taken to himself the glory that belonged to the One "higher than the highest." Ecclesiastes 5:8. Even to this day the temple of which Solomon declared, "This house which I have built is called by Thy name" (2 Chronicles 6:33), is oftenest spoken of, not as the temple of Jehovah, but as "Solomon's temple."

Man cannot show greater weakness than by allowing men to ascribe to him the honor for gifts that are Heaven-bestowed.

The true Christian will make God first and last and best in everything. No ambitious motives will chill his love for God; steadily, perseveringly, will he cause honor to redound to his heavenly Father. It is when we are faithful in exalting the name of God that our impulses are under divine supervision, and we are enabled to develop spiritual and intellectual power.

Jesus, the divine Master, ever exalted the name of His heavenly Father. He taught His disciples to pray, "Our Father who art in heaven, hallowed by Thy name." Matthew 6:9, A.R.V. And they were not to forget to acknowledge, "Thine is . . . the glory." Verse 13. So careful was the great Healer to direct attention from Himself to the Source of His power, that the wondering multitude, "when they saw the dumb to speak, the maimed to be whole, the lame to walk, and the blind to see," did not glorify Him, but "glorified the God of Israel." Matthew 15:31. In the wonderful prayer that Christ offered just before His crucifixion, He declared, "I have glorified Thee on the earth." "Glorify Thy Son," He pleaded, "that Thy Son also may glorify Thee." "O righteous Father, the world hath not known Thee: but I have known Thee, and these have known that Thou hast sent Me. And I have declared unto them Thy name, and will declare it: that the love wherewith Thou hast loved Me may be in them, and I in them." John 17:1, 4, 25, 26.

"Thus saith the Lord, Let not the wise man glory in his wisdom, neither let the mighty man glory in his might, let not the rich man glory in his riches: but let him that glorieth glory in this, that he understandeth and knoweth Me, that I am the Lord which exercise loving-kindness, judgment, and righteousness, in the earth: for in these things I delight, saith the Lord." Jeremiah 9:23, 24.

> "I will praise the name of God, . . .
> And will magnify Him with thanksgiving."

> "Thou art worthy, O Lord, to receive glory and honor
> and power."

> "I will praise Thee, O Lord my God, with all my heart:
> And I will glorify Thy name forevermore."

> "O magnify the Lord with me,
> And let us exalt His name together."
> Psalm 69:30; Revelation 4:11; Psalms 86:12; 34:3.

The introduction of principles leading away from a spirit of sacrifice and tending toward self-glorification, was accompanied by yet another gross perversion of the divine plan for Israel. God had designed that His people should be the light of the world. From them was to shine forth the glory of His law as revealed in the life practice. For the carrying out of this design, He had caused the chosen nation to occupy a strategic position among the nations of earth.

In the days of Solomon the kingdom of Israel extended from Hamath on the north to Egypt on the south, and from the Mediterranean Sea to the river Euphrates. Through this territory ran many natural highways of the world's commerce, and caravans from distant lands were constantly passing to and fro. Thus there was given to Solomon and his people opportunity to reveal to men of all nations the character of the King of kings, and to teach them to reverence and obey Him. To all the world this knowledge was to be given. Through the teaching of the sacrificial offerings, Christ was to be uplifted before the nations, that all who would might live.

Placed at the head of a nation that had been set as a beacon light to the surrounding nations, Solomon should have used his God-given wisdom and power of influence in organizing and directing a great movement for the enlightenment of those who were ignorant of God and His truth. Thus multitudes would have been won to allegiance to the divine precepts, Israel would have been shielded from the evils practiced by the heathen, and the Lord of glory would have been greatly honored. But Solomon lost sight of this high purpose. He failed of improving his splendid opportunities for enlightening those who were continually passing through his territory or tarrying at the principal cities.

The missionary spirit that God had implanted in the heart of Solomon and in the hearts of all true Israelites was supplanted by a spirit of commercialism. The opportunities afforded by contact with many nations were used for personal aggrandizement. Solomon sought to strengthen his position politically by building fortified cities at the gateways of commerce. He rebuilt Gezer, near Joppa, lying along the road between Egypt and Syria; Beth-horon, to the westward of Jerusalem, commanding the passes of the highway leading from the heart of Judea to Gezer and the seacoast; Megiddo, situated on the caravan road from Damascus to Egypt, and from Jerusalem to the northward; and "Tadmor in the wilderness" (2 Chronicles 8:4), along the route of caravans from the east. All these cities were strongly fortified. The commercial advantages of an outlet at the head of the Red Sea were developed by the construction of "a navy of ships in Ezion-geber, . . . on the shore of the Red Sea, in the land of Edom." Trained sailors from Tyre, "with the servants of Solomon," manned these vessels on voyages "to Ophir, and fetched from thence gold," and "great plenty of almug trees, and precious stones." Verse 18; 1 Kings 9:26, 28; 10:11.

The revenue of the king and of many of his subjects was greatly increased, but at what a cost! Through the cupidity and shortsightedness of those to whom had been entrusted the oracles of God, the countless multitudes who thronged the highways of travel were allowed to remain in ignorance of Jehovah.

In striking contrast to the course pursued by Solomon was the course followed by Christ when He was on this earth. The Saviour, though possessing "all power," never used this power for self-aggrandizement. No dream of earthly conquest, of worldly greatness, marred the perfection of His service for mankind. "Foxes have holes, and the birds of the air have nests," He said; "but the Son of man hath not where to lay His head." Matthew 8:20. Those who, in response to the call of the hour, have entered the service of the Master Worker, may well study His methods. He took advantage of the opportunities to be found along the great thoroughfares of travel.

In the intervals of His journeys to and fro, Jesus dwelt at Capernaum, which came to be known as "His own city." Matthew 9:1. Situated on the highway from Damascus to Jerusalem and Egypt and to the Mediterranean Sea, it was well adapted to be the center of the Saviour's work. People from many lands passed through the city or tarried for rest. There Jesus met with those of all nations and all ranks, and thus His lessons were carried to other countries and into many households. By this means interest was aroused in the prophecies pointing forward to the Messiah, attention was directed to the Saviour, and His mission was brought before the world.

In this our day the opportunities for coming into contact with men and women of all classes and many nationalities are much greater than in the days of Israel. The thoroughfares of travel have multiplied a thousandfold.

Like Christ, the messengers of the Most High today should take their position in these great thoroughfares, where they can meet the passing multitudes from all parts of the world. Like Him, hiding self in God, they are to sow the gospel seed, presenting before others the precious truths of Holy Scripture that will take deep root in mind and heart, and spring up unto life eternal.

Solemn are the lessons of Israel's failure during the years when ruler and people turned from the high purpose they had been called to fulfill. Wherein they were weak, even to the point of failure, the Israel of God today, the representatives of heaven that make up the true church of Christ, must be strong; for upon them devolves the task of finishing the work that has been committed to man, and of ushering in the day of final awards. Yet the same influences that prevailed against Israel in the time when Solomon reigned are to be met with still. The forces of the enemy of all righteousness are strongly entrenched; only by the power of God can the victory be gained. The conflict before us calls for the exercise of a spirit of self-denial, for distrust of self and for dependence on God alone, for the wise use of every opportunity for the saving of souls. The Lord's blessing will attend

His church as they advance unitedly, revealing to a world lying in the darkness of error the beauty of holiness as manifested in a Christlike spirit of self-sacrifice, in an exaltation of the divine rather than the human, and in loving and untiring service for those so much in need of the blessings of the gospel.

chapter 5

Solomon's Repentance

TWICE during Solomon's reign the Lord had appeared to him with words of approval and counsel—in the night vision at Gibeon, when the promise of wisdom, riches, and honor was accompanied by an admonition to remain humble and obedient; and after the dedication of the temple, when once more the Lord exhorted him to faithfulness. Plain were the admonitions, wonderful the promises, given to Solomon; yet of him who in circumstances, in character, and in life seemed abundantly fitted to heed the charge and meet the expectation of Heaven, it is recorded: "He kept not that which the Lord commanded." "His heart was turned from the Lord God of Israel, which had appeared unto him twice, and had commanded him concerning this thing, that he should not go after other gods." 1 Kings 11:9, 10. And so complete was his apostasy, so hardened his heart in transgression, that his case seemed well-nigh hopeless.

From the joy of divine communion, Solomon turned to

find satisfaction in the pleasures of sense. Of this experience he says:

"I made me great works; I builded me houses; I planted me vineyards: I made me gardens and orchards: . . . I got me servants and maidens: . . . I gathered me also silver and gold, and the peculiar treasure of kings and of the provinces: I gat me men singers and women singers, and the delights of the sons of men, as musical instruments, and that of all sorts. So I was great, and increased more than all that were before me in Jerusalem. . . .

"And whatsoever mine eyes desired I kept not from them, I withheld not my heart from any joy; for my heart rejoiced in all my labor. . . . Then I looked on all the works that my hands had wrought, and on the labor that I had labored to do: and, behold, all was vanity and vexation of spirit, and there was no profit under the sun.

"And I turned myself to behold wisdom, and madness, and folly: for what can the man do that cometh after the king? even that which hath been already done. . . . I hated life. . . . Yea, I hated all my labor which I had taken under the sun." Ecclesiastes 2:4-18.

By his own bitter experience, Solomon learned the emptiness of a life that seeks in earthly things its highest good. He erected altars to heathen gods, only to learn how vain is their promise of rest to the spirit. Gloomy and soul-harassing thoughts troubled him night and day. For him there was no longer any joy of life or peace of mind, and the future was dark with despair.

Yet the Lord forsook him not. By messages of reproof and by severe judgments, He sought to arouse the king to a realization of the sinfulness of his course. He removed His protecting care and permitted adversaries to harass and weaken the kingdom. "The Lord stirred up an adversary unto Solomon, Hadad the Edomite. . . . And God stirred him up another adversary, Rezon, . . . captain over a band," who "abhorred Israel, and reigned over Syria. And Jeroboam, . . . Solomon's servant," "a mighty man of valor," "even he lifted up his hand against the king." 1 Kings 11:14-28.

At last the Lord, through a prophet, delivered to Solomon the startling message: "Forasmuch as this is done of thee, and thou hast not kept My covenant and My statutes, which I have commanded thee, I will surely rend the kingdom from thee, and will give it to thy servant. Notwithstanding in thy days I will not do it for David thy father's sake: but I will rend it out of the hand of thy son." Verses 11, 12.

Awakened as from a dream by this sentence of judgment pronounced against him and his house, Solomon with quickened conscience began to see his folly in its true light. Chastened in spirit, with mind and body enfeebled, he turned wearied and thirsting from earth's broken cisterns, to drink once more at the fountain of life. For him at last the discipline of suffering had accomplished its work. Long had he been harassed by the fear of utter ruin because of inability to turn from folly; but now he discerned in the message given him a ray of hope. God had not utterly cut him off, but stood ready to deliver him from a bondage more cruel than the grave, and from which he had had no power to free himself.

In gratitude Solomon acknowledged the power and the loving-kindness of the One who is "higher than the highest" (Ecclesiastes 5:8); in penitence he began to retrace his steps

toward the exalted plane of purity and holiness from whence he had fallen so far. He could never hope to escape the blasting results of sin, he could never free his mind from all remembrance of the self-indulgent course he had been pursuing, but he would endeavor earnestly to dissuade others from following after folly. He would humbly confess the error of his ways and lift his voice in warning lest others be lost irretrievably because of the influences for evil he had been setting in operation.

The true penitent does not put his past sins from his remembrance. He does not, as soon as he has obtained peace, grow unconcerned in regard to the mistakes he has made. He thinks of those who have been led into evil by his course, and tries in every possible way to lead them back into the true path. The clearer the light that he has entered into, the stronger is his desire to set the feet of others in the right way. He does not gloss over his wayward course, making his wrong a light thing, but lifts the danger signal, that others may take warning.

Solomon acknowledged that "the heart of the sons of men is full of evil, and madness is in their heart." Ecclesiastes 9:3. And again he declared, "Because sentence against an evil work is not executed speedily, therefore the heart of the sons of men is fully set in them to do evil. Though a sinner do evil an hundred times, and his days be prolonged, yet surely I know that it shall be well with them that fear God, which fear before Him: but it shall not be well with the wicked, neither shall he prolong his days, which are as a shadow; because he feareth not before God." Ecclesiastes 8:11-13.

By the spirit of inspiration the king recorded for after

In his old age Solomon looked back upon his days of luxury, fame, and riches, and he said, "All is vanity."

© P.P.P.A.   JOHN STEEL, ARTIST

generations the history of his wasted years with their lessons of warning. And thus, although the seed of his sowing was reaped by his people in harvests of evil, his lifework was not wholly lost. With meekness and lowliness Solomon in his later years "taught the people knowledge; yea, he gave good heed, and sought out, and set in order many proverbs." He "sought to find out acceptable words: and that which was written was upright, even words of truth." "The words of the wise are as goads, and as nails fastened by the masters of assemblies, which are given from one shepherd. And further, by these, my son, be admonished." Ecclesiastes 12:9-12.

"Let us hear the conclusion of the whole matter," he wrote: "Fear God, and keep His commandments: for this is the whole duty of man. For God shall bring every work into judgment, with every secret thing, whether it be good, or whether it be evil." Verses 13, 14.

Solomon's later writings reveal that as he realized more and still more the wickedness of his course, he gave special attention to warning the youth against falling into the errors that had led him to squander for nought Heaven's choicest gifts. With sorrow and shame he confessed that in the prime of manhood, when he should have found God his comfort, his support, his life, he turned from the light of Heaven and the wisdom of God, and put idolatry in the place of the worship of Jehovah. And now, having learned through sad experience the folly of such a life, his yearning desire was to save others from entering into the bitter experience through which he had passed.

With touching pathos he wrote concerning the privileges and responsibilities before the youth in God's service:

"Truly the light is sweet, and a pleasant thing it is for the eyes to behold the sun: but if a man live many years, and rejoice in them all; yet let him remember the days of darkness; for they shall be many. All that cometh is vanity. Rejoice, O young man, in thy youth; and let thy heart cheer thee in the days of thy youth, and walk in the ways of thine heart, and in the sight of thine eyes: but know thou, that for all these things God will bring thee into judgment. Therefore remove sorrow from thy heart, and put away evil from thy flesh: for childhood and youth are vanity." Ecclesiastes 11:7-10.

"Remember now thy Creator in the days of thy youth,
  While the evil days come not,
  Nor the years draw nigh,
    When thou shalt say, I have no pleasure in them;

"While the sun,
  Or the light,
  Or the moon,
  Or the stars,
Be not darkened,
Nor the clouds return after the rain:

  "In the day when the keepers of the house shall tremble,
  And the strong men shall bow themselves,
  And the grinders cease because they are few,
  And those that look out of the windows be darkened,
  And the doors shall be shut in the streets,

  "When the sound of the grinding is low,
  And he shall rise up at the voice of the bird,
  And all the daughters of music shall be brought low;

  "Also when they shall be afraid of that which is high,
  And fears shall be in the way,

"And the almond tree shall flourish,
   And the grasshopper shall be a burden,
   And desire shall fail:

"Because man goeth to his long home,
   And the mourners go about the streets:

"Or ever the silver cord be loosed,
   Or the golden bowl be broken,
   Or the pitcher be broken at the fountain,
   Or the wheel broken at the cistern.

"Then shall the dust return to the earth
      As it was:
   And the spirit shall return unto God
      Who gave it."
                                    Ecclesiastes 12:1-7.

Not only to the youth, but to those of mature years, and to those who are descending the hill of life and facing the western sun, the life of Solomon is full of warning. We see and hear of unsteadiness in youth, the young wavering between right and wrong, and the current of evil passions proving too strong for them. In those of maturer years, we do not look for this unsteadiness and unfaithfulness; we expect the character to be established, the principles firmly rooted. But this is not always so. When Solomon should have been in character as a sturdy oak, he fell from his steadfastness under the power of temptation. When his strength should have been the firmest, he was found to be the weakest.

From such examples we should learn that in watchfulness and prayer is the only safety for both young and old. Security does not lie in exalted position and great privileges. One may for many years have enjoyed a genuine Christian experience, but he is still exposed to Satan's attacks. In the battle with inward sin and outward temptation, even the wise and powerful Solomon was vanquished. His failure teaches us that, whatever a man's intellectual qualities may be, and however faithfully he may have served God in the past, he can never with safety trust in his own wisdom and integrity.

In every generation and in every land the true foundation and pattern for character building have been the same. The divine law, "Thou shalt love the Lord thy God with all thy heart, . . . and thy neighbor as thyself," the great principle made manifest in the character and life of our Saviour, is the only secure foundation, the only sure guide. Luke 10:27. "Wisdom and knowledge shall be the stability of thy times, and strength of salvation," the wisdom and knowledge which God's word alone can impart. Isaiah 33:6.

It is as true now as when the words were spoken to Israel of obedience to His commandments: "This is your wisdom and your understanding in the sight of the nations." Deuteronomy 4:6. Here is the only safeguard for individual integrity, for the purity of the home, the well-being of society, or the stability of the nation. Amidst all life's perplexities and dangers and conflicting claims, the one safe and sure rule is to do what God says. "The statutes of the Lord are right," and "he that doeth these things shall never be moved." Psalms 19:8; 15:5.

Those who heed the warning of Solomon's apostasy will shun the first approach of those sins that overcame him. Only obedience to the requirements of Heaven will keep man from apostasy. God has bestowed upon man great light and many blessings; but unless this light and these blessings are accepted, they are no security against disobedience and apostasy. When those whom God has exalted to positions of high trust turn from Him to human wisdom, their light becomes darkness. Their entrusted capabilities become a snare.

Till the conflict is ended, there will be those who will depart from God. Satan will so shape circumstances that unless we are kept by divine power, they will almost imperceptibly weaken the fortifications of the soul. We need to inquire at every step, "Is this the way of the Lord?" So long as life shall last, there will be need of guarding the affections and the passions with a firm purpose. Not one moment can we be secure except as we rely upon God, the life hidden with Christ. Watchfulness and prayer are the safeguards of purity.

All who enter the City of God will enter through the strait gate—by agonizing effort; for "there shall in no wise enter into it anything that defileth." Revelation 21:27. But none who have fallen need give up to despair. Aged men, once honored of God, may have defiled their souls, sacrificing virtue on the altar of lust; but if they repent, forsake sin, and turn to God, there is still hope for them. He who declares, "Be thou faithful unto death, and I will give thee a crown of life," also gives the invitation, "Let the wicked forsake his way, and the unrighteous man his thoughts: and let him return unto the Lord, and He will have mercy upon him; and to our God, for He will abundantly pardon." Revelation 2:10; Isaiah 55:7. God hates sin, but He loves the sinner. "I will heal their backsliding," He declares; "I will love them freely." Hosea 14:4.

Solomon's repentance was sincere; but the harm that his example of evil-doing had wrought could not be undone.

During his apostasy there were in the kingdom men who remained true to their trust, maintaining their purity and loyalty. But many were led astray; and the forces of evil set in operation by the introduction of idolatry and worldly practices could not easily be stayed by the penitent king. His influence for good was greatly weakened. Many hesitated to place full confidence in his leadership. Though the king confessed his sin and wrote out for the benefit of after generations a record of his folly and repentance, he could never hope entirely to destroy the baleful influence of his wrong deeds. Emboldened by his apostasy, many continued to do evil, and evil only. And in the downward course of many of the rulers who followed him may be traced the sad influence of the prostitution of his God-given powers.

In the anguish of bitter reflection on the evil of his course, Solomon was constrained to declare, "Wisdom is better than weapons of war: but one sinner destroyeth much good." "There is an evil which I have seen under the sun, as an error which proceedeth from the ruler: folly is set in great dignity."

"Dead flies cause the ointment of the apothecary to send forth a stinking savor: so doth a little folly him that is in reputation for wisdom and honor." Ecclesiastes 9:18; 10:5, 6, 1.

Among the many lessons taught by Solomon's life, none is more strongly emphasized than the power of influence for good or for ill. However contracted may be our sphere, we still exert an influence for weal or woe. Beyond our knowledge or control, it tells upon others in blessing or cursing. It may be heavy with the gloom of discontent and selfishness, or poisonous with the deadly taint of some cherished sin; or it may be charged with the life-giving power of faith, courage, and hope, and sweet with the fragrance of love. But potent for good or for ill it will surely be.

That our influence should be a savor of death unto death is a fearful thought, yet it is possible. One soul misled, forfeiting eternal bliss—who can estimate the loss! And yet one rash act, one thoughtless word, on our part may exert so deep an influence on the life of another that it will prove the ruin of his soul. One blemish on the character may turn many away from Christ.

As the seed sown produces a harvest, and this in turn is sown, the harvest is multiplied. In our relation to others, this law holds true. Every act, every word, is a seed that will bear fruit. Every deed of thoughtful kindness, of obedience, of self-denial, will reproduce itself in others, and through them in still others. So every act of envy, malice, or dissension is a seed that will spring up in a "root of bitterness" whereby many shall be defiled. Hebrews 12:15. And how much larger number will the "many" poison! Thus the sowing of good and evil goes on for time and for eternity.

chapter 6

The Rending of the Kingdom

"SOLOMON slept with his fathers, and was buried in the City of David his father: and Rehoboam his son reigned in his stead." 1 Kings 11:43.

Soon after his accession to the throne, Rehoboam went to Shechem, where he expected to receive formal recognition from all the tribes. "To Shechem were all Israel come to make him king." 2 Chronicles 10:1.

Among those present was Jeroboam the son of Nebat—the same Jeroboam who during Solomon's reign had been known as "a mighty man of valor," and to whom the prophet Ahijah the Shilonite had delivered the startling message, "Behold, I will rend the kingdom out of the hand of Solomon, and will give ten tribes to thee." 1 Kings 11:28, 31.

The Lord through His messenger had spoken plainly to Jeroboam regarding the necessity of dividing the kingdom. This division must take place, He had declared, "because that they have forsaken Me, and have worshiped Ashtoreth the goddess of the Zidonians, Chemosh the god of the Moabites, and Milcom the god of the children of Ammon, and have not walked in My ways, to do that which is right in Mine eyes, and to keep My statutes and My judgments, as did David." Verse 33.

Jeroboam had been further instructed that the kingdom was not to be divided before the close of Solomon's reign. "I will not take the whole kingdom out of his hand," the Lord had declared; "but I will make him prince all the days of his life for David My servant's sake, whom I chose, because he kept My commandments and My statutes: but I will take the kingdom out of his son's hand, and will give it unto thee, even ten tribes." Verses 34, 35.

Although Solomon had longed to prepare the mind of Rehoboam, his chosen successor, to meet with wisdom the crisis foretold by the prophet of God, he had never been able to exert a strong molding influence for good over the mind of his son, whose early training had been so grossly neglected. Rehoboam had received from his mother, an Ammonitess, the stamp of a vacillating character. At times he endeavored to serve God and was granted a measure of prosperity; but he was not steadfast, and at last he yielded to the influences for evil that had surrounded him from infancy. In the mistakes of Rehoboam's life and in his final apostasy is revealed the fearful result of Solomon's union with idolatrous women.

The tribes had long suffered grievous wrongs under the oppressive measures of their former ruler. The extravagance of Solomon's reign during his apostasy had led him to tax the people heavily and to require of them much menial service. Before going forward with the coronation of a new ruler, the leading men from among the tribes determined to ascertain whether or not it was the purpose of Solomon's son to lessen these burdens. "So Jeroboam and all Israel came and spake to Rehoboam, saying, Thy father made our yoke grievous: now therefore ease thou somewhat the grievous servitude of thy father, and his heavy yoke that he put upon us, and we will serve thee."

Desirous of taking counsel with his advisers before outlining his policy, Rehoboam answered, "Come again unto me after three days. And the people departed.

"And King Rehoboam took counsel with the old men that had stood before Solomon his father while he yet lived, saying, What counsel give ye me to return answer to this people? And they spake unto him, saying, If thou be kind to this people, and please them, and speak good words to them, they will be thy servants forever." 2 Chronicles 10:3-7.

Dissatisfied, Rehoboam turned to the younger men with whom he had associated during his youth and early manhood, and inquired of them, "What counsel give ye that we may answer this people, who have spoken to me, saying, Make the yoke which thy father did put upon us lighter?" 1 Kings 12:9. The young men suggested that he deal sternly with the subjects of his kingdom and make plain to them that from the very beginning he would brook no interference with his personal wishes.

Flattered by the prospect of exercising supreme authority, Rehoboam determined to disregard the counsel of the older men of his realm, and to make the younger men his advisers. Thus it came to pass that on the day appointed, when "Jeroboam and all the people came to Rehoboam" for a statement concerning the policy he intended to pursue, Rehoboam "answered the people roughly, . . . saying, My father made your yoke heavy, and I will add to your yoke: my father also chastised you with whips, but I will chastise you with scorpions." Verses 12-14.

Had Rehoboam and his inexperienced counselors understood the divine will concerning Israel, they would have listened to the request of the people for decided reforms in the administration of the government. But in the hour of opportunity that came to them during the meeting in Shechem, they failed to reason from cause to effect, and thus forever weakened their influence over a large number of the people. Their expressed determination to perpetuate and add to the oppression introduced during Solomon's reign was in direct conflict with God's plan for Israel, and gave the people ample occasion to doubt the sincerity of their motives. In this unwise and unfeeling attempt to exercise power, the king and his chosen counselors revealed the pride of position and authority.

The Lord did not allow Rehoboam to carry out the policy he had outlined. Among the tribes were many thousands who had become thoroughly aroused over the oppressive measures of Solomon's reign, and these now felt that they could not do otherwise than rebel against the house of David. "When all Israel saw that the king hearkened not unto them, the people answered the king, saying, What portion have we in David? neither have we inheritance in the son of Jesse: to your tents, O Israel: now see to thine own house, David. So Israel departed unto their tents." Verse 16.

The breach created by the rash speech of Rehoboam proved irreparable. Thenceforth the twelve tribes of Israel were divided, the tribes of Judah and Benjamin composing the lower or southern kingdom of Judah, under the rulership of Rehoboam; while the ten northern tribes formed and maintained a separate government, known as the kingdom of Israel, with Jeroboam as their ruler. Thus was fulfilled the prediction of the prophet concerning the rending of the kingdom. "The cause was from the Lord." Verse 15.

When Rehoboam saw the ten tribes withdrawing their allegiance from him, he was aroused to action. Through one of the influential men of his kingdom, "Adoram, who was over the tribute," he made an effort to conciliate them. But the ambassador of peace received treatment which bore witness to the feeling against Rehoboam. "All Israel stoned him with stones, that he died." Startled by this evidence of the strength of revolt, "King Rehoboam made speed to get him up to his chariot, to flee to Jerusalem." Verse 18.

At Jerusalem "he assembled all the house of Judah, with the tribe of Benjamin, an hundred and fourscore thousand chosen men, which were warriors, to fight against the house of Israel, to bring the kingdom again to Rehoboam the son of Solomon. But the word of God came unto Shemaiah the man of God, saying, Speak unto Rehoboam, the son of Solomon, king of Judah, and unto all the house of Judah and Benjamin, and to the remnant of the people, saying, Thus saith the Lord, Ye shall not go up, nor fight against your brethren the children of Israel: return every man to his house; for this thing is from Me. They hearkened therefore to the word of the Lord, and returned to depart, according to the word of the Lord." Verses 21-24.

For three years Rehoboam tried to profit by his sad experience at the beginning of his reign; and in this effort he was prospered. He "built cities for defense in Judah," and "fortified the strongholds, and put captains in them, and store of victual, and of oil and wine." He was careful to make these fortified cities "exceeding strong." 2 Chronicles 11:5, 11, 12. But the secret of Judah's prosperity during the first years of Rehoboam's reign lay not in these measures. It was their recognition of God as the Supreme Ruler that placed the tribes of Judah and Benjamin on vantage ground. To their number were added many God-fearing men from the northern tribes. "Out of all the tribes of Israel," the record reads, "such as set their hearts to seek the Lord God of Israel came to Jerusalem, to sacrifice unto the Lord God of their fathers. So they strengthened the kingdom of Judah, and made Rehoboam the son of Solomon strong, three years: for three years they walked in the way of David and Solomon." Verses 16, 17.

In continuing this course lay Rehoboam's opportunity to redeem in large measure the mistakes of the past and to restore confidence in his ability to rule with discretion. But the pen of inspiration has traced the sad record of Solomon's successor as one who failed to exert a strong influence for loyalty to Jehovah. Naturally headstrong, confident, self-willed, and inclined to idolatry, nevertheless, had he placed his trust wholly in God, he would have developed strength of character, steadfast faith, and submission to the divine requirements. But as time passed, the king put his trust in the power of position and in the strongholds he had fortified. Little by little he gave way to inherited weaknesses, until he threw his influence wholly on the side of idolatry. "It came to pass, when Rehoboam had established the kingdom, and had strengthened himself, he forsook the law of the Lord, and all Israel with him." 2 Chronicles 12:1.

How sad, how filled with significance, the words, "And all Israel with him"! The people whom God had chosen to stand as a light to the surrounding nations were turning from their Source of strength and seeking to become like the nations about them. As with Solomon, so with Rehoboam—the influence of wrong example led many astray. And as with them, so to a greater or less degree is it today with everyone who gives himself up to work evil—the influence of wrongdoing is not confined to the doer. No man liveth unto himself. None perish alone in their iniquity. Every life is a light that brightens and cheers the pathway of others, or a dark and desolating influence that tends toward despair and ruin. We lead others either upward to happiness and immortal life, or downward to sorrow and eternal death. And if by our deeds we strengthen or force into activity the evil powers of those around us, we share their sin.

God did not allow the apostasy of Judah's ruler to remain unpunished. "In the fifth year of King Rehoboam Shishak king of Egypt came up against Jerusalem, because they had transgressed against the Lord, with twelve hundred chariots, and three score thousand horsemen: and the people were without number that came with him out of Egypt. . . . And he took the fenced cities which pertained to Judah, and came to Jerusalem.

"Then came Shemaiah the prophet to Rehoboam, and to the princes of Judah, that were gathered together to Jerusalem because of Shishak, and said unto them, Thus saith the Lord,

Ye have forsaken Me, and therefore have I also left you in the hand of Shishak." Verses 2-5.

The people had not yet gone to such lengths in apostasy that they despised the judgments of God. In the losses sustained by the invasion of Shishak, they recognized the hand of God and for a time humbled themselves. "The Lord is righteous," they acknowledged.

"And when the Lord saw that they humbled themselves, the word of the Lord came to Shemaiah, saying, They have humbled themselves; therefore I will not destroy them, but I will grant them some deliverance; and My wrath shall not be poured out upon Jerusalem by the hand of Shishak. Nevertheless they shall be his servants; that they may know My service, and the service of the kingdoms of the countries.

"So Shishak king of Egypt came up against Jerusalem, and took away the treasures of the house of the Lord, and the treasures of the king's house; he took all: he carried away also the shields of gold which Solomon had made. Instead of which King Rehoboam made shields of brass, and committed them to the hands of the chief of the guard, that kept the entrance of the king's house. . . . And when he humbled himself, the wrath of the Lord turned from him, that He would not destroy him altogether: and also in Judah things went well." Verses 6-12.

But as the hand of affliction was removed, and the nation prospered once more, many forgot their fears and turned again to idolatry. Among these was King Rehoboam himself. Though humbled by the calamity that had befallen him, he failed to make this experience a decisive turning point in his life. Forgetting the lesson that God had endeavored to teach him, he relapsed into the sins that had brought judgments on the nation. After a few inglorious years, during which the king "did evil, because he prepared not his heart to seek the Lord," "Rehoboam slept with his fathers, and was buried in the City of David: and Abijah his son reigned in his stead." Verses 14, 16.

With the rending of the kingdom early in Rehoboam's reign the glory of Israel began to depart, never again to be regained in its fullness. At times during the centuries that followed, the throne of David was occupied by men of moral worth and far-seeing judgment, and under the rulership of these sovereigns the blessings resting upon the men of Judah were extended to the surrounding nations. At times the name of Jehovah was exalted above every false god, and His law was held in reverence. From time to time mighty prophets arose to strengthen the hands of the rulers and to encourage the people to continued faithfulness. But the seeds of evil already springing up when Rehoboam ascended the throne were never to be wholly uprooted; and at times the once-favored people of God were to fall so low as to become a byword among the heathen.

Yet notwithstanding the perversity of those who leaned toward idolatrous practices, God in mercy would do everything in His power to save the divided kingdom from utter ruin. And as the years rolled on and His purpose concerning Israel seemed to be utterly thwarted by the devices of men inspired by satanic agencies, He still manifested His beneficent designs through the captivity and restoration of the chosen nation.

The rending of the kingdom was but the beginning of a

wonderful history, wherein are revealed the long-sufferance and tender mercy of God. From the crucible of affliction through which they were to pass because of hereditary and cultivated tendencies to evil, those whom God was seeking to purify unto Himself a peculiar people, zealous of good works, were finally to acknowledge:

"There is none like unto Thee, O Lord; Thou art great, and Thy name is great in might. Who would not fear Thee, O King of nations? . . . Among all the wise men of the nations, and in all their kingdoms, there is none like unto Thee." "The Lord is the true God, He is the living God, and an everlasting King." Jeremiah 10:6, 7, 10.

And the worshipers of idols were at last to learn the lesson that false gods are powerless to uplift and save. "The gods that have not made the heavens and the earth, even they shall perish from the earth, and from under these heavens." Verse 11. Only in allegiance to the living God, the Creator of all and the Ruler over all, can man find rest and peace.

With one accord the chastened and penitent of Israel and Judah were at last to renew their covenant relationship with Jehovah of hosts, the God of their fathers; and of Him they were to declare:

> "He hath made the earth by His power,
>   He hath established the world by His wisdom,
>   And hath stretched out the heavens by His discretion.
>
> "When He uttereth His voice, there is a multitude of waters
>   in the heavens,
>
>   And He causeth the vapors to ascend from the ends of the
>   earth;

He maketh lightnings with rain, and bringeth forth the wind
out of His treasures.

"Every man is brutish in his knowledge:
Every founder is confounded by the graven image:
For his molten image is falsehood, and there is no breath in
them.

"They are vanity, and the work of errors:
In the time of their visitation they shall perish.
The portion of Jacob is not like them:

"For He is the former of all things;
And Israel is the rod of His inheritance:
The Lord of hosts is His name."

Verses 12-16.

chapter 7

Jeroboam

PLACED on the throne by the ten tribes of Israel who had rebelled against the house of David, Jeroboam, the former servant of Solomon, was in a position to bring about wise reforms in both civil and religious affairs. Under the rulership of Solomon he had shown aptitude and sound judgment; and the knowledge he had gained during years of faithful service fitted him to rule with discretion. But Jeroboam failed to make God his trust.

Jeroboam's greatest fear was that at some future time the hearts of his subjects might be won over by the ruler occupying the throne of David. He reasoned that if the ten tribes should be permitted to visit often the ancient seat of the Jewish monarchy, where the services of the temple were still conducted as in the years of Solomon's reign, many might feel inclined to renew their allegiance to the government centering at Jerusalem. Taking counsel with his advisers, Jeroboam determined by one bold stroke to lessen, so far as possible, the probability of a revolt from his rule. He would

As the prophet appeared before the pagan altar and denounced idolatry, the altar cracked asunder and fell.

[*99-100*] 79

bring this about by creating within the borders of his newly formed kingdom two centers of worship, one at Bethel and the other at Dan. In these places the ten tribes should be invited to assemble, instead of at Jerusalem, to worship God.

In arranging this transfer, Jeroboam thought to appeal to the imagination of the Israelites by setting before them some visible representation to symbolize the presence of the invisible God. Accordingly he caused to be made two calves of gold, and these were placed within shrines at the appointed centers of worship. In this effort to represent the Deity, Jeroboam violated the plain command of Jehovah: "Thou shalt not make unto thee any graven image. . . . Thou shalt not bow down thyself to them, nor serve them." Exodus 20:4, 5.

So strong was Jeroboam's desire to keep the ten tribes away from Jerusalem that he lost sight of the fundamental weakness of his plan. He failed to take into consideration the great peril to which he was exposing the Israelites by setting before them the idolatrous symbol of the deity with which their ancestors had been so familiar during the centuries of Egyptian bondage. Jeroboam's recent residence in Egypt should have taught him the folly of placing before the people such heathen representations. But his set purpose of inducing the northern tribes to discontinue their annual visits to the Holy City led him to adopt the most imprudent of measures. "It is too much for you to go up to Jerusalem," he urged; "behold thy gods, O Israel, which brought thee up out of the land of Egypt." 1 Kings 12:28. Thus they were invited to bow down before the golden images and adopt strange forms of worship.

The king tried to persuade the Levites, some of whom were living within his realm, to serve as priests in the newly erected shrines at Bethel and Dan; but in this effort he met with failure. He was therefore compelled to elevate to the priesthood men from "the lowest of the people." Verse 31. Alarmed over the prospect, many of the faithful, including a great number of the Levites, fled to Jerusalem, where they might worship in harmony with the divine requirements.

"Jeroboam ordained a feast in the eighth month, on the fifteenth day of the month, like unto the feast that is in Judah, and he offered upon the altar. So did he in Bethel, sacrificing unto the calves that he had made: and he placed in Bethel the priests of the high places which he had made." Verse 32.

The king's bold defiance of God in thus setting aside divinely appointed institutions was not allowed to pass unrebuked. Even while he was officiating and burning incense during the dedication of the strange altar he had set up at Bethel, there appeared before him a man of God from the kingdom of Judah, sent to denounce him for presuming to introduce new forms of worship. The prophet "cried against the altar, . . . and said, O altar, altar, thus saith the Lord; Behold, a child shall be born unto the house of David, Josiah by name; and upon thee shall he offer the priests of the high places that burn incense upon thee, and men's bones shall be burnt upon thee.

"And he gave a sign the same day, saying, This is the sign which the Lord hath spoken; Behold, the altar shall be rent, and the ashes that are upon it shall be poured out." Immediately the altar "was rent, and the ashes poured out from the altar, according to the sign which the man of God had given by the word of the Lord." 1 Kings 13:2, 3, 5.

On seeing this, Jeroboam was filled with a spirit of defiance against God and attempted to restrain the one who had delivered the message. In wrath "he put forth his hand from the altar" and cried out, "Lay hold on him." His impetuous act met with swift rebuke. The hand outstretched against the messenger of Jehovah suddenly became powerless and withered, and could not be withdrawn.

Terror-stricken, the king appealed to the prophet to intercede with God in his behalf. "Entreat now the face of the Lord thy God," he pleaded, "and pray for me, that my hand may be restored me again. And the man of God besought the Lord, and the king's hand was restored him again, and became as it was before." Verses 4, 6.

Vain had been Jeroboam's effort to invest with solemnity the dedication of a strange altar, respect for which would have led to disrespect for the worship of Jehovah in the temple at Jerusalem. By the message of the prophet, the king of Israel should have been led to repent and to renounce his wicked purposes, which were turning the people away from the true worship of God. But he hardened his heart and determined to follow a way of his own choosing.

At the time of the feast at Bethel the hearts of the Israelites were not fully hardened. Many were susceptible to the influence of the Holy Spirit. The Lord designed that those who were taking rapid steps in apostasy should be checked in their course before it should be too late. He sent His messenger to interrupt the idolatrous proceedings and to reveal to king and people what the outworking of this apostasy would be. The rending of the altar was a sign of God's displeasure at the abomination that was being wrought in Israel.

The Lord seeks to save, not to destroy. He delights in the rescue of sinners. "As I live, saith the Lord God, I have no pleasure in the death of the wicked." Ezekiel 33:11. By warnings and entreaties He calls the wayward to cease from their evil-doing and to turn to Him and live. He gives His chosen messengers a holy boldness, that those who hear may fear and be brought to repentance. How firmly the man of God rebuked the king! And this firmness was essential; in no other way could the existing evils have been rebuked. The Lord gave His servant boldness, that an abiding impression might be made on those who heard. The messengers of the Lord are never to fear the face of man, but are to stand unflinchingly for the right. So long as they put their trust in God, they need not fear; for He who gives them their commission gives them also the assurance of His protecting care.

Having delivered his message, the prophet was about to return, when Jeroboam said to him, "Come home with me, and refresh thyself, and I will give thee a reward." "If thou wilt give me half thine house," the prophet replied, "I will not go in with thee, neither will I eat bread nor drink water in this place: for so was it charged me by the word of the Lord, saying, Eat no bread, nor drink water, nor turn again by the same way that thou camest." 1 Kings 13:7-9.

Well would it have been for the prophet had he adhered to his purpose to return to Judea without delay. While traveling homeward by another route, he was overtaken by an aged man who claimed to be a prophet and who made false representations to the man of God, declaring, "I am a prophet also as thou art; and an angel spake unto me by the word of the Lord, saying, Bring him back with thee into thine house, that he may eat bread and drink water." Again and again the lie was repeated and the invitation urged until the man of God was persuaded to return.

Because the true prophet allowed himself to take a course contrary to the line of duty, God permitted him to suffer the penalty of transgression. While he and the one who had invited him to return to Bethel were sitting together at the table, the inspiration of the Almighty came upon the false prophet, "and he cried unto the man of God that came from Judah, saying, Thus saith the Lord, Forasmuch as thou hast disobeyed the mouth of the Lord, and hast not kept the commandment which the Lord thy God commanded thee, . . . thy carcass shall not come unto the sepulcher of thy fathers." Verses 18-22.

This prophecy of doom was soon literally fulfilled. "It came to pass, after he had eaten bread, and after he had drunk, that he saddled for him the ass. . . . And when he was gone, a lion met him by the way, and slew him: and his carcass was cast in the way, and the ass stood by it, the lion also stood by the carcass. And, behold, men passed by, and saw the carcass cast in the way, . . . and they came and told it in the city where the old prophet dwelt. And when the prophet that brought him back from the way heard thereof, he said, It is the man of God, who was disobedient unto the word of the Lord." Verses 23-26.

The penalty that overtook the unfaithful messenger was a still further evidence of the truth of the prophecy uttered over the altar. If, after disobeying the word of the Lord, the prophet had been permitted to go on in safety, the king would have used this fact in an attempt to vindicate his own disobedience. In the rent altar, in the palsied arm, and in the terrible fate of the one who dared disobey an express command of Jehovah, Jeroboam should have discerned the swift displeasure of an offended God, and these judgments should have warned him not to persist in wrongdoing. But, far from repenting, Jeroboam "made again of the lowest of the people priests of the high places: whosoever would, he consecrated him, and he became one of the priests of the high places." Thus he not only sinned greatly himself, but "made Israel to sin;" and "this thing became sin unto the house of Jeroboam, even to cut it off, and to destroy it from off the face of the earth." Verses 33, 34; 14:16.

Toward the close of a troubled reign of twenty-two years, Jeroboam met with a disastrous defeat in a war with Abijah, the successor of Rehoboam. "Neither did Jeroboam recover strength again in the days of Abijah: and the Lord struck him, and he died." 2 Chronicles 13:20.

The apostasy introduced during Jeroboam's reign became more and more marked, until finally it resulted in the utter ruin of the kingdom of Israel. Even before the death of Jeroboam, Ahijah, the aged prophet at Shiloh who many years before had predicted the elevation of Jeroboam to the throne, declared: "The Lord shall smite Israel, as a reed is shaken in the water, and He shall root up Israel out of this good land, which He gave to their fathers, and shall scatter them beyond the river, because they have made their groves, provoking the Lord to anger. And He shall give Israel up because of the sins of Jeroboam, who did sin, and who made Israel to sin." 1 Kings 14:15, 16.

Yet the Lord did not give Israel up without first doing all that could be done to lead them back to their allegiance to Him. Through long, dark years when ruler after ruler stood up in bold defiance of Heaven and led Israel deeper and still deeper into idolatry, God sent message after message to His backslidden people. Through His prophets He gave them every opportunity to stay the tide of apostasy and to return to Him. During the years that were to follow the rending of the kingdom, Elijah and Elisha were to live and labor, and the tender appeals of Hosea and Amos and Obadiah were to be heard in the land. Never was the kingdom of Israel to be left without noble witnesses to the mighty power of God to save from sin. Even in the darkest hours some would remain true to their divine Ruler and in the midst of idolatry would live blameless in the sight of a holy God. These faithful ones were numbered among the goodly remnant through whom the eternal purpose of Jehovah was finally to be fulfilled.

chapter 8

National Apostasy

FROM the time of Jeroboam's death to Elijah's appearance before Ahab the people of Israel suffered a steady spiritual decline. Ruled by men who did not fear Jehovah and who encouraged strange forms of worship, the larger number of the people rapidly lost sight of their duty to serve the living God and adopted many of the practices of idolatry.

Nadab, the son of Jeroboam, occupied the throne of Israel for only a few months. His career of evil was suddenly stopped by a conspiracy headed by Baasha, one of his generals, to gain control of the government. Nadab was slain, with all his kindred in the line of succession, "according unto the saying of the Lord, which He spake by His servant Ahijah the Shilonite: because of the sins of Jeroboam which he sinned, and which he made Israel sin." 1 Kings 15:29, 30.

Thus perished the house of Jeroboam. The idolatrous worship introduced by him had brought upon the guilty offenders the retributive judgments of Heaven; and yet the rulers who followed—Baasha, Elah, Zimri, and Omri—during a period

Under the influence and leadership of Jezebel, Ahab introduced Baal worship throughout the kingdom of Israel.

© P.P.P.A.   JOHN STEEL, ARTIST

of nearly forty years, continued in the same fatal course of evil-doing.

During the greater part of this time of apostasy in Israel, Asa was ruling in the kingdom of Judah. For many years "Asa did that which was good and right in the eyes of the Lord his God: for he took away the altars of the strange gods, and the high places, and brake down the images, and cut down the groves: and commanded Judah to seek the Lord God of their fathers, and to do the law and the commandment. Also he took away out of all the cities of Judah the high places and the sun [margin] images: and the kingdom was quiet before him." 2 Chronicles 14:2-5.

The faith of Asa was put to a severe test when "Zerah the Ethiopian with an host of a thousand thousand, and three hundred chariots," invaded his kingdom. Verse 9. In this crisis Asa did not put his trust in the "fenced cities in Judah" that he had built, with "walls, and towers, gates, and bars," nor in the "mighty men of valor" in his carefully trained army. Verses 6-8. The king's trust was in Jehovah of hosts, in whose name marvelous deliverances had been wrought in behalf of Israel of old. Setting his forces in battle array, he sought the help of God.

The opposing armies now stood face to face. It was a time of test and trial to those who served the Lord. Had every sin been confessed? Had the men of Judah full confidence in God's power to deliver? Such thoughts as these were in the minds of the leaders. From every human viewpoint the vast host from Egypt would sweep everything before it. But in time of peace Asa had not been giving himself to amusement and pleasure; he had been preparing for any emergency. He had an army trained for conflict; he had endeavored to lead his people to make their peace with God. And now, although his forces were fewer in number than the enemy, his faith in the One whom he had made his trust did not weaken.

Having sought the Lord in the days of prosperity, the king could now rely upon Him in the day of adversity. His petitions showed that he was not a stranger to God's wonderful power. "It is nothing with Thee to help," he pleaded, "whether with many, or with them that have no power: help us, O Lord our God; for we rest on Thee, and in Thy name we go against this multitude. O Lord, Thou art our God; let not man prevail against Thee." Verse 11.

The prayer of Asa is one that every Christian believer may fittingly offer. We fight in a warfare, not against flesh and blood, but against principalities and powers, and against spiritual wickedness in high places. See Ephesians 6:12. In life's conflict we must meet evil agencies that have arrayed themselves against the right. Our hope is not in man, but in the living God. With full assurance of faith we may expect that He will unite His omnipotence with the efforts of human instrumentalities, for the glory of His name. Clad with the armor of His righteousness, we may gain the victory over every foe.

King Asa's faith was signally rewarded. "The Lord smote the Ethiopians before Asa, and before Judah; and the Ethiopians fled. And Asa and the people that were with him pursued them unto Gerar: and the Ethiopians were overthrown, that they could not recover themselves; for they were destroyed before the Lord, and before His host." 2 Chronicles 14:12, 13.

As the victorious armies of Judah and Benjamin were returning to Jerusalem, "the Spirit of God came upon Azariah the son of Oded: and he went out to meet Asa, and said unto him, Hear ye me, Asa, and all Judah and Benjamin; The Lord is with you, while ye be with Him; and if ye seek Him, He will be found of you; but if ye forsake Him, He will forsake you." "Be ye strong therefore, and let not your hands be weak: for your work shall be rewarded." 2 Chronicles 15:1, 2, 7.

Greatly encouraged by these words, Asa soon led out in a second reformation in Judah. He "put away the abominable idols out of all the land of Judah and Benjamin, and out of the cities which he had taken from Mount Ephraim, and renewed the altar of the Lord, that was before the porch of the Lord.

"And he gathered all Judah and Benjamin, and the strangers with them out of Ephraim and Manasseh, and out of Simeon: for they fell to him out of Israel in abundance, when they saw that the Lord his God was with him. So they gathered themselves together at Jerusalem in the third month, in the fifteenth year of the reign of Asa. And they offered unto the Lord the same time, of the spoil which they had brought, seven hundred oxen and seven thousand sheep. And they entered into a covenant to seek the Lord God of their fathers with all their heart and with all their soul." "And He was found of them: and the Lord gave them rest round about." Verses 8-12, 15.

Asa's long record of faithful service was marred by some mistakes, made at times when he failed to put his trust fully in God. When, on one occasion, the king of Israel entered the kingdom of Judah and seized Ramah, a fortified city only five miles from Jerusalem, Asa sought deliverance by forming an alliance with Benhadad, king of Syria. This failure to trust God alone in time of need was sternly rebuked by Hanani the prophet, who appeared before Asa with the message:

"Because thou hast relied on the king of Syria, and not relied on the Lord thy God, therefore is the host of the king of Syria escaped out of thine hand. Were not the Ethiopians and the Lubims a huge host, with very many chariots and horsemen? yet, because thou didst rely on the Lord, He delivered them into thine hand. For the eyes of the Lord run to and fro throughout the whole earth, to show Himself strong in the behalf of them whose heart is perfect toward Him. Herein thou hast done foolishly: therefore from henceforth thou shalt have wars." 2 Chronicles 16:7-9.

Instead of humbling himself before God because of his mistake, "Asa was wroth with the seer, and put him in a prison house; for he was in a rage with him because of this thing. And Asa oppressed some of the people the same time." Verse 10.

"In the thirty and ninth year of his reign," Asa was "diseased in his feet, until his disease was exceeding great: yet in his disease he sought not to the Lord, but to the physicians." Verse 12. The king died in the forty-first year of his reign and was succeeded by Jehoshaphat, his son.

Two years before the death of Asa, Ahab began to rule in the kingdom of Israel. From the beginning his reign was marked by a strange and terrible apostasy. His father, Omri, the founder of Samaria, had "wrought evil in the eyes of the Lord, and did worse than all that were before him" (1 Kings 16:25); but the sins of Ahab were even greater. He "did more to provoke the Lord God of Israel to anger than all the kings of Israel that were before him," acting "as if it had been a light thing for him to walk in the sins of Jeroboam the son of Nebat." Verses 33, 31. Not content with encouraging the forms of religious service followed at Bethel and Dan, he boldly led the people into the grossest heathenism, by setting aside the worship of Jehovah for Baal worship.

Taking to wife Jezebel, "the daughter of Ethbaal king of the Zidonians" and high priest of Baal, Ahab "served Baal, and worshiped him. And he reared up an altar for Baal in the house of Baal, which he had built in Samaria." Verses 31, 32.

Not only did Ahab introduce Baal worship at the capital city, but under the leadership of Jezebel he erected heathen altars in many "high places," where in the shelter of surrounding groves the priests and others connected with this seductive form of idolatry exerted their baleful influence, until well-nigh all Israel were following after Baal. "There was none like unto Ahab," who "did sell himself to work wickedness in the sight of the Lord, whom Jezebel his wife stirred up. And he did very abominably in following idols, according to all things as did the Amorites, whom the Lord cast out before the children of Israel." 1 Kings 21:25, 26.

Ahab was weak in moral power. His union by marriage with an idolatrous woman of decided character and positive temperament resulted disastrously both to himself and to the nation. Unprincipled, and with no high standard of right-doing, his character was easily molded by the determined spirit of Jezebel. His selfish nature was incapable of appreciating the mercies of God to Israel and his own obligations as the guardian and leader of the chosen people.

Under the blighting influence of Ahab's rule, Israel wandered far from the living God and corrupted their ways before Him. For many years they had been losing their sense of reverence and godly fear; and now it seemed as if there were none who dared expose their lives by openly standing forth in opposition to the prevailing blasphemy. The dark shadow of apostasy covered the whole land. Images of Baalim and Ashtoreth were everywhere to be seen. Idolatrous temples and consecrated groves, wherein were worshiped the works of men's hands, were multiplied. The air was polluted with the smoke of the sacrifices offered to false gods. Hill and vale resounded with the drunken cries of a heathen priesthood who sacrificed to the sun, moon, and stars.

Through the influence of Jezebel and her impious priests, the people were taught that the idol gods that had been set up were deities, ruling by their mystic power the elements of earth, fire, and water. All the bounties of heaven—the running brooks, the streams of living water, the gentle dew, the showers of rain which refreshed the earth and caused the fields to bring forth abundantly—were ascribed to the favor of Baal and Ashtoreth, instead of to the Giver of every good and perfect gift. The people forgot that the hills and valleys, the streams and fountains, were in the hand of the living God, that He controlled the sun, the clouds of heaven, and all the powers of nature.

Through faithful messengers the Lord sent repeated warnings to the apostate king and the people, but in vain were these words of reproof. In vain did the inspired messengers assert Jehovah's right to be the only God in Israel; in vain did they exalt the laws that He had entrusted to them. Captivated by the gorgeous display and the fascinating rites of idol worship, the people followed the example of the king and his court, and gave themselves up to the intoxicating, degrading pleasures of a sensual worship. In their blind folly they chose to reject God and His worship. The light so graciously given them had become darkness. The fine gold had become dim.

Alas, how had the glory of Israel departed! Never before had the chosen people of God fallen so low in apostasy. Of "the prophets of Baal" there were "four hundred and fifty," besides four hundred "prophets of the groves." 1 Kings 18:19. Nothing short of the miracle-working power of God could preserve the nation from utter destruction. Israel had voluntarily separated herself from Jehovah, yet the Lord in compassion still yearned after those who had been led into sin, and He was about to send to them one of the mightiest of His prophets, through whom many were to be led back to allegiance to the God of their fathers.

chapter 9

This chapter is based on 1 Kings 17:1-7.

Elijah the Tishbite

AMONG the mountains of Gilead, east of the Jordan, there dwelt in the days of Ahab a man of faith and prayer whose fearless ministry was destined to check the rapid spread of apostasy in Israel. Far removed from any city of renown, and occupying no high station in life, Elijah the Tishbite nevertheless entered upon his mission confident in God's purpose to prepare the way before him and to give him abundant success. The word of faith and power was upon his lips, and his whole life was devoted to the work of reform. His was the voice of one crying in the wilderness to rebuke sin and press back the tide of evil. And while he came to the people as a reprover of sin, his message offered the balm of Gilead to the sin-sick souls of all who desired to be healed.

As Elijah saw Israel going deeper and deeper into idolatry, his soul was distressed and his indignation aroused. God had done great things for His people. He had delivered them from bondage and given them "the lands of the heathen, . . . that they might observe His statutes, and keep His laws." Psalm 105:44, 45. But the beneficent designs of Jehovah were now well-nigh forgotten. Unbelief was fast separating the chosen nation from the Source of their strength. Viewing this apostasy from his mountain retreat, Elijah was overwhelmed with sorrow. In anguish of soul he besought God to arrest the once-favored people in their wicked course, to visit them with judgments, if need be, that they might be led to see in its true light their departure from Heaven. He longed to see them brought to repentance before they should go to such lengths in evil-doing as to provoke the Lord to destroy them utterly.

Elijah's prayer was answered. Oft-repeated appeals, remonstrances, and warnings had failed to bring Israel to repentance. The time had come when God must speak to them by means of judgments. Inasmuch as the worshipers of Baal claimed that the treasures of heaven, the dew and the rain, came not from Jehovah, but from the ruling forces of nature, and that it was through the creative energy of the sun that the earth was enriched and made to bring forth abundantly, the curse of God was to rest heavily upon the polluted land. The apostate tribes of Israel were to be shown the folly of trusting to the power of Baal for temporal blessings. Until they should turn to God with repentance, and acknowledge Him as the source of all blessing, there should fall upon the land neither dew nor rain.

To Elijah was entrusted the mission of delivering to Ahab Heaven's message of judgment. He did not seek to be the Lord's messenger; the word of the Lord came to him. And

jealous for the honor of God's cause, he did not hesitate to obey the divine summons, though to obey seemed to invite swift destruction at the hand of the wicked king. The prophet set out at once and traveled night and day until he reached Samaria. At the palace he solicited no admission, nor waited to be formally announced. Clad in the coarse garments usually worn by the prophets of that time, he passed the guards, apparently unnoticed, and stood for a moment before the astonished king.

Elijah made no apology for his abrupt appearance. A Greater than the ruler of Israel had commissioned him to speak; and, lifting his hand toward heaven, he solemnly affirmed by the living God that the judgments of the Most High were about to fall upon Israel. "As the Lord God of Israel liveth, before whom I stand," he declared, "there shall not be dew nor rain these years, but according to my word."

It was only by the exercise of strong faith in the unfailing power of God's word that Elijah delivered his message. Had he not possessed implicit confidence in the One whom he served, he would never have appeared before Ahab. On his way to Samaria, Elijah had passed by ever-flowing streams, hills covered with verdure, and stately forests that seemed beyond the reach of drought. Everything on which the eye rested was clothed with beauty. The prophet might have wondered how the streams that had never ceased their flow could become dry, or how those hills and valleys could be burned with drought. But he gave no place to unbelief. He fully believed that God would humble apostate Israel, and that through judgments they would be brought to repentance. The fiat of Heaven had gone forth; God's word could not

To Elijah, fearless prophet of Jehovah, was entrusted the mission of delivering Heaven's message of judgment to Ahab.

fail; and at the peril of his life Elijah fearlessly fulfilled his commission. Like a thunderbolt from a clear sky, the message of impending judgment fell upon the ears of the wicked king; but before Ahab could recover from his astonishment, or frame a reply, Elijah disappeared as abruptly as he had come, without waiting to witness the effect of his message. And the Lord went before him, making plain the way. "Turn thee eastward," the prophet was bidden, "and hide thyself by the brook Cherith, that is before Jordan. And it shall be, that thou shalt drink of the brook; and I have commanded the ravens to feed thee."

The king made diligent inquiry, but the prophet was not to be found. Queen Jezebel, angered over the message that had locked up the treasures of heaven, lost no time in conferring with the priests of Baal, who united with her in cursing the prophet and in defying the wrath of Jehovah. But notwithstanding their desire to find him who had uttered the word of woe, they were destined to meet with disappointment. Nor could they conceal from others a knowledge of the judgment pronounced in consequence of the prevailing apostasy. Tidings of Elijah's denunciation of the sins of Israel, and of his prophecy of swift-coming punishment, quickly spread throughout the land. The fears of some were aroused, but in general the heavenly message was received with scorn and ridicule.

The prophet's words went into immediate effect. Those who were at first inclined to scoff at the thought of calamity, soon had occasion for serious reflection; for after a few months the earth, unrefreshed by dew or rain, became dry, and vegetation withered. As time passed, streams that had never been known to fail began to decrease, and brooks began to dry up. Yet the people were urged by their leaders to have confidence in the power of Baal and to set aside as idle words the prophecy of Elijah. The priests still insisted that it was through the power of Baal that the showers of rain fell. Fear not the God of Elijah, nor tremble at His word, they urged, it is Baal that brings forth the harvest in its season and provides for man and beast.

God's message to Ahab gave Jezebel and her priests and all the followers of Baal and Ashtoreth opportunity to test the power of their gods, and, if possible, to prove the word of Elijah false. Against the assurances of hundreds of idolatrous priests, the prophecy of Elijah stood alone. If, notwithstanding the prophet's declaration, Baal could still give dew and rain, causing the streams to continue to flow and vegetation to flourish, then let the king of Israel worship him and the people say that he is God.

Determined to keep the people in deception, the priests of Baal continue to offer sacrifices to their gods and to call upon them night and day to refresh the earth. With costly offerings the priests attempt to appease the anger of their gods; with a zeal and a perseverance worthy of a better cause they linger round their pagan altars and pray earnestly for rain. Night after night, throughout the doomed land, their cries and entreaties arise. But no clouds appear in the heavens by day to hide the burning rays of the sun. No dew or rain refreshes the thirsty earth. The word of Jehovah stands unchanged by anything the priests of Baal can do.

A year passes, and yet there is no rain. The earth is parched as if with fire. The scorching heat of the sun destroys what little vegetation has survived. Streams dry up, and lowing herds and bleating flocks wander hither and thither in distress. Once-flourishing fields have become like burning desert sands, a desolate waste. The groves dedicated to idol worship are leafless; the forest trees, gaunt skeletons of nature, afford no shade. The air is dry and suffocating; dust storms blind the eyes and nearly stop the breath. Once-prosperous cities and villages have become places of mourning. Hunger and thirst are telling upon man and beast with fearful mortality. Famine, with all its horrors, comes closer and still closer.

Yet notwithstanding these evidences of God's power, Israel repented not, nor learned the lesson that God would have them learn. They did not see that He who created nature controls her laws, and can make of them instruments of blessing or of destruction. Proudhearted, enamored of their false worship, they were unwilling to humble themselves under the mighty hand of God, and they began to cast about for some other cause to which to attribute their sufferings.

Jezebel utterly refused to recognize the drought as a judgment from Jehovah. Unyielding in her determination to defy the God of heaven, she, with nearly the whole of Israel, united in denouncing Elijah as the cause of all their misery. Had he not borne testimony against their forms of worship? If only he could be put out of the way, she argued, the anger of their gods would be appeased, and their troubles would end.

Urged on by the queen, Ahab instituted a most diligent search for the hiding place of the prophet. To the surrounding nations, far and near, he sent messengers to seek for the man whom he hated, yet feared; and in his anxiety to make the search as thorough as possible, he required of these kingdoms and nations an oath that they knew nothing of the whereabouts of the prophet. But the search was in vain. The prophet was safe from the malice of the king whose sins had brought upon the land the denunciation of an offended God.

Failing in her efforts against Elijah, Jezebel determined to avenge herself by slaying all the prophets of Jehovah in Israel. Not one should be left alive. The infuriated woman carried out her purpose in the massacre of many of God's servants. Not all, however, perished. Obadiah, the governor of Ahab's house, yet faithful to God, "took an hundred prophets," and at the risk of his own life, "hid them by fifty in a cave, and fed them with bread and water." 1 Kings 18:4.

The second year of famine passed, and still the pitiless heavens gave no sign of rain. Drought and famine continued their devastation throughout the kingdom. Fathers and mothers, powerless to relieve the sufferings of their children, were forced to see them die. Yet still apostate Israel refused to humble their hearts before God and continued to murmur against the man by whose word these terrible judgments had been brought upon them. They seemed unable to discern in their suffering and distress a call to repentance, a divine interposition to save them from taking the fatal step beyond the boundary of Heaven's forgiveness.

The apostasy of Israel was an evil more dreadful than all the multiplied horrors of famine. God was seeking to free the people from their delusion and lead them to understand their accountability to the One to whom they owed their life and all things. He was trying to help them to recover their lost faith, and He must needs bring upon them great affliction.

"Have I any pleasure at all that the wicked should die? saith the Lord God: and not that he should return from his ways, and live?" "Cast away from you all your transgressions, whereby ye have transgressed; and make you a new heart and a new spirit: for why will ye die, O house of Israel? For I have no pleasure in the death of him that dieth, saith the Lord God: wherefore turn yourselves, and live ye." "Turn ye, turn ye from your evil ways; for why will ye die, O house of Israel?" Ezekiel 18:23, 31, 32; 33:11.

God had sent messengers to Israel, with appeals to return to their allegiance. Had they heeded these appeals, had they turned from Baal to the living God, Elijah's message of judgment would never have been given. But the warnings that might have been a savor of life unto life had proved to them a savor of death unto death. Their pride had been wounded, their anger had been aroused against the messengers, and now they regarded with intense hatred the prophet Elijah. If only he should fall into their hands, gladly they would deliver him to Jezebel—as if by silencing his voice they could stay the fulfillment of his words! In the face of calamity they continued to stand firm in their idolatry. Thus they were adding to the guilt that had brought the judgments of Heaven upon the land.

For stricken Israel there was but one remedy—a turning away from the sins that had brought upon them the chastening hand of the Almighty, and a turning to the Lord with full purpose of heart. To them had been given the assurance, "If I shut up heaven that there be no rain, or if I command the locusts to devour the land, or if I send pestilence among My people; if My people, which are called by My name, shall humble themselves, and pray, and seek My face, and turn from their wicked ways; then will I hear from heaven, and will forgive their sin, and will heal their land." 2 Chronicles 7:13, 14. It was to bring to pass this blessed result that God continued to withhold from them the dew and the rain until a decided reformation should take place.

chapter 10

This chapter is based on 1 Kings 17:8-24; 18:1-19.

The Voice of Stern Rebuke

FOR a time Elijah remained hidden in the mountains by the brook Cherith. There for many months he was miraculously provided with food. Later on, when, because of the continued drought, the brook became dry, God bade His servant find refuge in a heathen land. "Arise," He bade him, "get thee to Zarephath, [known in New Testament times as Sarepta], which belongeth to Zidon, and dwell there: behold, I have commanded a widow woman there to sustain thee."

This woman was not an Israelite. She had never had the privileges and blessings that the chosen people of God had enjoyed; but she was a believer in the true God and had walked in all the light that was shining on her pathway. And now, when there was no safety for Elijah in the land of Israel, God sent him to this woman to find an asylum in her home.

"So he arose and went to Zarephath. And when he came to the gate of the city, behold, the widow woman was there gathering of sticks: and he called to her, and said, Fetch

In surroundings showing severe effects
of Israel's prolonged drought, the king
and the prophet meet face to face.
© P.P.P.A.   JOHN STEEL, ARTIST

me, I pray thee, a little water in a vessel, that I may drink. And as she was going to fetch it, he called to her, and said, Bring me, I pray thee, a morsel of bread in thine hand."

In this poverty-stricken home the famine pressed sore, and the pitifully meager fare seemed about to fail. The coming of Elijah on the very day when the widow feared that she must give up the struggle to sustain life tested to the utmost her faith in the power of the living God to provide for her necessities. But even in her dire extremity she bore witness to her faith by a compliance with the request of the stranger who was asking her to share her last morsel with him.

In response to Elijah's request for food and drink, the widow said, "As the Lord thy God liveth, I have not a cake, but an handful of meal in a barrel, and a little oil in a cruse: and, behold, I am gathering two sticks, that I may go in and dress it for me and my son, that we may eat it, and die." Elijah said to her, "Fear not; go and do as thou hast said: but make me thereof a little cake first, and bring it unto me, and after make for thee and for thy son. For thus saith the Lord God of Israel, The barrel of meal shall not waste, neither shall the cruse of oil fail, until the day that the Lord sendeth rain upon the earth."

No greater test of faith than this could have been required. The widow had hitherto treated all strangers with kindness and liberality. Now, regardless of the suffering that might result to herself and child, and trusting in the God of Israel to supply her every need, she met this supreme test of hospitality by doing "according to the saying of Elijah."

Wonderful was the hospitality shown to God's prophet by this Phoenician woman, and wonderfully were her faith and generosity rewarded. "She, and he, and her house, did eat many days. And the barrel of meal wasted not, neither did the cruse of oil fail, according to the word of the Lord, which He spake by Elijah.

"And it came to pass after these things, that the son of the woman, the mistress of the house, fell sick; and his sickness was so sore, that there was no breath left in him. And she said unto Elijah, What have I to do with thee, O thou man of God? art thou come unto me to call my sin to remembrance, and to slay my son?

"And he said unto her, Give me thy son. And he took him out of her bosom, and carried him up into a loft, where he abode, and laid him upon his own bed. . . . And he stretched himself upon the child three times, and cried unto the Lord. . . . And the Lord heard the voice of Elijah; and the soul of the child came into him again, and he revived.

"And Elijah took the child, and brought him down out of the chamber into the house, and delivered him unto his mother: and Elijah said, See, thy son liveth. And the woman said to Elijah, Now by this I know that thou art a man of God, and that the word of the Lord in thy mouth is truth."

The widow of Zarephath shared her morsel with Elijah, and in return her life and that of her son were preserved. And to all who, in time of trial and want, give sympathy and assistance to others more needy, God has promised great blessing. He has not changed. His power is no less now than in the days of Elijah. No less sure now than when spoken by our Saviour is the promise, "He that receiveth a prophet in the name of a prophet shall receive a prophet's reward." Matthew 10:41.

"Be not forgetful to entertain strangers: for thereby some have entertained angels unawares." Hebrews 13:2. These words have lost none of their force through the lapse of time. Our heavenly Father still continues to place in the pathway of His children opportunities that are blessings in disguise; and those who improve these opportunities find great joy. "If thou draw out thy soul to the hungry, and satisfy the afflicted soul; then shall thy light rise in obscurity, and thy darkness be as the noonday: and the Lord shall guide thee continually, and satisfy thy soul in drought, and make fat thy bones: and thou shalt be like a watered garden, and like a spring of water, whose waters fail not." Isaiah 58:10, 11.

To His faithful servants today Christ says, "He that receiveth you receiveth Me, and he that receiveth Me receiveth Him that sent Me." No act of kindness shown in His name will fail to be recognized and rewarded. And in the same tender recognition Christ includes even the feeblest and lowliest of the family of God. "Whosoever shall give to drink," He says, "unto one of these little ones"—those who are as children in their faith and their knowledge of Christ—"a cup of cold water only in the name of a disciple, verily I say unto you, he shall in no wise lose his reward." Matthew 10:40, 42.

Through the long years of drought and famine, Elijah prayed earnestly that the hearts of Israel might be turned from idolatry to allegiance to God. Patiently the prophet waited, while the hand of the Lord rested heavily on the stricken land. As he saw evidences of suffering and want multiplying on every side, his heart was wrung with sorrow, and he longed for power to bring about a reformation quickly. But God Himself was working out His plan, and all that

His servant could do was to pray on in faith and await the time for decided action.

The apostasy prevailing in Ahab's day was the result of many years of evil-doing. Step by step, year after year, Israel had been departing from the right way. For generation after generation they had refused to make straight paths for their feet, and at last the great majority of the people had yielded themselves to the leadership of the powers of darkness.

About a century had passed since, under the rulership of King David, Israel had joyfully united in chanting hymns of praise to the Most High, in recognition of their entire dependence on Him for daily mercies. Listen to their words of adoration as then they sang:

"O God of our salvation, . . .
> Thou makest the outgoings of the morning and evening to rejoice.
Thou visitest the earth, and waterest it:
> Thou greatly enrichest it with the river of God, which is full of water:
Thou preparest them corn, when Thou hast so provided for it.
Thou waterest the ridges thereof abundantly: Thou causest rain to descend into the furrows thereof:
> Thou makest it soft with showers: Thou blessest the springing thereof.
Thou crownest the year with Thy goodness;
> And Thy paths drop fatness.
They drop upon the pastures of the wilderness:
> And the little hills rejoice on every side.
The pastures are clothed with flocks;
The valleys also are covered over with corn;
> They shout for joy, they also sing."
> > Psalm 65:5, 8-13, margin.

Israel had then recognized God as the One who "laid the

foundations of the earth." In expression of their faith they had sung:

"Thou coveredst it with the deep as with a garment:
The waters stood above the mountains.
At Thy rebuke they fled;
At the voice of Thy thunder they hasted away.
They go up by the mountains; they go down by the valleys
Unto the place which Thou hast founded for them.
Thou hast set a bound that they may not pass over;
That they turn not again to cover the earth."
Psalm 104:5-9.

It is by the mighty power of the Infinite One that the elements of nature in earth and sea and sky are kept within bounds. And these elements He uses for the happiness of His creatures. "His good treasure" is freely expended "to give the rain . . . in his season, and to bless all the work" of man's hands. Deuteronomy 28:12.

"He sendeth the springs into the valleys,
Which run among the hills.
They give drink to every beast of the field:
The wild asses quench their thirst.
By them shall the fowls of the heaven have their habitation,
Which sing among the branches. . . .
He causeth the grass to grow for the cattle,
And herb for the service of man:
That He may bring forth food out of the earth;
And wine that maketh glad the heart of man,
And oil to make his face to shine,
And bread which strengtheneth man's heart. . . .

"O Lord, how manifold are Thy works!
In wisdom hast Thou made them all:
The earth is full of Thy riches.
So is this great and wide sea,

Wherein are things creeping innumerable,
  Both small and great beasts. . . .
These wait all upon Thee;
That Thou mayest give them their meat in due season.
  That Thou givest them they gather:

"Thou openest Thine hand,
  They are filled with good."
                Psalm 104: 10-15, 24-28.

Israel had had abundant occasion for rejoicing. The land to which the Lord had brought them was a land flowing with milk and honey. During the wilderness wandering, God had assured them that He was guiding them to a country where they need never suffer for lack of rain. "The land, whither thou goest in to possess it," He had told them, "is not as the land of Egypt, from whence ye came out, where thou sowedst thy seed, and wateredst it with thy foot, as a garden of herbs: but the land, whither ye go to possess it, is a land of hills and valleys, and drinketh water of the rain of heaven: a land which the Lord thy God careth for: the eyes of the Lord thy God are always upon it, from the beginning of the year even unto the end of the year."

The promise of abundance of rain had been given on condition of obedience. "It shall come to pass," the Lord had declared, "if ye shall hearken diligently unto My commandments which I command you this day, to love the Lord your God, and to serve Him with all your heart and with all your soul, that I will give you the rain of your land in his due season, the first rain and the latter rain, that thou mayest gather in thy corn, and thy wine, and thine oil. And I will send grass in thy fields for thy cattle, that thou mayest eat and be full.

"Take heed to yourselves," the Lord had admonished His people, "that your heart be not deceived, and ye turn aside, and serve other gods, and worship them; and then the Lord's wrath be kindled against you, and He shut up the heaven, that there be no rain, and that the land yield not her fruit; and lest ye perish quickly from off the good land which the Lord giveth you." Deuteronomy 11:10-17.

"If thou wilt not hearken unto the voice of the Lord thy God, to observe to do all His commandments and His statutes," the Israelites had been warned, "thy heaven that is over thy head shall be brass, and the earth that is under thee shall be iron. The Lord shall make the rain of thy land powder and dust: from heaven shall it come down upon thee, until thou be destroyed." Deuteronomy 28:15, 23, 24.

These were among the wise counsels of Jehovah to ancient Israel. "Lay up these My words in your heart and in your soul," He had commanded His chosen people, "and bind them for a sign upon your hand, that they may be as frontlets between your eyes. And ye shall teach them your children, speaking of them when thou sittest in thine house, and when thou walkest by the way, when thou liest down, and when thou risest up." Deuteronomy 11:18, 19. Plain were these commands, yet as the centuries passed, and generation after generation lost sight of the provisions made for their spiritual welfare, the ruinous influences of apostasy threatened to sweep aside every barrier of divine grace.

Thus it had come to pass that God was now visiting His people with the severest of His judgments. The prediction of Elijah was meeting with terrible fulfillment. For three years the messenger of woe was sought for in city after city

and nation after nation. At the mandate of Ahab, many rulers
had given their oath of honor that the strange prophet could
not be found in their dominions. Yet the search was continued, for Jezebel and the prophets of Baal hated Elijah with
a deadly hatred, and they spared no effort to bring him within
reach of their power. And still there was no rain.

At last, "after many days," the word of the Lord came to
Elijah, "Go, show thyself unto Ahab; and I will send rain
upon the earth."

In obedience to the command, "Elijah went to show himself unto Ahab." About the time that the prophet set forth on
his journey to Samaria, Ahab had proposed to Obadiah, the
governor of his household, that they make thorough search
for springs and brooks of water, in the hope of finding pasture
for their starving flocks and herds. Even in the royal court
the effect of the long-continued drought was keenly felt. The
king, deeply concerned over the outlook for his household,
decided to unite personally with his servant in a search for
some favored spots where pasture might be had. "So they
divided the land between them to pass throughout it: Ahab

went one way by himself, and Obadiah went another way by himself."

"As Obadiah was in the way, behold, Elijah met him: and he knew him, and fell on his face, and said, Art thou that my lord Elijah?"

During the apostasy of Israel, Obadiah had remained faithful. His master, the king, had been unable to turn him from his allegiance to the living God. Now he was honored with a commission from Elijah, who said, "Go, tell thy lord, Behold, Elijah is here."

Greatly terrified, Obadiah exclaimed, "What have I sinned, that thou wouldest deliver thy servant into the hand of Ahab, to slay me?" To take such a message as this to Ahab was to court certain death. "As the Lord thy God liveth," he explained to the prophet, "there is no nation or kingdom, whither my lord hath not sent to seek thee: and when they said, He is not there; he took an oath of the kingdom and nation, that they found thee not. And now thou sayest, Go, tell thy lord, Behold, Elijah is here. And it shall come to pass, as soon as I am gone from thee, that the Spirit of the Lord shall carry thee whither I know not; and so when I come and tell Ahab, and he cannot find thee, he shall slay me."

Earnestly Obadiah pleaded with the prophet not to urge him. "I thy servant," he urged, "fear the Lord from my youth. Was it not told my lord what I did when Jezebel slew the prophets of the Lord, how I hid an hundred men of the Lord's prophets by fifty in a cave, and fed them with bread and water? And now thou sayest, Go, tell thy lord, Behold, Elijah is here: and he shall slay me."

With a solemn oath Elijah promised Obadiah that the

errand should not be in vain. "As the Lord of hosts liveth, before whom I stand," he declared, "I will surely show myself unto him today." Thus assured, "Obadiah went to meet Ahab, and told him."

In astonishment mingled with terror the king listened to the message from the man whom he feared and hated, and for whom he had sought so untiringly. Well he knew that Elijah would not endanger his life merely for the sake of meeting him. Could it be possible that the prophet was about to utter another woe against Israel? The king's heart was seized with dread. He remembered the withered arm of Jeroboam. Ahab could not avoid obeying the summons, neither dared he lift up his hand against the messenger of God. And so, accompanied by a bodyguard of soldiers, the trembling monarch went to meet the prophet.

The king and the prophet stand face to face. Though Ahab

is filled with passionate hatred, yet in the presence of Elijah he seems unmanned, powerless. In his first faltering words, "Art thou he that troubleth Israel?" he unconsciously reveals the inmost feelings of his heart. Ahab knew that it was by the word of God that the heavens had become as brass, yet he sought to cast upon the prophet the blame for the heavy judgments resting on the land.

It is natural for the wrongdoer to hold the messengers of God responsible for the calamities that come as the sure result of a departure from the way of righteousness. Those who place themselves in Satan's power are unable to see things as God sees them. When the mirror of truth is held up before them, they become indignant at the thought of receiving reproof. Blinded by sin, they refuse to repent; they feel that God's servants have turned against them and are worthy of severest censure.

Standing in conscious innocence before Ahab, Elijah makes no attempt to excuse himself or to flatter the king. Nor does he seek to evade the king's wrath by the good news that the drought is almost over. He has no apology to offer. Indignant, and jealous for the honor of God, he casts back the imputation of Ahab, fearlessly declaring to the king that it is *his* sins, and the sins of *his* fathers, that have brought upon Israel this terrible calamity. "I have not troubled Israel," Elijah boldly asserts, "but thou, and thy father's house, in that ye have forsaken the commandments of the Lord, and thou hast followed Baalim."

Today there is need of the voice of stern rebuke; for grievous sins have separated the people from God. Infidelity is fast becoming fashionable. "We will not have this man to reign over us," is the language of thousands. Luke 19:14. The smooth sermons so often preached make no lasting impression; the trumpet does not give a certain sound. Men are not cut to the heart by the plain, sharp truths of God's word.

There are many professed Christians who, if they should express their real feelings, would say, What need is there of speaking so plainly? They might as well ask, Why need John the Baptist have said to the Pharisees, "O generation of vipers, who hath warned you to flee from the wrath to come?" Luke 3:7. Why need he have provoked the anger of Herodias by telling Herod that it was unlawful for him to live with his brother's wife? The forerunner of Christ lost his life by his plain speaking. Why could he not have moved along without incurring the displeasure of those who were living in sin?

So men who should be standing as faithful guardians of God's law have argued, till policy has taken the place of faithfulness, and sin is allowed to go unreproved. When will the voice of faithful rebuke be heard once more in the church?

"Thou art the man." 2 Samuel 12:7. Words as unmistakably plain as these spoken by Nathan to David are seldom heard in the pulpits of today, seldom seen in the public press. If they were not so rare, we should see more of the power of God revealed among men. The Lord's messengers should not complain that their efforts are without fruit until they repent of their own love of approbation and their desire to please men, which leads them to suppress truth.

Those ministers who are men pleasers, who cry, Peace, peace, when God has not spoken peace, might well humble their hearts before God, asking pardon for their insincerity and their lack of moral courage. It is not from love for their neighbor that they smooth down the message entrusted to them, but because they are self-indulgent and ease-loving. True love seeks first the honor of God and the salvation of souls. Those who have this love will not evade the truth to save themselves from the unpleasant results of plain speaking. When souls are in peril, God's ministers will not consider self, but will speak the word given them to speak, refusing to excuse or palliate evil.

Would that every minister might realize the sacredness of his office and the holiness of his work, and show the courage that Elijah showed! As divinely appointed messengers, ministers are in a position of awful responsibility. They are to "reprove, rebuke, exhort with all long-suffering." 2 Timothy 4:2. In Christ's stead they are to labor as stewards of the mysteries of heaven, encouraging the obedient and warning the disobedient. With them worldly policy is to have no weight. Never are they to swerve from the path in which Jesus has bidden them walk. They are to go forward in faith, remembering that they are surrounded by a cloud of witnesses. They are not to speak their own words, but words which One greater than the potentates of earth has bidden them speak. Their message is to be, "Thus saith the Lord." God calls for men like Elijah, Nathan, and John the Baptist —men who will bear His message with faithfulness, regardless of the consequences; men who will speak the truth bravely, though it call for the sacrifice of all they have.

God cannot use men who, in time of peril, when the strength, courage, and influence of all are needed, are afraid to take a firm stand for the right. He calls for men who will do faithful battle against wrong, warring against principalities and powers, against the rulers of the darkness of this world, against spiritual wickedness in high places. It is to such as these that He will speak the words: "Well done, good and faithful servant; . . . enter thou into the joy of thy Lord." Matthew 25:23.

chapter 11

This chapter is based on 1 Kings 18:19-40.

Carmel

STANDING before Ahab, Elijah demanded that all Israel be assembled to meet him and the prophets of Baal and Ashtoreth on Mount Carmel. "Send," he commanded, "and gather to me all Israel unto Mount Carmel, and the prophets of Baal four hundred and fifty, and the prophets of the groves four hundred, which eat at Jezebel's table."

The command was issued by one who seemed to stand in the very presence of Jehovah; and Ahab obeyed at once, as if the prophet were monarch, and the king a subject. Swift messengers were sent throughout the kingdom with the summons to meet Elijah and the prophets of Baal and Ashtoreth. In every town and village the people prepared to assemble at the appointed time. As they journeyed toward the place, the hearts of many were filled with strange forebodings. Something unusual was about to happen; else why this summons to gather at Carmel? What new calamity was about to fall upon the people and the land?

Before the throng and the priests of
Baal on Mount Carmel, Elijah cried out,
"How long halt ye between two opinions?"

Before the drought, Mount Carmel had been a place of beauty, its streams fed from never-failing springs, and its fertile slopes covered with fair flowers and flourishing groves. But now its beauty languished under a withering curse. The altars erected to the worship of Baal and Ashtoreth stood now in leafless groves. On the summit of one of the highest ridges, in sharp contrast with these was the broken-down altar of Jehovah.

Carmel overlooked a wide expanse of country; its heights were visible from many parts of the kingdom of Israel. At the foot of the mount there were vantage points from which could be seen much of what took place above. God had been signally dishonored by the idolatrous worship carried on under cover of its wooded slopes; and Elijah chose this elevation as the most conspicuous place for the display of God's power and for the vindication of the honor of His name.

Early on the morning of the day appointed, the hosts of apostate Israel, in eager expectancy, gather near the top of the mountain. Jezebel's prophets march up in imposing array. In regal pomp the king appears and takes his position at the head of the priests, and the idolaters shout his welcome. But there is apprehension in the hearts of the priests as they remember that at the word of the prophet the land of Israel for three years and a half has been destitute of dew and rain. Some fearful crisis is at hand, they feel sure. The gods in whom they have trusted have been unable to prove Elijah a false prophet. To their frantic cries, their prayers, their tears, their humiliation, their revolting ceremonies, their costly and ceaseless sacrifices, the objects of their worship have been strangely indifferent.

Facing King Ahab and the false prophets, and surrounded by the assembled hosts of Israel, Elijah stands, the only one who has appeared to vindicate the honor of Jehovah. He whom the whole kingdom has charged with its weight of woe is now before them, apparently defenseless in the presence of the monarch of Israel, the prophets of Baal, the men of war, and the surrounding thousands. But Elijah is not alone. Above and around him are the protecting hosts of heaven, angels that excel in strength.

Unashamed, unterrified, the prophet stands before the multitude, fully aware of his commission to execute the divine command. His countenance is lighted with an awful solemnity. In anxious expectancy the people wait for him to speak. Looking first upon the broken-down altar of Jehovah, and then upon the multitude, Elijah cries out in clear, trumpet-like tones, "How long halt ye between two opinions? if the Lord be God, follow Him: but if Baal, then follow him."

The people answer him not a word. Not one in that vast assembly dare reveal loyalty to Jehovah. Like a dark cloud, deception and blindness had overspread Israel. Not all at once had this fatal apostasy closed about them, but gradually, as from time to time they had failed to heed the words of warning and reproof that the Lord sent them. Each departure from rightdoing, each refusal to repent, had deepened their guilt and driven them farther from Heaven. And now, in this crisis, they persisted in refusing to take their stand for God.

The Lord abhors indifference and disloyalty in a time of crisis in His work. The whole universe is watching with inexpressible interest the closing scenes of the great controversy between good and evil. The people of God are nearing the borders of the eternal world; what can be of more importance to them than that they be loyal to the God of heaven? All through the ages, God has had moral heroes, and He has them now—those who, like Joseph and Elijah and Daniel, are not ashamed to acknowledge themselves His peculiar people. His special blessing accompanies the labors of men of action, men who will not be swerved from the straight line of duty, but who with divine energy will inquire, "Who is on the Lord's side?" (Exodus 32:26), men who will not stop merely with the inquiry, but who will demand that those who choose to identify themselves with the people of God shall step forward and reveal unmistakably their allegiance to the King of kings and Lord of lords. Such men make their wills and plans subordinate to the law of God. For love of Him they count not their lives dear unto themselves. Their work is to catch the light from the Word and let it shine forth to the world in clear, steady rays. Fidelity to God is their motto.

While Israel on Carmel doubt and hesitate, the voice of Elijah again breaks the silence: "I, even I only, remain a prophet of the Lord; but Baal's prophets are four hundred and fifty men. Let them therefore give us two bullocks; and let them choose one bullock for themselves, and cut it in pieces, and lay it on wood, and put no fire under: and I will dress the other bullock, and lay it on wood, and put no fire under: and call ye on the name of your gods, and I will call on the name of the Lord: and the God that answereth by fire, let him be God."

The proposal of Elijah is so reasonable that the people cannot well evade it, so they find courage to answer, "It is well spoken." The prophets of Baal dare not lift their voices in dissent; and, addressing them, Elijah directs, "Choose you one bullock for yourselves, and dress it first; for ye are many; and call on the name of your gods, but put no fire under."

Outwardly bold and defiant, but with terror in their guilty hearts, the false priests prepare their altar, laying on the wood and the victim; and then they begin their incantations. Their shrill cries echo and re-echo through the forests and the surrounding heights, as they call on the name of their god, saying, "O Baal, hear us." The priests gather about their altar, and with leaping and writhing and screaming, with tearing of hair and cutting of flesh, they beseech their god to help them.

The morning passes, noon comes, and yet there is no evidence that Baal hears the cries of his deluded followers. There is no voice, no reply to their frantic prayers. The sacrifice remains unconsumed.

As they continue their frenzied devotions, the crafty priests are continually trying to devise some means by which they may kindle a fire upon the altar and lead the people to believe that the fire has come direct from Baal. But Elijah watches every movement; and the priests, hoping against hope for some opportunity to deceive, continue to carry on their senseless ceremonies.

"It came to pass at noon, that Elijah mocked them, and said, Cry aloud: for he is a god; either he is talking, or he is pursuing, or he is in a journey, or peradventure he sleepeth, and must be awaked. And they cried aloud, and cut themselves after their manner with knives and lancets, till the blood gushed out upon them. And it came to pass, when midday was past, and they prophesied until the time of the offering of the evening sacrifice, that there was neither voice, nor any to answer, nor any that regarded."

Gladly would Satan have come to the help of those whom he had deceived, and who were devoted to his service. Gladly would he have sent the lightning to kindle their sacrifice. But Jehovah has set Satan's bounds, restrained his power, and not all the enemy's devices can convey one spark to Baal's altar.

At last, their voices hoarse with shouting, their garments stained with blood from self-inflicted wounds, the priests become desperate. With unabated frenzy they now mingle with their pleading terrible cursings of their sun-god, and Elijah continues to watch intently; for he knows that if by any device the priests should succeed in kindling their altar fire, he would instantly be torn in pieces.

Evening draws on. The prophets of Baal are weary, faint, confused. One suggests one thing, and another something else, until finally they cease their efforts. Their shrieks and curses no longer resound over Carmel. In despair they retire from the contest.

All day long the people have witnessed the demonstrations of the baffled priests. They have beheld their wild leaping round the altar, as if they would grasp the burning rays of the sun to serve their purpose. They have looked with horror on the frightful, self-inflicted mutilations of the priests, and have had opportunity to reflect on the follies of idol worship. Many in the throng are weary of the exhibitions of demonism, and they now await with deepest interest the movements of Elijah.

It is the hour of the evening sacrifice, and Elijah bids the people, "Come near unto me." As they tremblingly draw near, he turns to the broken-down altar where once men worshiped the God of heaven, and repairs it. To him this heap of ruins is more precious than all the magnificent altars of heathendom.

In the reconstruction of this ancient altar, Elijah revealed his respect for the covenant that the Lord made with Israel when they crossed the Jordan into the Promised Land. Choosing "twelve stones, according to the number of the tribes of the sons of Jacob, . . . he built an altar in the name of the Lord."

The disappointed priests of Baal, exhausted by their vain efforts, wait to see what Elijah will do. They hate the prophet for proposing a test that has exposed the weakness and inefficiency of their gods; yet they fear his power. The people, fearful also, and almost breathless with expectancy, watch while Elijah continues his preparations. The calm demeanor of the prophet stands out in sharp contrast with the fanatical, senseless frenzy of the followers of Baal.

The altar completed, the prophet makes a trench about it, and, having put the wood in order and prepared the bullock, he lays the victim on the altar and commands the people to flood the sacrifice and the altar with water. "Fill four barrels," he directed, "and pour it on the burnt sacrifice, and on the wood. And he said, Do it the second time. And they did it the second time. And he said, Do it the third time. And they did it the third time. And the water ran round about the altar; and he filled the trench also with water."

Reminding the people of the long-continued apostasy that has awakened the wrath of Jehovah, Elijah calls upon them to humble their hearts and turn to the God of their fathers, that the curse upon the land of Israel may be removed. Then, bowing reverently before the unseen God, he raises his hands toward heaven and offers a simple prayer. Baal's priests have screamed and foamed and leaped, from early morning until late in the afternoon; but as Elijah prays, no senseless shrieks resound over Carmel's height. He prays as if he knows Jehovah is there, a witness to the scene, a listener to his appeal. The prophets of Baal have prayed wildly, incoherently. Elijah prays simply and fervently, asking God to show His superiority over Baal, that Israel may be led to turn to Him.

"Lord God of Abraham, Isaac, and of Israel," the prophet pleads, "let it be known this day that Thou art God in Israel, and that I am Thy servant, and that I have done all these things at Thy word. Hear me, O Lord, hear me, that this people may know that Thou art the Lord God, and that Thou hast turned their heart back again."

In the crisis the dauntless prophet Elijah saw his faith rewarded as God sent fire to burn the offering.
© P.P.P.A.   JOHN STEEL, ARTIST

A silence, oppressive in its solemnity, rests upon all. The priests of Baal tremble with terror. Conscious of their guilt, they look for swift retribution.

No sooner is the prayer of Elijah ended than flames of fire, like brilliant flashes of lightning, descend from heaven upon the upreared altar, consuming the sacrifice, licking up the water in the trench, and consuming even the stones of the altar. The brilliancy of the blaze illumines the mountain and dazzles the eyes of the multitude. In the valleys below, where many are watching in anxious suspense the movements of those above, the descent of fire is clearly seen, and all are amazed at the sight. It resembles the pillar of fire which at the Red Sea separated the children of Israel from the Egyptian host.

The people on the mount prostrate themselves in awe before the unseen God. They dare not continue to look upon the Heaven-sent fire. They fear that they themselves will be consumed; and, convicted of their duty to acknowledge the God of Elijah as the God of their fathers, to whom they owe allegiance, they cry out together as with one voice, "The Lord, He is the God; the Lord, He is the God." With startling distinctness the cry resounds over the mountain and echoes in the plain below. At last Israel is aroused, undeceived, penitent. At last the people see how greatly they have dishonored God. The character of Baal worship, in contrast with the reasonable service required by the true God, stands fully revealed. The people recognize God's justice and mercy in withholding the dew and the rain until they have been brought to confess His name. They are ready now to admit that the God of Elijah is above every idol.

The priests of Baal witness with consternation the wonderful revelation of Jehovah's power. Yet even in their discomfiture and in the presence of divine glory, they refuse to repent of their evil-doing. They would still remain the prophets of Baal. Thus they showed themselves ripe for destruction. That repentant Israel may be protected from the allurements of those who have taught them to worship Baal, Elijah is directed by the Lord to destroy these false teachers. The anger of the people has already been aroused against the leaders in transgression; and when Elijah gives the command, "Take the prophets of Baal; let not one of them escape," they are ready to obey. They seize the priests, and take them to the brook Kishon, and there, before the close of the day that marked the beginning of decided reform, the ministers of Baal are slain. Not one is permitted to live.

chapter 12

This chapter is based on 1 Kings 18:41-46; 19:1-8.

From Jezreel to Horeb

WITH the slaying of the prophets of Baal, the way was opened for carrying forward a mighty spiritual reformation among the ten tribes of the northern kingdom. Elijah had set before the people their apostasy; he had called upon them to humble their hearts and turn to the Lord. The judgments of Heaven had been executed; the people had confessed their sins, and had acknowledged the God of their fathers as the living God; and now the curse of Heaven was to be withdrawn, and the temporal blessings of life renewed. The land was to be refreshed with rain. "Get thee up, eat and drink," Elijah said to Ahab; "for there is a sound of abundance of rain." Then the prophet went to the top of the mount to pray.

It was not because of any outward evidence that the showers were about to fall, that Elijah could so confidently bid Ahab prepare for rain. The prophet saw no clouds in the heavens; he heard no thunder. He simply spoke the word that the Spirit of the Lord had moved him to speak in response to his own strong faith. Throughout the day he had unflinchingly performed the will of God and had revealed his implicit confidence in the prophecies of God's word; and now, having done all that was in his power to do, he knew that Heaven would freely bestow the blessings foretold. The same God who had sent the drought had promised an abundance of rain as the reward of rightdoing; and now Elijah waited for the promised outpouring. In an attitude of humility, "his face between his knees," he interceded with God in behalf of penitent Israel.

Again and again Elijah sent his servant to a point overlooking the Mediterranean, to learn whether there were any visible token that God had heard his prayer. Each time the servant returned with the word, "There is nothing." The prophet did not become impatient or lose faith, but continued his earnest pleading. Six times the servant returned with the word that there was no sign of rain in the brassy heavens. Undaunted, Elijah sent him forth once more; and this time the servant returned with the word, "Behold, there ariseth a little cloud out of the sea, like a man's hand."

This was enough. Elijah did not wait for the heavens to gather blackness. In that small cloud he beheld by faith an abundance of rain; and he acted in harmony with his faith, sending his servant quickly to Ahab with the message, "Prepare thy chariot, and get thee down, that the rain stop thee not."

It was because Elijah was a man of large faith that God could use him in this grave crisis in the history of Israel. As he prayed, his faith reached out and grasped the promises of Heaven, and he persevered in prayer until his petitions were answered. He did not wait for the full evidence that God had heard him, but was willing to venture all on the slightest token of divine favor. And yet what he was enabled to do under God, all may do in their sphere of activity in God's service; for of the prophet from the mountains of Gilead it is written: "Elias was a man subject to like passions as we are, and he prayed earnestly that it might not rain: and it rained not on the earth by the space of three years and six months." James 5:17.

Faith such as this is needed in the world today—faith that will lay hold on the promises of God's word and refuse to let go until Heaven hears. Faith such as this connects us closely with Heaven, and brings us strength for coping with the powers of darkness. Through faith God's children have "subdued kingdoms, wrought righteousness, obtained promises, stopped the mouths of lions, quenched the violence of fire, escaped the edge of the sword, out of weakness were made strong, waxed valiant in fight, turned to flight the armies of the aliens." Hebrews 11:33, 34. And through faith we today are to reach the heights of God's purpose for us. "If thou canst believe, all things are possible to him that believeth." Mark 9:23.

Faith is an essential element of prevailing prayer. "He that cometh to God must believe that He is, and that He is a rewarder of them that diligently seek Him." "If we ask anything according to His will, He heareth us: and if we know that He hear us, whatsoever we ask, we know that we have the petitions that we desired of Him." Hebrews 11:6; 1 John 5:14, 15. With the persevering faith of Jacob, with the unyielding persistence of Elijah, we may present our petitions to the Father, claiming all that He has promised. The honor of His throne is staked for the fulfillment of His word.

The shades of night were gathering about Mount Carmel as Ahab prepared for the descent. "It came to pass in the meanwhile, that the heaven was black with clouds and wind, and there was a great rain. And Ahab rode, and went to Jezreel." As he journeyed toward the royal city through the darkness and the blinding rain, Ahab was unable to see his way before him. Elijah, who, as the prophet of God, had that day humiliated Ahab before his subjects and slain his idolatrous priests, still acknowledged him as Israel's king; and now, as an act of homage, and strengthened by the power of God, he ran before the royal chariot, guiding the king to the entrance of the city.

In this gracious act of God's messenger shown to a wicked king is a lesson for all who claim to be servants of God, but who are exalted in their own estimation. There are those who feel above performing duties that to them appear menial. They hesitate to perform even needful service, fearing that they will be found doing the work of a servant. These have much to learn from the example of Elijah. By his word the treasures of heaven had been for three years withheld from the earth; he had been signally honored of God as, in answer to his prayer on Carmel, fire had flashed from heaven and consumed the sacrifice; his hand had executed the judgment of God in slaying the idolatrous prophets; his petition for rain had been granted. And yet, after the signal triumphs with which God had been pleased to honor his public ministry, he was willing to perform the service of a menial.

At the gate of Jezreel, Elijah and Ahab separated. The prophet, choosing to remain outside the walls, wrapped himself in his mantle, and lay down upon the bare earth to sleep. The king, passing within, soon reached the shelter of his palace and there related to his wife the wonderful events of the day and the marvelous revelation of divine power that had proved to Israel that Jehovah is the true God and Elijah His chosen messenger. As Ahab told the queen of the slaying of the idolatrous prophets, Jezebel, hardened and impenitent, became infuriated. She refused to recognize in the events on Carmel the overruling providence of God, and, still defiant, she boldly declared that Elijah should die.

That night a messenger aroused the weary prophet and delivered to him the word of Jezebel: "So let the gods do to me, and more also, if I make not thy life as the life of one of them by tomorrow about this time."

It would seem that after showing courage so undaunted, after triumphing so completely over king and priests and people, Elijah could never afterward have given way to despondency nor been awed into timidity. But he who had been blessed with so many evidences of God's loving care was not above the frailties of mankind, and in this dark hour his faith and courage forsook him. Bewildered, he started from his slumber. The rain was pouring from the heavens, and darkness was on every side. Forgetting that three years before, God had directed his course to a place of refuge from the hatred of Jezebel and the search of Ahab, the prophet now fled for his life. Reaching Beersheba, he "left his servant there. But he himself went a day's journey into the wilderness."

Elijah should not have fled from his post of duty. He should have met the threat of Jezebel with an appeal for protection to the One who had commissioned him to vindicate the honor of Jehovah. He should have told the messenger that the God in whom he trusted would protect him against the hatred of the queen. Only a few hours had passed since he had witnessed a wonderful manifestation of divine power, and this should have given him assurance that he would not now be forsaken. Had he remained where he was, had he made God his refuge and strength, standing steadfast for the truth, he would have been shielded from harm. The Lord would have given him another signal victory by sending His judgments on Jezebel; and the impression made on the king and the people would have wrought a great reformation.

Elijah had expected much from the miracle wrought on Carmel. He had hoped that after this display of God's power, Jezebel would no longer have influence over the mind of Ahab, and that there would be a speedy reform throughout

Israel. All day on Carmel's height he had toiled without food. Yet when he guided the chariot of Ahab to the gate of Jezreel, his courage was strong, despite the physical strain under which he had labored.

But a reaction such as frequently follows high faith and glorious success was pressing upon Elijah. He feared that the reformation begun on Carmel might not be lasting; and depression seized him. He had been exalted to Pisgah's top; now he was in the valley. While under the inspiration of the Almighty, he had stood the severest trial of faith; but in this time of discouragement, with Jezebel's threat sounding in his ears, and Satan still apparently prevailing through the plotting of this wicked woman, he lost his hold on God. He had been exalted above measure, and the reaction was tremendous. Forgetting God, Elijah fled on and on, until he found himself in a dreary waste, alone. Utterly wearied, he sat down to rest under a juniper tree. And sitting there, he requested for himself that he might die. "It is enough; now, O Lord," he said, "take away my life; for I am not better than my fathers." A fugitive, far from the dwelling places of men, his spirits crushed by bitter disappointment, he desired never again to look upon the face of man. At last, utterly exhausted, he fell asleep.

Into the experience of all there come times of keen disappointment and utter discouragement—days when sorrow is the portion, and it is hard to believe that God is still the kind benefactor of His earthborn children; days when troubles harass the soul, till death seems preferable to life. It is then that many lose their hold on God and are brought into the slavery of doubt, the bondage of unbelief. Could we at such times discern with spiritual insight the meaning of God's providences we should see angels seeking to save us from ourselves, striving to plant our feet upon a foundation more firm than the everlasting hills, and new faith, new life, would spring into being.

The faithful Job, in the day of his affliction and darkness, declared:

"Let the day perish wherein I was born."
"O that my grief were throughly weighed,
  And my calamity laid in the balances together!"

"O that I might have my request;
  And that God would grant me the thing that I long for!
  Even that it would please God to destroy me;
  That He would let loose His hand, and cut me off!
  Then should I yet have comfort."

"I will not refrain my mouth;
  I will speak in the anguish of my spirit;
  I will complain in the bitterness of my soul."

"My soul chooseth . . . death rather than my life.
  I loathe it;
  I would not live alway:
  Let me alone;
  For my days are vanity."
            Job 3:3; 6:2, 8-10; 7:11, 15, 16.

But though weary of life, Job was not allowed to die. To him were pointed out the possibilities of the future, and there was given him the message of hope:

"Thou shalt be steadfast, and shalt not fear:
  Because thou shalt forget thy misery,
  And remember it as waters that pass away:

And thine age shall be clearer than the noonday;
Thou shalt shine forth, thou shalt be as the morning.
And thou shalt be secure,
Because there is hope. . . .
Thou shalt lie down,
And none shall make thee afraid;
Yea, many shall make suit unto thee.
But the eyes of the wicked shall fail,
And they shall not escape,
And their hope shall be as the giving up of the ghost."

Job 11:15-20.

From the depths of discouragement and despondency Job rose to the heights of implicit trust in the mercy and the saving power of God. Triumphantly he declared:

"Though He slay me, yet will I trust in Him: . . .
He also shall be my salvation."

"I know that my Redeemer liveth,
And that He shall stand at the latter day upon the earth:
And though after my skin worms destroy this body,
Yet in my flesh shall I see God:
Whom I shall see for myself,
And mine eyes shall behold, and not another."

Job 13:15, 16; 19:25-27.

"The Lord answered Job out of the whirlwind" (Job 38:1), and revealed to His servant the might of His power. When Job caught a glimpse of his Creator, he abhorred himself and repented in dust and ashes. Then the Lord was able to bless him abundantly and to make his last years the best of his life.

Hope and courage are essential to perfect service for God. These are the fruit of faith. Despondency is sinful and unreasonable. God is able and willing "more abundantly"

Out of suffering and loss, Job learned
such firm reliance on God that he said,
"Though He slay me, yet will I trust in Him."

(Hebrews 6:17) to bestow upon His servants the strength they need for test and trial. The plans of the enemies of His work may seem to be well laid and firmly established, but God can overthrow the strongest of these. And this He does in His own time and way, when He sees that the faith of His servants has been sufficiently tested.

For the disheartened there is a sure remedy—faith, prayer, work. Faith and activity will impart assurance and satisfaction that will increase day by day. Are you tempted to give way to feelings of anxious foreboding or utter despondency? In the darkest days, when appearances seem most forbidding, fear not. Have faith in God. He knows your need. He has all power. His infinite love and compassion never weary. Fear not that He will fail of fulfilling His promise. He is eternal truth. Never will He change the covenant He has made with those who love Him. And He will bestow upon His faithful servants the measure of efficiency that their need demands. The apostle Paul has testified: "He said unto me, My grace is sufficient for thee: for My strength is made perfect in weakness. . . . Therefore I take pleasure in infirmities, in reproaches, in necessities, in persecutions, in distresses for Christ's sake: for when I am weak, then am I strong." 2 Corinthians 12:9, 10.

Did God forsake Elijah in his hour of trial? Oh, no! He loved His servant no less when Elijah felt himself forsaken of God and man than when, in answer to his prayer, fire flashed from heaven and illuminated the mountaintop. And now, as Elijah slept, a soft touch and a pleasant voice awoke him. He started up in terror, as if to flee, fearing that the enemy had discovered him. But the pitying face bending over him was not the face of an enemy, but of a friend. God had sent an angel from heaven with food for His servant. "Arise and eat," the angel said. "And he looked, and, behold, there was a cake baken on the coals, and a cruse of water at his head."

After Elijah had partaken of the refreshment prepared for him, he slept again. A second time the angel came. Touching the exhausted man, he said with pitying tenderness, "Arise and eat; because the journey is too great for thee." "And he arose, and did eat and drink;" and in the strength of that food he was able to journey "forty days and forty nights unto Horeb the mount of God," where he found refuge in a cave.

chapter 13

This chapter is based on 1 Kings 19:9-18.

"What Doest Thou Here?"

ELIJAH'S retreat on Mount Horeb, though hidden from man, was known to God; and the weary and discouraged prophet was not left to struggle alone with the powers of darkness that were pressing upon him. At the entrance to the cave wherein Elijah had taken refuge, God met with him, through a mighty angel sent to inquire into his needs and to make plain the divine purpose for Israel.

Not until Elijah had learned to trust wholly in God could he complete his work for those who had been seduced into Baal worship. The signal triumph on the heights of Carmel had opened the way for still greater victories; yet from the wonderful opportunities opening before him, Elijah had been turned away by the threat of Jezebel. The man of God must be made to understand the weakness of his present position as compared with the vantage ground the Lord would have him occupy.

God met His tried servant with the inquiry, "What doest thou here, Elijah?" I sent you to the brook Cherith and after-

Elijah, standing at the mouth of the
cave, waited through tempest and
earthquake for God's promised word.

ward to the widow of Sarepta. I commissioned you to return to Israel and to stand before the idolatrous priests on Carmel, and I girded you with strength to guide the chariot of the king to the gate of Jezreel. But who sent you on this hasty flight into the wilderness? What errand have you here?

In bitterness of soul Elijah mourned out his complaint: "I have been very jealous for the Lord God of hosts: for the children of Israel have forsaken Thy covenant, thrown down Thine altars, and slain Thy prophets with the sword; and I, even I only, am left; and they seek my life, to take it away."

Calling upon the prophet to leave the cave, the angel bade him stand before the Lord on the mount, and listen to His word. "And, behold, the Lord passed by, and a great and strong wind rent the mountains, and brake in pieces the rocks before the Lord; but the Lord was not in the wind: and after the wind an earthquake; but the Lord was not in the earthquake: and after the earthquake a fire; but the Lord was not in the fire: and after the fire a still small voice. And it was so, when Elijah heard it, that he wrapped his face in his mantle, and went out, and stood in the entering in of the cave."

Not in mighty manifestations of divine power, but by "a still small voice," did God choose to reveal Himself to His servant. He desired to teach Elijah that it is not always the work that makes the greatest demonstration that is most successful in accomplishing His purpose. While Elijah waited for the revelation of the Lord, a tempest rolled, the lightnings flashed, and a devouring fire swept by; but God was not in all this. Then there came a still, small voice, and the prophet covered his head before the presence of the Lord. His petulance was silenced, his spirit softened and subdued. He now knew that a quiet trust, a firm reliance on God, would ever find for him a present help in time of need.

It is not always the most learned presentation of God's truth that convicts and converts the soul. Not by eloquence or logic are men's hearts reached, but by the sweet influences of the Holy Spirit, which operate quietly yet surely in transforming and developing character. It is the still, small voice of the Spirit of God that has power to change the heart.

"What doest thou here, Elijah?" the voice inquired; and again the prophet answered, "I have been very jealous for the Lord God of hosts: because the children of Israel have forsaken Thy covenant, thrown down Thine altars, and slain Thy prophets with the sword; and I, even I only, am left; and they seek my life, to take it away."

The Lord answered Elijah that the wrongdoers in Israel should not go unpunished. Men were to be especially chosen to fulfill the divine purpose in the punishment of the idolatrous kingdom. There was stern work to be done, that all might be given opportunity to take their position on the side of the true God. Elijah himself was to return to Israel, and share with others the burden of bringing about a reformation.

"Go," the Lord commanded Elijah, "return on thy way to the wilderness of Damascus: and when thou comest, anoint Hazael to be king over Syria: and Jehu the son of Nimshi shalt thou anoint to be king over Israel: and Elisha the son of Shaphat of Abel-meholah shalt thou anoint to be prophet in thy room. And it shall come to pass, that him that escapeth the sword of Hazael shall Jehu slay: and him that escapeth from the sword of Jehu shall Elisha slay."

Elijah had thought that he alone in Israel was a worshiper

of the true God. But He who reads the hearts of all revealed to the prophet that there were many others who, through the long years of apostasy, had remained true to Him. "I have left Me," God said, "seven thousand in Israel, all the knees which have not bowed unto Baal, and every mouth which hath not kissed him."

From Elijah's experience during those days of discouragement and apparent defeat there are many lessons to be drawn, lessons invaluable to the servants of God in this age, marked as it is by general departure from right. The apostasy prevailing today is similar to that which in the prophet's day overspread Israel. In the exaltation of the human above the divine, in the praise of popular leaders, in the worship of mammon, and in the placing of the teachings of science above the truths of revelation, multitudes today are following after Baal. Doubt and unbelief are exercising their baleful influence over mind and heart, and many are substituting for the oracles of God the theories of men. It is publicly taught that we have reached a time when human reason should be exalted above the teachings of the Word. The law of God, the divine standard of righteousness, is declared to be of no effect. The enemy of all truth is working with deceptive power to cause men and women to place human institutions where God should be, and to forget that which was ordained for the happiness and salvation of mankind.

Yet this apostasy, widespread as it has come to be, is not universal. Not all in the world are lawless and sinful; not all have taken sides with the enemy. God has many thousands who have not bowed the knee to Baal, many who long to understand more fully in regard to Christ and the law, many who are hoping against hope that Jesus will come soon to end the reign of sin and death. And there are many who have been worshiping Baal ignorantly, but with whom the Spirit of God is still striving.

These need the personal help of those who have learned to know God and the power of His word. In such a time as this, every child of God should be actively engaged in helping others. As those who have an understanding of Bible truth try to seek out the men and women who are longing for light, angels of God will attend them. And where angels go, none need fear to move forward. As a result of the faithful efforts of consecrated workers, many will be turned from idolatry to the worship of the living God. Many will cease to pay homage to man-made institutions and will take their stand fearlessly on the side of God and His law.

Much depends on the unceasing activity of those who are true and loyal, and for this reason Satan puts forth every possible effort to thwart the divine purpose to be wrought out through the obedient. He causes some to lose sight of their high and holy mission, and to become satisfied with the pleasures of this life. He leads them to settle down at ease, or, for the sake of greater worldly advantages, to remove from places where they might be a power for good. Others he causes to flee in discouragement from duty, because of opposition or persecution. But all such are regarded by Heaven with tenderest pity. To every child of God whose voice the enemy of souls had succeeded in silencing, the question is addressed, "What doest thou here?" I commissioned you to go into all the world and preach the gospel, to prepare a people for the day of God. Why are you here? Who sent you?

The joy set before Christ, the joy that sustained Him through sacrifice and suffering, was the joy of seeing sinners saved. This should be the joy of every follower of His, the spur to his ambition. Those who realize, even in a limited degree, what redemption means to them and to their fellow men, will comprehend in some measure the vast needs of humanity. Their hearts will be moved to compassion as they see the moral and spiritual destitution of thousands who are under the shadow of a terrible doom, in comparison with which physical suffering fades into nothingness.

Of families, as of individuals, the question is asked, "What doest thou here?" In many churches there are families well instructed in the truths of God's word, who might widen the sphere of their influence by moving to places in need of the ministry they are capable of giving. God calls for Christian families to go into the dark places of the earth and work wisely and perseveringly for those who are enshrouded in spiritual gloom. To answer this call requires self-sacrifice. While many are waiting to have every obstacle removed, souls are dying, without hope and without God. For the sake of worldly advantage, for the sake of acquiring scientific knowledge, men are willing to venture into pestilential regions and to endure hardship and privation. Where are those who are willing to do as much for the sake of telling others of the Saviour?

If, under trying circumstances, men of spiritual power, pressed beyond measure, become discouraged and desponding, if at times they see nothing desirable in life, that they should choose it, this is nothing strange or new. Let all such remember that one of the mightiest of the prophets fled for his life before the rage of an infuriated woman. A fugitive, weary and travel-worn, bitter disappointment crushing his spirits, he asked that he might die. But it was when hope was gone and his lifework seemed threatened with defeat, that he learned one of the most precious lessons of his life. In the hour of his greatest weakness he learned the need and the possibility of trusting God under circumstances the most forbidding.

Those who, while spending their life energies in self-sacrificing labor, are tempted to give way to despondency and distrust, may gather courage from the experience of Elijah. God's watchful care, His love, His power, are especially manifest in behalf of His servants whose zeal is misunderstood or unappreciated, whose counsels and reproofs are slighted, and whose efforts toward reform are repaid with hatred and opposition.

It is at the time of greatest weakness that Satan assails the soul with the fiercest temptations. It was thus that he hoped to prevail over the Son of God; for by this policy he had gained many victories over man. When the willpower weakened and faith failed, then those who had stood long and valiantly for the right yielded to temptation. Moses, wearied with forty years of wandering and unbelief, lost for a moment his hold on Infinite Power. He failed just on the borders of the Promised Land. So with Elijah. He who had maintained his trust in Jehovah during the years of drought and famine, he who had stood undaunted before Ahab, he who throughout that trying day on Carmel had stood before the whole nation of Israel the sole witness to the true God, in a moment of weariness allowed the fear of death to overcome his faith in God.

And so it is today. When we are encompassed with doubt, perplexed by circumstances, or afflicted by poverty or distress, Satan seeks to shake our confidence in Jehovah. It is then that he arrays before us our mistakes and tempts us to distrust God, to question His love. He hopes to discourage the soul and break our hold on God.

Those who, standing in the forefront of the conflict, are impelled by the Holy Spirit to do a special work, will frequently feel a reaction when the pressure is removed. Despondency may shake the most heroic faith and weaken the most steadfast will. But God understands, and He still pities and loves. He reads the motives and the purposes of the heart. To wait patiently, to trust when everything looks dark, is the lesson that the leaders in God's work need to learn. Heaven will not fail them in their day of adversity. Nothing is apparently more helpless, yet really more invincible, than the soul that feels its nothingness and relies wholly on God.

Not alone for men in positions of large responsibility is the lesson of Elijah's experience in learning anew how to trust God in the hour of trial. He who was Elijah's strength is strong to uphold every struggling child of His, no matter how weak. Of everyone He expects loyalty, and to everyone He grants power according to the need. In his own strength man is strengthless; but in the might of God he may be strong to overcome evil and to help others to overcome. Satan can never gain advantage of him who makes God his defense. "Surely, shall one say, in the Lord have I righteousness and strength." Isaiah 45:24.

Fellow Christian, Satan knows your weakness; therefore cling to Jesus. Abiding in God's love, you may stand every test. The righteousness of Christ alone can give you power to stem the tide of evil that is sweeping over the world. Bring faith into your experience. Faith lightens every burden, relieves every weariness. Providences that are now mysterious you may solve by continued trust in God. Walk by faith in the path He marks out. Trials will come, but go forward. This will strengthen your faith and fit you for service. The records of sacred history are written, not merely that we may read and wonder, but that the same faith which wrought in God's servants of old may work in us. In no less marked manner will the Lord work now, wherever there are hearts of faith to be channels of His power.

To us, as to Peter, the word is spoken, "Satan hath desired to have you, that he may sift you as wheat: but I have prayed for thee, that thy faith fail not." Luke 22:31, 32. Christ will never abandon those for whom He has died. We may leave Him and be overwhelmed with temptation, but Christ can never turn from one for whom He has paid the ransom of His own life. Could our spiritual vision be quickened, we should see souls bowed under oppression and burdened with grief, pressed as a cart beneath sheaves, and ready to die in discouragement. We should see angels flying quickly to the aid of these tempted ones, forcing back the hosts of evil that encompass them, and placing their feet on the sure foundation. The battles waging between the two armies are as real as those fought by the armies of this world, and on the issue of the spiritual conflict eternal destinies depend.

In the vision of the prophet Ezekiel there was the appearance of a hand beneath the wings of the cherubim. This is to teach God's servants that it is divine power that gives success. Those whom God employs as His messengers are not to feel that His work is dependent on them. Finite beings are not left to carry this burden of responsibility. He who slumbers not, who is continually at work for the accomplishment of His designs, will carry forward His work. He will thwart the purposes of wicked men and will bring to confusion the counsels of those who plot mischief against His people. He who is the King, the Lord of hosts, sitteth between the cherubim, and amidst the strife and tumult of nations He guards His children still. When the strongholds of kings shall be overthrown, when the arrows of wrath shall strike through the hearts of His enemies, His people will be safe in His hands.

chapter 14

"In the Spirit and Power of Elias"

THROUGH the long centuries that have passed since Elijah's time, the record of his lifework has brought inspiration and courage to those who have been called to stand for the right in the midst of apostasy. And for us, "upon whom the ends of the world are come" (1 Corinthians 10:11), it has special significance. History is being repeated. The world today has its Ahabs and its Jezebels. The present age is one of idolatry, as verily as was that in which Elijah lived. No outward shrine may be visible; there may be no image for the eye to rest upon; yet thousands are following after the gods of this world—after riches, fame, pleasure, and the pleasing fables that permit man to follow the inclinations of the unregenerate heart. Multitudes have a wrong conception of God and His attributes, and are as truly serving a false god as were the worshipers of Baal. Many even of those who claim to be Christians have allied themselves with influences that are unalterably opposed to God and His truth. Thus they are led to turn away from the divine and to exalt the human.

12—P.A.K.

The prevailing spirit of our time is one of infidelity and apostasy—a spirit of avowed illumination because of a knowledge of truth, but in reality of the blindest presumption. Human theories are exalted and placed where God and His law should be. Satan tempts men and women to disobey, with the promise that in disobedience they will find liberty and freedom that will make them as gods. There is seen a spirit of opposition to the plain word of God, of idolatrous exaltation of human wisdom above divine revelation. Men have allowed their minds to become so darkened and confused by conformity to worldly customs and influences that they seem to have lost all power to discriminate between light and darkness, truth and error. So far have they departed from the right way that they hold the opinions of a few philosophers, so-called, to be more trustworthy than the truths of the Bible. The entreaties and promises of God's word, its threatenings against disobedience and idolatry—these seem powerless to melt their hearts. A faith such as actuated Paul, Peter, and John they regard as old-fashioned, mystical, and unworthy of the intelligence of modern thinkers.

In the beginning, God gave His law to mankind as a means of attaining happiness and eternal life. Satan's only hope of thwarting the purpose of God is to lead men and women to disobey this law, and his constant effort has been to misrepresent its teachings and belittle its importance. His master stroke has been an attempt to change the law itself, so as to lead men to violate its precepts while professing to obey it.

One writer has likened the attempt to change the law of God to an ancient mischievous practice of turning in a wrong direction a signpost erected at an important junction where two roads met. The perplexity and hardship which this practice often caused was great.

A signpost was erected by God for those journeying through this world. One arm of this signpost pointed out willing obedience to the Creator as the road to felicity and life, while the other arm indicated disobedience as the path to misery and death. The way to happiness was as clearly defined as was the way to the city of refuge under the Jewish dispensation. But in an evil hour for our race, the great enemy of all good turned the signpost around, and multitudes have mistaken the way.

Through Moses the Lord instructed the Israelites: "Verily My Sabbaths ye shall keep: for it is a sign between Me and you throughout your generations; that ye may know that I am the Lord that doth sanctify you. Ye shall keep the Sabbath therefore; for it is holy unto you: everyone that defileth it shall surely be put to death: for whosoever doeth any work . . . in the Sabbath day, he shall surely be put to death. Wherefore the children of Israel shall keep the Sabbath, to observe the Sabbath throughout their generations, for a perpetual covenant. It is a sign between Me and the children of Israel forever: for in six days the Lord made heaven and earth, and on the seventh day He rested, and was refreshed." Exodus 31:13-17.

In these words the Lord clearly defined obedience as the way to the City of God; but the man of sin has changed the signpost, making it point in the wrong direction. He has set up a false sabbath and has caused men and women to think that by resting on it they were obeying the command of the Creator.

God has declared that the seventh day is the Sabbath of the Lord. When "the heavens and the earth were finished," He exalted this day as a memorial of His creative work. Resting on the seventh day "from all His work which He had made," "God blessed the seventh day, and sanctified it." Genesis 2:1-3.

At the time of the Exodus from Egypt, the Sabbath institution was brought prominently before the people of God. While they were still in bondage, their taskmasters had attempted to force them to labor on the Sabbath by increasing the amount of work required each week. Again and again the conditions of labor had been made harder and more exacting. But the Israelites were delivered from bondage and brought to a place where they might observe unmolested all the precepts of Jehovah. At Sinai the law was spoken; and a copy of it, on two tables of stone, "written with the finger of God" was delivered to Moses. Exodus 31:18. And through nearly forty years of wandering the Israelites were constantly reminded of God's appointed rest day, by the withholding of the manna every seventh day and the miraculous preservation of the double portion that fell on the preparation day.

Before entering the Promised Land, the Israelites were admonished by Moses to "keep the Sabbath day to sanctify it." Deuteronomy 5:12. The Lord designed that by a faithful observance of the Sabbath command, Israel should continually be reminded of their accountability to Him as their Creator and their Redeemer. While they should keep the Sabbath in the proper spirit, idolatry could not exist; but should the claims of this precept of the Decalogue be set aside as no longer binding, the Creator would be forgotten and men would worship other gods. "I gave them My Sabbaths," God declared, "to be a sign between Me and them, that they might know that I am the Lord that sanctify them." Yet "they despised My judgments, and walked not in My statutes, but polluted My Sabbaths: for their heart went after their idols." And in His appeal to them to return to Him, He called their attention anew to the importance of keeping the Sabbath holy. "I am the Lord your God," He said; "walk in My statutes, and keep My judgments, and do them; and hallow My Sabbaths; and they shall be a sign between Me and you, that ye may know that I am the Lord your God." Ezekiel 20:12, 16, 19, 20.

In calling the attention of Judah to the sins that finally brought upon them the Babylonian Captivity, the Lord declared: "Thou hast . . . profaned My Sabbaths." "Therefore have I poured out Mine indignation upon them; I have consumed them with the fire of My wrath: their own way have I recompensed upon their heads." Ezekiel 22:8, 31.

At the restoration of Jerusalem, in the days of Nehemiah, Sabbathbreaking was met with the stern inquiry, "Did not your fathers thus, and did not our God bring all this evil upon us, and upon this city? yet ye bring more wrath upon Israel by profaning the Sabbath." Nehemiah 13:18.

Christ, during His earthly ministry, emphasized the binding claims of the Sabbath; in all His teaching He showed reverence for the institution He Himself had given. In His days the Sabbath had become so perverted that its observance reflected the character of selfish and arbitrary men rather than the character of God. Christ set aside the false teaching by which those who claimed to know God had misrepresented Him. Although followed with merciless hostility by the rabbis,

He did not even appear to conform to their requirements, but went straight forward keeping the Sabbath according to the law of God.

In unmistakable language He testified to His regard for the law of Jehovah. "Think not that I am come to destroy the law, or the prophets," He said; "I am not come to destroy, but to fulfill. For verily I say unto you, Till heaven and earth pass, one jot or one tittle shall in no wise pass from the law, till all be fulfilled. Whosoever therefore shall break one of these least commandments, and shall teach men so, he shall be called the least in the kingdom of heaven: but whosoever shall do and teach them, the same shall be called great in the kingdom of heaven." Matthew 5:17-19.

During the Christian dispensation, the great enemy of man's happiness has made the Sabbath of the fourth commandment an object of special attack. Satan says, "I will work at cross purposes with God. I will empower my followers to set aside God's memorial, the seventh-day Sabbath. Thus I will show the world that the day sanctified and blessed by God has been changed. That day shall not live in the minds of the people. I will obliterate the memory of it. I will place in its stead a day that does not bear the credentials of God, a day that cannot be a sign between God and His people. I will lead those who accept this day to place upon it the sanctity that God placed upon the seventh day.

"Through my vicegerent, I will exalt myself. The first day will be extolled, and the Protestant world will receive this spurious sabbath as genuine. Through the nonobservance of the Sabbath that God instituted, I will bring His law into contempt. The words, 'A sign between Me and you through-

While in Egyptian bondage the Israelites observed the Sabbath under hardship, frequently suffering extreme cruelty.

© P.P.P.A.   JOHN STEEL, ARTIST

out your generations,' I will make to serve on the side of my sabbath.

"Thus the world will become mine. I will be the ruler of the earth, the prince of the world. I will so control the minds under my power that God's Sabbath shall be a special object of contempt. A sign? I will make the observance of the seventh day a sign of disloyalty to the authorities of earth. Human laws will be made so stringent that men and women will not dare to observe the seventh-day Sabbath. For fear of wanting food and clothing, they will join with the world in transgressing God's law. The earth will be wholly under my dominion."

Through the setting up of a false sabbath, the enemy thought to change times and laws. But has he really succeeded in changing God's law? The words of the thirty-first chapter of Exodus are the answer. He who is the same yesterday, today, and forever, has declared of the seventh-day Sabbath: "It is a sign between Me and you throughout your generations." "It is a sign . . . forever." Exodus 31:13, 17. The changed signpost is pointing the wrong way, but God has not changed. He is still the mighty God of Israel. "Behold, the nations are as a drop of a bucket, and are counted as the small dust of the balance: behold, He taketh up the isles as a very little thing. And Lebanon is not sufficient to burn, nor the beasts thereof sufficient for a burnt offering. All nations before Him are as nothing; and they are counted to Him less than nothing, and vanity." Isaiah 40:15-17. And He is just as jealous for His law now as He was in the days of Ahab and Elijah.

But how is that law disregarded! Behold the world today in open rebellion against God. This is in truth a froward generation, filled with ingratitude, formalism, insincerity, pride, and apostasy. Men neglect the Bible and hate truth. Jesus sees His law rejected, His love despised, His ambassadors treated with indifference. He has spoken by His mercies, but these have been unacknowledged; He has spoken by warnings, but these have been unheeded. The temple courts of the human soul have been turned into places of unholy traffic. Selfishness, envy, pride, malice—all are cherished.

Many do not hesitate to sneer at the word of God. Those who believe that word just as it reads are held up to ridicule. There is a growing contempt for law and order, directly traceable to a violation of the plain commands of Jehovah. Violence and crime are the result of turning aside from the path of obedience. Behold the wretchedness and misery of multitudes who worship at the shrine of idols and who seek in vain for happiness and peace.

Behold the well-nigh universal disregard of the Sabbath commandment. Behold also the daring impiety of those who, while enacting laws to safeguard the supposed sanctity of the first day of the week, at the same time are making laws legalizing the liquor traffic. Wise above that which is written, they attempt to coerce the consciences of men, while lending their sanction to an evil that brutalizes and destroys the beings created in the image of God. It is Satan himself who inspires such legislation. He well knows that the curse of God will rest on those who exalt human enactments above the divine, and he does all in his power to lead men into the broad road that ends in destruction.

So long have men worshiped human opinions and human institutions that almost the whole world is following after idols. And he who has endeavored to change God's law is using every deceptive artifice to induce men and women to array themselves against God and against the sign by which the righteous are known. But the Lord will not always suffer His law to be broken and despised with impunity. There is a time coming when "the lofty looks of man shall be humbled, and the haughtiness of men shall be bowed down, and the Lord alone shall be exalted in that day." Isaiah 2:11. Skepticism may treat the claims of God's law with jest, scoffing, and denial. The spirit of worldliness may contaminate the many and control the few, the cause of God may hold its ground only by great exertion and continual sacrifice, yet in the end the truth will triumph gloriously.

In the closing work of God in the earth, the standard of His law will be again exalted. False religion may prevail, iniquity may abound, the love of many may wax cold, the cross of Calvary may be lost sight of, and darkness, like the pall of death, may spread over the world; the whole force of the popular current may be turned against the truth; plot after plot may be formed to overthrow the people of God; but in the hour of greatest peril the God of Elijah will raise up human instrumentalities to bear a message that will not be silenced. In the populous cities of the land, and in the places where men have gone to the greatest lengths in speaking against the Most High, the voice of stern rebuke will be heard. Boldly will men of God's appointment denounce the union of the church with the world. Earnestly will they call upon men and women to turn from the observance of a man-made institution to the observance of the true Sabbath. "Fear God, and give glory to Him," they will proclaim to every nation;

"for the hour of His judgment is come: and worship Him that made heaven, and earth, and the sea, and the fountains of waters. . . . If any man worship the beast and his image, and receive his mark in his forehead, or in his hand, the same shall drink of the wine of the wrath of God, which is poured out without mixture into the cup of His indignation." Revelation 14:7-10.

God will not break His covenant, nor alter the thing that has gone out of His lips. His word will stand fast forever as unalterable as His throne. At the judgment this covenant will be brought forth, plainly written with the finger of God, and the world will be arraigned before the bar of Infinite Justice to receive sentence.

Today, as in the days of Elijah, the line of demarcation between God's commandment-keeping people and the worshipers of false gods is clearly drawn. "How long halt ye between two opinions?" Elijah cried; "if the Lord be God, follow Him: but if Baal, then follow him." 1 Kings 18:21. And the message for today is: "Babylon the great is fallen, is fallen. . . . Come out of her, My people, that ye be not partakers of her sins, and that ye receive not of her plagues. For her sins have reached unto heaven, and God hath remembered her iniquities." Revelation 18:2, 4, 5.

The time is not far distant when the test will come to every soul. The observance of the false sabbath will be urged upon us. The contest will be between the commandments of God and the commandments of men. Those who have yielded step by step to worldly demands and conformed to worldly customs will then yield to the powers that be, rather than subject themselves to derision, insult, threatened imprisonment, and death. At that time the gold will be separated from the dross. True godliness will be clearly distinguished from the appearance and tinsel of it. Many a star that we have admired for its brilliance will then go out in darkness. Those who have assumed the ornaments of the sanctuary, but are not clothed with Christ's righteousness, will then appear in the shame of their own nakedness.

Among earth's inhabitants, scattered in every land, there are those who have not bowed the knee to Baal. Like the stars of heaven, which appear only at night, these faithful ones will shine forth when darkness covers the earth and gross darkness the people. In heathen Africa, in the Catholic lands of Europe and of South America, in China, in India, in the islands of the sea, and in all the dark corners of the earth, God has in reserve a firmanent of chosen ones that will yet shine forth amidst the darkness, revealing clearly to an apostate world the transforming power of obedience to His law. Even now they are appearing in every nation, among every tongue and people; and in the hour of deepest apostasy, when Satan's supreme effort is made to cause "all, both small and great, rich and poor, free and bond," to receive, under penalty of death, the sign of allegiance to a false rest day, these faithful ones, "blameless and harmless, the sons of God, without rebuke," will "shine as lights in the world." Revelation 13:16; Philippians 2:15. The darker the night, the more brilliantly will they shine.

What strange work Elijah would have done in numbering Israel at the time when God's judgments were falling upon the backsliding people! He could count only one on the Lord's side. But when he said, "I, even I only, am left; and they seek my life," the word of the Lord surprised him, "Yet I have left Me seven thousand in Israel, all the knees which have not bowed unto Baal." 1 Kings 19:14, 18.

Then let no man attempt to number Israel today, but let everyone have a heart of flesh, a heart of tender sympathy, a heart that, like the heart of Christ, reaches out for the salvation of a lost world.

John Steel

chapter 15

Jehoshaphat

UNTIL called to the throne at the age of thirty-five, Jehoshaphat had before him the example of good King Asa, who in nearly every crisis had done "that which was right in the eyes of the Lord." 1 Kings 15:11. During a prosperous reign of twenty-five years, Jehoshaphat sought to walk "in all the ways of Asa his father; he turned not aside."

In his efforts to rule wisely, Jehoshaphat endeavored to persuade his subjects to take a firm stand against idolatrous practices. Many of the people in his realm "offered and burnt incense yet in the high places." 1 Kings 22:43. The king did not at once destroy these shrines; but from the beginning he tried to safeguard Judah from the sins characterizing the northern kingdom under the rule of Ahab, of whom he was a contemporary for many years. Jehoshaphat himself was loyal to God. He "sought not unto Baalim; but sought to the

Because Jehoshaphat sought the Lord and walked in His ways, God blessed him and established the kingdom in his hands.

Lord God of his father, and walked in His commandments, and not after the doings of Israel." Because of his integrity, the Lord was with him, and "stablished the kingdom in his hand." 2 Chronicles 17:3-5.

"All Judah brought to Jehoshaphat presents; and he had riches and honor in abundance. And his heart was lifted up in the ways of the Lord." As time passed and reformations were wrought, the king "took away the high places and groves out of Judah." Verses 5, 6. "And the remnant of the Sodomites, which remained in the days of his father Asa, he took out of the land." 1 Kings 22:46. Thus gradually the inhabitants of Judah were freed from many of the perils that had been threatening to retard seriously their spiritual development.

Throughout the kingdom the people were in need of instruction in the law of God. In an understanding of this law lay their safety; by conforming their lives to its requirements they would become loyal both to God and to man. Knowing this, Jehoshaphat took steps to ensure to his people thorough instruction in the Holy Scriptures. The princes in charge of the different portions of his realm were directed to arrange for the faithful ministry of teaching priests. By royal appointment these instructors, working under the direct supervision of the princes, "went about throughout all the cities of Judah, and taught the people." 2 Chronicles 17:7-9. And as many endeavored to understand God's requirements and to put away sin, a revival was effected.

To this wise provision for the spiritual needs of his subjects, Jehoshaphat owed much of his prosperity as a ruler. In obedience to God's law there is great gain. In conformity to the divine requirements there is a transforming power that brings peace and good will among men. If the teachings of God's word were made the controlling influence in the life of every man and woman, if mind and heart were brought under its restraining power, the evils that now exist in national and in social life would find no place. From every home would go forth an influence that would make men and women strong in spiritual insight and in moral power, and thus nations and individuals would be placed on vantage ground.

For many years Jehoshaphat lived in peace, unmolested by surrounding nations. "The fear of the Lord fell upon all the kingdoms of the lands that were round about Judah." Verse 10. From Philistia he received tribute money and presents; from Arabia, large flocks of sheep and goats. "Jehoshaphat waxed great exceedingly; and he built in Judah castles, and cities of store. . . . Men of war, mighty men of valor, . . . waited on the king, beside those whom the king put in the fenced cities throughout all Judah." Verses 12-19. Blessed abundantly with "riches and honor," he was enabled to wield a mighty influence for truth and righteousness. 2 Chronicles 18:1.

Some years after coming to the throne, Jehoshaphat, now in the height of his prosperity, consented to the marriage of his son, Jehoram, to Athaliah, daughter of Ahab and Jezebel. By this union there was formed between the kingdoms of Judah and Israel an alliance which was not in the order of God and which in a time of crisis brought disaster to the king and to many of his subjects.

On one occasion Jehoshaphat visited the king of Israel at

Samaria. Special honor was shown the royal guest from Jerusalem, and before the close of his visit he was persuaded to unite with the king of Israel in war against the Syrians. Ahab hoped that by joining his forces with those of Judah he might regain Ramoth, one of the old cities of refuge, which, he contended, rightfully belonged to the Israelites.

Although Jehoshaphat in a moment of weakness had rashly promised to join the king of Israel in his war against the Syrians, yet his better judgment led him to seek to learn the will of God concerning the undertaking. "Inquire, I pray thee, at the word of the Lord today," he suggested to Ahab. In response, Ahab called together four hundred of the false prophets of Samaria, and asked of them, "Shall we go to Ramothgilead to battle, or shall I forbear?" And they answered, "Go up; for God will deliver it into the king's hand." Verses 4, 5.

Unsatisfied, Jehoshaphat sought to learn for a certainty the will of God. "Is there not here a prophet of the Lord," he asked, "that we might inquire of him?" Verse 6. "There is yet one man, Micaiah the son of Imlah, by whom we may inquire of the Lord," Ahab answered; "but I hate him; for he doth not prophesy good concerning me, but evil." 1 Kings 22:8. Jehoshaphat was firm in his request that the man of God be called; and upon appearing before them and being adjured by Ahab to tell "nothing but that which is true in the name of the Lord," Micaiah said: "I saw all Israel scattered upon the hills, as sheep that have not a shepherd: and the Lord said, These have no master: let them return every man to his house in peace." Verses 16, 17.

The words of the prophet should have been enough to

show the kings that their project was not favored by Heaven, but neither ruler felt inclined to heed the warning. Ahab had marked out his course, and he was determined to follow it. Jehoshaphat had given his word of honor, "We will be with thee in the war;" and after making such a promise, he was reluctant to withdraw his forces. 2 Chronicles 18:3. "So the king of Israel and Jehoshaphat the king of Judah went up to Ramothgilead." 1 Kings 22:29.

During the battle that followed, Ahab was shot by an arrow, and at eventide he died. "About the going down of the sun," "there went a proclamation throughout the host," "Every man to his city, and every man to his own country." Verse 36. Thus was fulfilled the word of the prophet.

From this disastrous battle Jehoshaphat returned to Jerusalem. As he approached the city, the prophet Jehu met him with the reproof: "Shouldest thou help the ungodly, and love them that hate the Lord? therefore is wrath upon thee from before the Lord. Nevertheless there are good things found in thee, in that thou hast taken away the groves out of the land, and hast prepared thine heart to seek God." 2 Chronicles 19:2, 3.

The later years of Jehoshaphat's reign were largely spent in strengthening the national and spiritual defenses of Judah. He "went out again through the people from Beersheba to Mount Ephraim, and brought them back unto the Lord God of their fathers." Verse 4.

One of the important steps taken by the king was the establishment and maintenance of efficient courts of justice. He "set judges in the land throughout all the fenced cities of Judah, city by city;" and in the charge given them he urged:

"Take heed what ye do: for ye judge not for man, but for the Lord, who is with you in the judgment. Wherefore now let the fear of the Lord be upon you; take heed and do it: for there is no iniquity with the Lord our God, nor respect of persons, nor taking of gifts." Verses 5-7.

The judicial system was perfected by the founding of a court of appeal at Jerusalem, where Jehoshaphat "set of the Levites, and of the priests, and of the chief of the fathers of Israel, for the judgment of the Lord, and for controversies." Verse 8.

The king exhorted these judges to be faithful. "Thus shall ye do in the fear of the Lord, faithfully, and with a perfect heart," he charged them. "And what cause soever shall come to you of your brethren that dwell in their cities, between blood and blood, between law and commandment, statutes and judgments, ye shall even warn them that they trespass not against the Lord, and so wrath come upon you, and upon your brethren: this do, and ye shall not trespass.

"And, behold, Amariah the chief priest is over you in all matters of the Lord; and Zebadiah the son of Ishmael, the ruler of the house of Judah, for all the king's matters: also the Levites shall be officers before you.

"Deal courageously, and the Lord shall be with the good." Verses 9-11.

In his careful safeguarding of the rights and liberties of his subjects, Jehoshaphat emphasized the consideration that every member of the human family receives from the God of justice, who rules over all. "God standeth in the congregation of the mighty; He judgeth among the gods." And those who are appointed to act as judges under Him, are

King Ahab, rashly rejecting Micaiah's counsel against attacking the Syrians, lost his life in the ensuing battle.

to "defend the poor and fatherless;" they are to "do justice to the afflicted and needy," and "rid them out of the hand of the wicked." Psalm 82:1, 3, 4.

Toward the close of Jehoshaphat's reign the kingdom of Judah was invaded by an army before whose approach the inhabitants of the land had reason to tremble. "The children of Moab, and the children of Ammon, and with them other beside the Ammonites, came against Jehoshaphat to battle." Tidings of this invasion reached the king through a messenger, who appeared with the startling word, "There cometh a great multitude against thee from beyond the sea on this side Syria; and, behold, they be in Hazazon-tamar, which is Engedi." 2 Chronicles 20:1, 2.

Jehoshaphat was a man of courage and valor. For years he had been strengthening his armies and his fortified cities. He was well prepared to meet almost any foe; yet in this crisis he put not his trust in the arm of flesh. Not by disciplined armies and fenced cities, but by a living faith in the God of Israel, could he hope to gain the victory over these heathen who boasted of their power to humble Judah in the eyes of the nations.

"Jehoshaphat feared, and set himself to seek the Lord, and proclaimed a fast throughout all Judah. And Judah gathered themselves together, to ask help of the Lord: even out of all the cities of Judah they came to seek the Lord.

Standing in the temple court before his people, Jehoshaphat poured out his soul in prayer, pleading God's promises, with confession of Israel's helplessness. "O Lord God of our fathers," he petitioned, "art not Thou God in heaven? and rulest not Thou over all the kingdoms of the heathen? and in Thine hand is there not power and might, so that none is able to withstand Thee? Art not Thou our God, who didst drive out the inhabitants of this land before Thy people Israel, and gavest it to the seed of Abraham Thy friend forever? And they dwelt therein, and have built Thee a sanctuary therein for Thy name, saying, If, when evil cometh upon us, as the sword, judgment, or pestilence, or famine, we stand before this house, and in Thy presence, (for Thy name is in this house,) and cry unto Thee in our affliction, then Thou wilt hear and help.

"And now, behold, the children of Ammon and Moab and Mount Seir, whom Thou wouldest not let Israel invade, when they came out of the land of Egypt, but they turned from them, and destroyed them not; behold, I say, how they reward us, to come to cast us out of Thy possession, which Thou hast given us to inherit. O our God, wilt Thou not judge them? for we have no might against this great company that cometh against us; neither know we what to do: but our eyes are upon Thee." Verses 3-12.

With confidence Jehoshaphat could say to the Lord, "Our eyes are upon Thee." For years he had taught the people to trust in the One who in past ages had so often interposed to save His chosen ones from utter destruction; and now, when the kingdom was in peril, Jehoshaphat did not stand alone; "all Judah stood before the Lord, with their little ones, their wives, and their children." Verse 13. Unitedly they fasted and prayed; unitedly they besought the Lord to put their enemies to confusion, that the name of Jehovah might be glorified.

"Keep not Thou silence, O God:
Hold not Thy peace, and be not still, O God.

> For, lo, Thine enemies make a tumult:
> And they that hate Thee have lifted up the head.
> They have taken crafty counsel against Thy people,
> And consulted against Thy hidden ones.
> They have said, Come, and let us cut them off from
>   being a nation;
> That the name of Israel may be no more in remembrance.
> For they have consulted together with one consent:
> They are confederate against Thee:
> The tabernacles of Edom, and the Ishmaelites;
> Of Moab, and the Hagarenes;
> Gebal, and Ammon, and Amalek. . . .
> Do unto them as unto the Midianites;
> As to Sisera, as to Jabin, at the brook of Kison: . . .
> Let them be confounded and troubled forever;
> Yea, let them be put to shame, and perish:
> That men may know that Thou, whose name alone is
>   Jehovah,
> Art the Most High over all the earth."
>
> Psalm 83.

As the people joined with their king in humbling themselves before God, and asking Him for help, the Spirit of the Lord came upon Jahaziel, "a Levite of the sons of Asaph," and he said:

"Hearken ye, all Judah, and ye inhabitants of Jerusalem, and thou King Jehoshaphat, Thus saith the Lord unto you, Be not afraid nor dismayed by reason of this great multitude; for the battle is not yours, but God's. Tomorrow go ye down against them: behold, they come up by the cliff of Ziz; and ye shall find them at the end of the brook, before the wilderness of Jeruel. Ye shall not need to fight in this battle: set yourselves, stand ye still, and see the salvation of the Lord with you, O Judah and Jerusalem: fear not, nor be dismayed;

tomorrow go out against them: for the Lord will be with you."

"Jehoshaphat bowed his head with his face to the ground: and all Judah and the inhabitants of Jerusalem fell before the Lord, worshiping the Lord. And the Levites, of the children of the Kohathites, and of the children of the Korhites, stood up to praise the Lord God of Israel with a loud voice on high."

Early in the morning they rose and went into the wilderness of Tekoa. As they advanced to the battle, Jehoshaphat said, "Hear me, O Judah, and ye inhabitants of Jerusalem; Believe in the Lord your God, so shall ye be established; believe His prophets, so shall ye prosper." "And when he had consulted with the people, he appointed singers unto the Lord, and that should praise the beauty of holiness." 2 Chronicles 20:14-21. These singers went before the army, lifting their voices in praise to God for the promise of victory.

It was a singular way of going to battle against the enemy's army—praising the Lord with singing, and exalting the God of Israel. This was their battle song. They possessed the beauty of holiness. If more praising of God were engaged in now, hope and courage and faith would steadily increase. And would not this strengthen the hands of the valiant soldiers who today are standing in defense of truth?

"The Lord set ambushments against the children of Ammon, Moab, and Mount Seir, which were come against Judah; and they were smitten. For the children of Ammon and Moab stood up against the inhabitants of Mount Seir, utterly to slay and destroy them: and when they had made an end of the inhabitants of Seir, everyone helped to destroy another.

"And when Judah came toward the watchtower in the

wilderness, they looked unto the multitude, and, behold, they were dead bodies fallen to the earth, and none escaped." Verses 22-24.

God was the strength of Judah in this crisis, and He is the strength of His people today. We are not to trust in princes, or to set men in the place of God. We are to remember that human beings are fallible and erring, and that He who has all power is our strong tower of defense. In every emergency we are to feel that the battle is His. His resources are limitless, and apparent impossibilities will make the victory all the greater.

> "Save us, O God of our salvation,
>   And gather us together,
> And deliver us from the heathen,
> That we may give thanks to Thy holy name,
> And glory in Thy praise."
>   1 Chronicles 16:35.

Laden with spoil, the armies of Judah returned "with joy; for the Lord had made them to rejoice over their enemies. And they came to Jerusalem with psalteries and harps and trumpets unto the house of the Lord." 2 Chronicles 20:27, 28. Great was their cause for rejoicing. In obedience to the command, "Stand ye still, and see the salvation of the Lord: . . . fear not, nor be dismayed," they had put their trust wholly in God, and He had proved to be their fortress and their deliverer. Verse 17. Now they could sing with understanding the inspired hymns of David:

> "God is our refuge and strength,
>   A very present help in trouble. . . .
> He breaketh the bow, and cutteth the spear in sunder;

He burneth the chariot in the fire.
Be still, and know that I am God:
I will be exalted among the heathen, I will be exalted
        in the earth.
    The Lord of hosts is with us;
    The God of Jacob is our refuge."
                            Psalm 46.

"According to Thy name, O God,
 So is Thy praise unto the ends of the earth:
 Thy right hand is full of righteousness.
 Let Mount Zion rejoice,
 Let the daughters of Judah be glad,
 Because of Thy judgments. . . .

"This God is our God for ever and ever:
    He will be our guide even unto death."
                            Psalm 48:10-14.

Through the faith of Judah's ruler and of his armies "the fear of God was on all the kingdoms of those countries, when they had heard that the Lord fought against the enemies of Israel. So the realm of Jehoshaphat was quiet: for his God gave him rest." 2 Chronicles 20:29, 30.

chapter 16

This chapter is based on 1 Kings 21; 2 Kings 1.

The Fall of the House of Ahab

THE evil influence that Jezebel had exercised from the first over Ahab continued during the later years of his life and bore fruit in deeds of shame and violence such as have seldom been equaled in sacred history. "There was none like unto Ahab, which did sell himself to work wickedness in the sight of the Lord, whom Jezebel his wife stirred up."

Naturally of a covetous disposition, Ahab, strengthened and sustained in wrongdoing by Jezebel, had followed the dictates of his evil heart until he was fully controlled by the spirit of selfishness. He could brook no refusal of his wishes; the things he desired he felt should by right be his.

This dominant trait in Ahab, which influenced so disastrously the fortunes of the kingdom under his successors, is revealed in an incident which took place while Elijah was still a prophet in Israel. Hard by the palace of the king was a vineyard belonging to Naboth, a Jezreelite. Ahab set his

The servants obeyed King Jehu's command
and threw the wicked and idolatrous
Jezebel from the window to her death.
© P.P.P.A.   JOHN STEEL, ARTIST

[*204*] 187

heart on possessing this vineyard, and he proposed to buy it or else to give in exchange for it another piece of land. "Give me thy vineyard," he said to Naboth, "that I may have it for a garden of herbs, because it is near unto my house: and I will give thee for it a better vineyard than it; or, if it seem good to thee, I will give thee the worth of it in money."

Naboth valued his vineyard highly because it had belonged to his fathers, and he refused to part with it. "The Lord forbid it me," he said to Ahab, "that I should give the inheritance of my fathers unto thee." According to the Levitical code no land could be transferred permanently by sale or exchange; every one of the children of Israel must "keep himself to the inheritance of the tribe of his fathers." Numbers 36:7.

Naboth's refusal made the selfish monarch ill. "Ahab came into his house heavy and displeased because of the word which Naboth the Jezreelite had spoken to him. . . . And he laid him down upon his bed, and turned away his face, and would eat no bread."

Jezebel soon learned the particulars, and, indignant that anyone should refuse the request of the king, she assured Ahab that he need no longer be sad. "Dost thou now govern the kingdom of Israel?" she said. "Arise, and eat bread, and let thine heart be merry: I will give thee the vinyard of Naboth the Jezreelite."

Ahab cared not by what means his wife might accomplish the desired object, and Jezebel immediately proceeded to carry out her wicked purpose. She wrote letters in the name of the king, sealed them with his signet, and sent them to the elders and nobles of the city where Naboth dwelt, saying: "Proclaim a fast, and set Naboth on high among the people:

and set two men, sons of Belial, before him, to bear witness against him, saying, Thou didst blaspheme God and the king. And then carry him out, and stone him, that he may die."

The command was obeyed. "The men of his city, even the elders and the nobles, . . . did as Jezebel had . . . written in the letters which she had sent unto them." Then Jezebel went to the king and bade him arise and take the vineyard. And Ahab, heedless of the consequences, blindly followed her counsel and went down to take possession of the coveted property.

The king was not allowed to enjoy unrebuked that which he had gained by fraud and bloodshed. "The word of the Lord came to Elijah the Tishbite, saying, Arise, go down to meet Ahab king of Israel, which is in Samaria: behold, he is in the vineyard of Naboth, whither he is gone down to possess it. And thou shalt speak unto him, saying, Thus saith the Lord, Hast thou killed, and also taken possession?" And the Lord further instructed Elijah to pronounce upon Ahab a terrible judgment.

The prophet hastened to carry out the divine command. The guilty ruler, meeting the stern messenger of Jehovah face to face in the vineyard, gave voice to his startled fear in the words, "Hast thou found me, O mine enemy?"

Without hesitation the messenger of the Lord replied, "I have found thee: because thou hast sold thyself to work evil in the sight of the Lord. Behold, I will bring evil upon thee, and will take away thy posterity." No mercy was to be shown. The house of Ahab was to be utterly destroyed, "like the house of Jeroboam the son of Nebat, and like the house of Baasha the son of Ahijah," the Lord declared through His servant, "for the provocation wherewith thou hast provoked Me to anger, and made Israel to sin."

And of Jezebel the Lord declared, "The dogs shall eat Jezebel by the wall of Jezreel. Him that dieth of Ahab in the city the dogs shall eat; and him that dieth in the field shall the fowls of the air eat."

When the king heard this fearful message, "he rent his clothes, and put sackcloth upon his flesh, and fasted, and lay in sackcloth, and went softly.

"And the word of the Lord came to Elijah the Tishbite, saying, Seest thou how Ahab humbleth himself before Me? because he humbleth himself before Me, I will not bring the evil in his days: but in his son's days will I bring the evil upon his house."

It was less than three years later that King Ahab met his death at the hands of the Syrians. Ahaziah, his successor, "did evil in the sight of the Lord, and walked in the way of his father, and in the way of his mother, and in the way of Jeroboam." "He served Baal, and worshiped him, and provoked to anger the Lord God of Israel," as his father Ahab had done. 1 Kings 22:52, 53. But judgments followed close upon the sins of the rebellious king. A disastrous war with Moab, and then an accident by which his own life was threatened, attested to God's wrath against him.

Having fallen "through a lattice in his upper chamber," Ahaziah, seriously injured, and fearful of the possible outcome, sent some of his servants to make inquiry of Baal-zebub, the god of Ekron, whether he should recover or not. The god of Ekron was supposed to give information, through the medium of its priests, concerning future events. Large numbers of people went to inquire of it; but the predictions there uttered, and the information given, proceeded from the prince of darkness.

Ahaziah's servants were met by a man of God, who directed them to return to the king with the message: "Is it because there is no God in Israel, that ye go to inquire of Baal-zebub, the god of Ekron? Now therefore thus saith Jehovah, Thou shalt not come down from the bed whither thou art gone up, but shalt surely die." Having delivered his message, the prophet departed.

The astonished servants hastened back to the king, and repeated to him the words of the man of God. The king inquired, "What manner of man was he?" They answered, "He was an hairy man, and girt with a girdle of leather about his loins." "It is Elijah the Tishbite," Ahaziah exclaimed. He knew that if the stranger whom his messengers had met was indeed Elijah, the words of doom pronounced would surely come to pass. Anxious to avert, if possible, the threatened judgment, he determined to send for the prophet.

Twice Ahaziah sent a company of soldiers to intimidate the prophet, and twice the wrath of God fell upon them in judgment. The third company of soldiers humbled themselves before God; and their captain, as he approached the Lord's messenger, "fell on his knees before Elijah, and besought him, and said unto him, O man of God, I pray thee, let my life, and the life of these fifty thy servants, be precious in thy sight."

"The angel of Jehovah said unto Elijah, Go down with him: be not afraid of him. And he arose, and went down with him unto the king. And he said unto him, Thus saith Jehovah,

Forasmuch as thou hast sent messengers to inquire of Baal-zebub, the god of Ekron, is it because there is no God in Israel to inquire of His word? therefore thou shalt not come down from the bed whither thou art gone up, but shalt surely die."

During his father's reign, Ahaziah had witnessed the wondrous works of the Most High. He had seen the terrible evidences that God had given apostate Israel of the way in which He regards those who set aside the binding claims of His law. Ahaziah had acted as if these awful realities were but idle tales. Instead of humbling his heart before the Lord, he had followed after Baal, and at last he had ventured upon this, his most daring act of impiety. Rebellious, and unwilling to repent, Ahaziah died, "according to the word of the Lord which Elijah had spoken."

The history of King Ahaziah's sin and its punishment has in it a warning which none can disregard with impunity. Men today may not pay homage to heathen gods, yet thousands are worshiping at Satan's shrine as verily as did the king of Israel. The spirit of idolatry is rife in the world today, although, under the influence of science and education, it has assumed forms more refined and attractive than in the days when Ahaziah sought to the god of Ekron. Every day adds its sorrowful evidence that faith in the sure word of prophecy is decreasing, and that in its stead superstition and satanic witchery are captivating the minds of many.

Today the mysteries of heathen worship are replaced by the secret associations and séances, the obscurities and wonders, of spiritistic mediums. The disclosures of these mediums are eagerly received by thousands who refuse to accept light from God's word or through His Spirit. Believers in spiritism may speak with scorn of the magicians of old, but the great deceiver laughs in triumph as they yield to his arts under a different form.

There are many who shrink with horror from the thought of consulting spirit mediums, but who are attracted by more pleasing forms of spiritism. Others are led astray by the teachings of Christian Science, and by the mysticism of Theosophy and other Oriental religions.

The apostles of nearly all forms of spiritism claim to have power to heal. They attribute this power to electricity, magnetism, the so-called "sympathetic remedies," or to latent forces within the mind of man. And there are not a few, even in this Christian age, who go to these healers, instead of trusting in the power of the living God and the skill of well-qualified physicians. The mother, watching by the sickbed of her child, exclaims, "I can do no more. Is there no physician who has power to restore my child?" She is told of the wonderful cures performed by some clairvoyant or magnetic healer, and she trusts her dear one to his charge, placing it as verily in the hand of Satan as if he were standing by her side. In many instances the future life of the child is controlled by a satanic power which it seems impossible to break.

God had cause for displeasure at Ahaziah's impiety. What had He not done to win the hearts of the people of Israel and to inspire them with confidence in Himself? For ages He had been giving His people manifestations of unexampled kindness and love. From the beginning He had shown that His "delights were with the sons of men." Proverbs 8:31. He had been a very present help to all who sought Him in sincerity. Yet now the king of Israel, turning from God to ask help of the worst enemy of his people, proclaimed to the heathen that he had more confidence in their idols than in the God of heaven. In the same manner do men and women dishonor Him when they turn from the Source of strength and wisdom to ask help or counsel from the powers of darkness. If God's wrath was kindled by Ahaziah's act, how does He regard those who, having still greater light, choose to follow a similar course?

Those who give themselves up to the sorcery of Satan, may boast of great benefit received; but does this prove their course to be wise or safe? What if life should be prolonged? What if temporal gain should be secured? Will it pay in the end to have disregarded the will of God? All such apparent gain will prove at last an irrecoverable loss. We cannot with impunity break down a single barrier which God has erected to guard His people from Satan's power.

As Ahaziah had no son, he was succeeded by Jehoram, his brother, who reigned over the ten tribes for twelve years. Throughout these years his mother, Jezebel, was still living, and she continued to exercise her evil influence over the affairs of the nation. Idolatrous customs were still practiced by many of the people. Jehoram himself "wrought evil in the sight of the Lord; but not like his father, and like his mother: for he put away the image of Baal that his father had made. Nevertheless he cleaved unto the sins of Jeroboam the son of Nebat, which made Israel to sin; he departed not therefrom." 2 Kings 3:2, 3.

It was during Jehoram's reign over Israel that Jehoshaphat died, and Jehoshaphat's son, also named Jehoram, ascended the throne of the kingdom of Judah. By his marriage with the daughter of Ahab and Jezebel, Jehoram of Judah was closely connected with the king of Israel; and in his reign he followed after Baal, "like as did the house of Ahab." "Moreover he made high places in the mountains of Judah, and caused the inhabitants of Jerusalem to commit fornication, and compelled Judah thereto." 2 Chronicles 21:6, 11.

The king of Judah was not permitted to continue his terrible apostasy unreproved. The prophet Elijah had not yet been translated, and he could not remain silent while the kingdom of Judah was pursuing the same course that had brought the northern kingdom to the verge of ruin. The prophet sent to Jehoram of Judah a written communication, in which the wicked king read the awful words:

"Thus saith the Lord God of David thy father, Because thou has not walked in the ways of Jehoshaphat thy father, nor in the ways of Asa king of Judah, but hast walked in the way of the kings of Israel, and hast made Judah and the inhabitants of Jerusalem to go a whoring, like to the whoredoms of the house of Ahab, and also hast slain thy brethren of thy father's house, which were better than thyself: behold, with a great plague will the Lord smite thy people, and thy children, and thy wives, and all thy goods: and thou shalt have great sickness."

In fulfillment of this prophecy "the Lord stirred up against Jehoram the spirit of the Philistines, and of the Arabians, that were near the Ethiopians: and they came up into Judah, and brake into it, and carried away all the substance that was found in the king's house, and his sons also, and his wives; so that there was never a son left him, save Jehoahaz [Ahaziah, Azariah], the youngest of his sons.

"And after all this the Lord smote him in his bowels with an incurable disease. And it came to pass, that in process of time, after the end of two years, . . . he died of sore diseases." "And Ahaziah [Jehoahaz] his son reigned in his stead." Verses 12-19; 2 Kings 8:24.

Jehoram the son of Ahab was still reigning in the kingdom of Israel when his nephew, Ahaziah, came to the throne of Judah. Ahaziah ruled only one year, and during this time, influenced by his mother, Athaliah, "his counselor to do wickedly," "he walked in the way of the house of Ahab, and did evil in the sight of the Lord." 2 Chronicles 22:3, 4; 2 Kings 8:27. Jezebel, his grandmother, was still living, and he allied himself boldly with Jehoram of Israel, his uncle.

Ahaziah of Judah soon met a tragic end. The surviving members of the house of Ahab were indeed "his counselors after the death of his father to his destruction." 2 Chronicles

22:3, 4. While Ahaziah was visiting his uncle at Jezreel, the prophet Elisha was divinely directed to send one of the sons of the prophets to Ramothgilead to anoint Jehu king of Israel. The combined forces of Judah and Israel were at that time engaged in a military campaign against the Syrians of Ramothgilead. Jehoram had been wounded in battle, and had returned to Jezreel, leaving Jehu in charge of the royal armies.

In anointing Jehu, the messenger of Elisha declared, "I have anointed thee king over the people of the Lord, even over Israel." And then he solemnly charged Jehu with a special commission from heaven. "Thou shalt smite the house of Ahab thy master," the Lord declared through His messenger, "that I may avenge the blood of My servants the prophets, and the blood of all the servants of the Lord, at the hand of Jezebel. For the whole house of Ahab shall perish." 2 Kings 9:6-8.

After he had been proclaimed king by the army, Jehu hastened to Jezreel, where he began his work of execution on those who had deliberately chosen to continue in sin and to lead others into sin. Jehoram of Israel, Ahaziah of Judah, and Jezebel the queen mother, with "all that remained of the house of Ahab in Jezreel, and all his great men, and his kinsfolks, and his priests," were slain. "All the prophets of Baal, all his servants, and all his priests" dwelling at the center of Baal worship near Samaria, were put to the sword. The idolatrous images were broken down and burned, and the temple of Baal was laid in ruins. "Thus Jehu destroyed Baal out of Israel." 2 Kings 10:11, 19, 28.

Tidings of this general execution reached Athaliah, Jezebel's daughter, who still occupied a commanding position in the kingdom of Judah. When she saw that her son, the king of Judah, was dead, "she arose and destroyed all the seed royal of the house of Judah." In this massacre all the descendants of David who were eligible to the throne were destroyed, save one, a babe named Joash, whom the wife of Jehoiada the high priest hid within the precincts of the temple. For six years the child remained hidden, while "Athaliah reigned over the land." 2 Chronicles 22:10, 12.

At the end of this time, "the Levites and all Judah" (2 Chronicles 23:8) united with Jehoiada the high priest in crowning and anointing the child Joash and acclaiming him their king. "And they clapped their hands, and said, God save the king." 2 Kings 11:12.

"Now when Athaliah heard the noise of the people running and praising the king, she came to the people into the house of the Lord." 2 Chronicles 23:12. "And when she looked, behold, the king stood by a pillar, as the manner was, and the princes and the trumpeters by the king, and all the people of the land rejoiced, and blew with trumpets."

"Athaliah rent her clothes, and cried, Treason, Treason." 2 Kings 11:14. But Jehoiada commanded the officers to lay hold of Athaliah and all her followers and lead them out of the temple to a place of execution, where they were to be slain.

Thus perished the last member of the house of Ahab. The terrible evil that had been wrought through his alliance with Jezebel, continued till the last of his descendants was destroyed. Even in the land of Judah, where the worship of the true God had never been formally set aside, Athaliah had succeeded in seducing many. Immediately after the execution of the impenitent queen "all the people of the land went into the house of Baal, and brake it down; his altars and his

After six years of Athaliah's oppressive reign the people revolted and crowned young Prince Joash as their king.
© P.P.P.A.   JOHN STEEL, ARTIST

images brake they in pieces thoroughly, and slew Mattan the priest of Baal before the altars." Verse 18.

A reformation followed. Those who took part in acclaiming Joash king, had solemnly covenanted "that they should be the Lord's people." And now that the evil influence of the daughter of Jezebel had been removed from the kingdom of Judah, and the priests of Baal had been slain and their temple destroyed, "all the people of the land rejoiced: and the city was quiet." 2 Chronicles 23:16, 21.

chapter 17

The Call of Elisha

GOD had bidden Elijah anoint another to be prophet in his stead. "Elisha the son of Shaphat . . . shalt thou anoint to be prophet in thy room" (1 Kings 19:16), He had said; and in obedience to the command, Elijah went to find Elisha. As he journeyed northward, how changed was the scene from what it had been only a short while before! Then the ground was parched, the farming districts unworked, for neither dew nor rain had fallen for three and a half years. Now on every hand vegetation was springing up as if to redeem the time of drought and famine.

Elisha's father was a wealthy farmer, a man whose household were among the number that in a time of almost universal apostasy had not bowed the knee to Baal. Theirs was a home where God was honored and where allegiance to the faith of ancient Israel was the rule of daily life. In such surroundings the early years of Elisha were passed. In the quietude of country life, under the teaching of God and nature and the discipline of useful work, he received the training in habits of simplicity and of obedience to his parents and to God that helped to fit him for the high position he was afterward to occupy.

The prophetic call came to Elisha while, with his father's servants, he was plowing in the field. He had taken up the work that lay nearest. He possessed both the capabilities of a leader among men and the meekness of one who is ready to serve. Of a quiet and gentle spirit, he was nevertheless energetic and steadfast. Integrity, fidelity, and the love and fear of God were his, and in the humble round of daily toil he gained strength of purpose and nobleness of character, constantly increasing in grace and knowledge. While co-operating with his father in the home-life duties, he was learning to co-operate with God.

By faithfulness in little things, Elisha was preparing for weightier trusts. Day by day, through practical experience, he gained a fitness for a broader, higher work. He learned to serve; and in learning this, he learned also how to instruct and lead. The lesson is for all. None can know what may be God's purpose in His discipline; but all may be certain that faithfulness in little things is the evidence of fitness for greater responsibilities. Every act of life is a revelation of character, and he only who in small duties proves himself "a workman that needeth not to be ashamed" can be honored by God with higher service. 2 Timothy 2:15.

He who feels that it is of no consequence how he performs the smaller tasks proves himself unfit for a more honored position. He may think himself fully competent to take up the larger duties; but God looks deeper than the surface. After test and trial, there is written against him the sentence, "Thou art weighed in the balances, and art found wanting." His unfaithfulness reacts upon himself. He fails of gaining the grace, the power, the force of character, which is received through unreserved surrender.

Because they are not connected with some directly religious work, many feel that their lives are useless, that they are doing nothing for the advancement of God's kingdom. If they could do some great thing how gladly they would undertake it! But because they can serve only in little things, they think themselves justified in doing nothing. In this they err. A man may be in the active service of God while engaged in the ordinary, everyday duties—while felling trees, clearing the ground, or following the plow. The mother who trains her children for Christ is as truly working for God as is the minister in the pulpit.

Many long for special talent with which to do a wonderful work, while the duties lying close at hand, the performance of which would make the life fragrant, are lost sight of. Let such ones take up the duties lying directly in their pathway. Success depends not so much on talent as on energy and willingness. It is not the possession of splendid talents that enables us to render acceptable service, but the conscientious performance of daily duties, the contented spirit, the unaffected, sincere interest in the welfare of others. In the humblest lot true excellence may be found. The commonest tasks, wrought with loving faithfulness, are beautiful in God's sight.

As Elijah, divinely directed in seeking a successor, passed the field in which Elisha was plowing, he cast upon the young man's shoulders the mantle of consecration. During the famine the family of Shaphat had become familiar with the work and mission of Elijah, and now the Spirit of God impressed Elisha's heart as to the meaning of the prophet's act. To him it was the signal that God had called him to be the successor of Elijah.

"And he left the oxen, and ran after Elijah, and said, Let me, I pray thee, kiss my father and my mother, and then I will follow thee." "Go back again," was Elijah's answer, "for what have I done to thee?" This was not a repulse, but a test of faith. Elisha must count the cost—decide for himself to accept or reject the call. If his desires clung to his home and its advantages, he was at liberty to remain there. But Elisha understood the meaning of the call. He knew it was from God, and he did not hesitate to obey. Not for any worldly advantage would he forgo the opportunity of becoming God's messenger or sacrifice the privilege of association with His servant. He "took a yoke of oxen, and slew them, and boiled their flesh with the instruments of the oxen, and gave unto the people, and they did eat. Then he arose, and went after Elijah, and ministered unto him." 1 Kings 19:20, 21. Without hesitation he left a home where he was beloved, to attend the prophet in his uncertain life.

Had Elisha asked Elijah what was expected of him,— what would be his work,—he would have been answered: God knows; He will make it known to you. If you wait upon the Lord, He will answer your every question. You may come with me if you have evidence that God has called you. Know for yourself that God stands back of me, and that it is His voice you hear. If you can count everything but dross that you may win the favor of God, come.

The prophet Elijah placed his mantle around Elisha, thus indicating to him that God had called him to His service.
© P.P.P.A.   JOHN STEEL, ARTIST

Similar to the call that came to Elisha was the answer given by Christ to the young ruler who asked Him the question, "What good thing shall I do, that I may have eternal life?" "If thou wilt be perfect," Christ replied, "go and sell that thou hast, and give to the poor, and thou shalt have treasure in heaven: and come and follow Me." Matthew 19:16, 21.

Elisha accepted the call to service, casting no backward glance at the pleasures and comforts he was leaving. The young ruler, when he heard the Saviour's words, "went away sorrowful: for he had great possessions." Verse 22. He was not willing to make the sacrifice. His love for his possessions was greater than his love for God. By his refusal to renounce all for Christ, he proved himself unworthy of a place in the Master's service.

The call to place all on the altar of service comes to each one. We are not all asked to serve as Elisha served, nor are we all bidden to sell everything we have; but God asks us to give His service the first place in our lives, to allow no day to pass without doing something to advance His work in the earth. He does not expect from all the same kind of service. One may be called to ministry in a foreign land; another may be asked to give of his means for the support of gospel work. God accepts the offering of each. It is the consecration of the life and all its interests, that is necessary. Those who make this consecration will hear and obey the call of Heaven.

To everyone who becomes a partaker of His grace, the Lord appoints a work for others. Individually we are to stand in our lot, saying, "Here am I; send me." Whether a man be a minister of the Word or a physician, whether he be merchant or farmer, professional man or mechanic, the responsibility rests upon him. It is his work to reveal to others the gospel of their salvation. Every enterprise in which he engages should be a means to this end.

It was no great work that was at first required of Elisha; commonplace duties still constituted his discipline. He is spoken of as pouring water on the hands of Elijah, his master. He was willing to do anything that the Lord directed, and at every step he learned lessons of humility and service. As the prophet's personal attendant, he continued to prove faithful in little things, while with daily strengthening purpose he devoted himself to the mission appointed him by God.

Elisha's life after uniting with Elijah was not without temptations. Trials he had in abundance; but in every emergency he relied on God. He was tempted to think of the home that he had left, but to this temptation he gave no heed. Having put his hand to the plow, he was resolved not to turn back, and through test and trial he proved true to his trust.

Ministry comprehends far more than preaching the word. It means training young men as Elijah trained Elisha, taking them from their ordinary duties, and giving them responsibilities to bear in God's work—small responsibilities at first, and larger ones as they gain strength and experience. There are in the ministry men of faith and prayer, men who can say, "That which was from the beginning, which we have heard, which we have seen with our eyes, which we have looked upon, and our hands have handled, of the Word of life; . . . that which we have seen and heard declare we unto you." 1 John 1:1-3. Young, inexperienced workers should be trained by actual labor in connection with these experienced servants of God. Thus they will learn how to bear burdens.

Those who undertake this training of young workers are doing noble service. The Lord Himself co-operates with their efforts. And the young men to whom the word of consecration has been spoken, whose privilege it is to be brought into close association with earnest, godly workers, should make the most of their opportunity. God has honored them by choosing them for His service and by placing them where they can gain greater fitness for it, and they should be humble, faithful, obedient, and willing to sacrifice. If they submit to God's discipline, carrying out His directions and choosing His servants as their counselors, they will develop into righteous, high-principled, steadfast men, whom God can entrust with responsibilities.

As the gospel is proclaimed in its purity, men will be called from the plow and from the common commercial business vocations that largely occupy the mind and will be educated in connection with men of experience. As they learn to labor effectively, they will proclaim the truth with power. Through most wonderful workings of divine providence, mountains of difficulty will be removed and cast into the sea. The message that means so much to the dwellers upon the earth will be heard and understood. Men will know what is truth. Onward and still onward the work will advance until the whole earth shall have been warned, and then shall the end come.

For several years after the call of Elisha, Elijah and Elisha labored together, the younger man daily gaining greater preparedness for his work. Elijah had been God's instrument for the overthrow of gigantic evils. The idolatry which, supported by Ahab and the heathen Jezebel, had seduced the nation, had been given a decided check. Baal's prophets had been slain. The whole people of Israel had been deeply stirred, and many were returning to the worship of God. As Elijah's successor, Elisha, by careful, patient instruction, must endeavor to guide Israel in safe paths. His association with Elijah, the greatest prophet since the days of Moses, prepared him for the work that he was soon to take up alone.

During these years of united ministry, Elijah from time to time was called upon to meet flagrant evils with stern rebuke. When wicked Ahab seized Naboth's vineyard, it was the voice of Elijah that prophesied his doom and the doom of all his house. And when Ahaziah, after the death of his father Ahab, turned from the living God to Baal-zebub, the god of Ekron, it was Elijah's voice that was heard once more in earnest protest.

The schools of the prophets, established by Samuel, had fallen into decay during the years of Israel's apostasy. Elijah re-established these schools, making provision for young men to gain an education that would lead them to magnify the law and make it honorable. Three of these schools, one at Gilgal, one at Bethel, and one at Jericho, are mentioned in the record. Just before Elijah was taken to heaven, he and Elisha visited these centers of training. The lessons that the prophet of God had given them on former visits, he now repeated. Especially did he instruct them concerning their high privilege of loyally maintaining their allegiance to the God of heaven. He also impressed upon their minds the importance of letting simplicity mark every feature of their education. Only in this way could they receive the mold of heaven and go forth to work in the ways of the Lord.

The heart of Elijah was cheered as he saw what was being accomplished by means of these schools. The work of reformation was not complete, but he could see throughout the kingdom a verification of the word of the Lord, "Yet I have left Me seven thousand in Israel, all the knees which have not bowed unto Baal." 1 Kings 19:18.

As Elisha accompanied the prophet on his round of service from school to school, his faith and resolution were once more tested. At Gilgal, and again at Bethel and Jericho, he was invited by the prophet to turn back. "Tarry here, I pray thee," Elijah said; "for the Lord hath sent me to Bethel." But in his early labor of guiding the plow, Elisha had learned not to fail or to become discouraged, and now that he had set his hand to the plow in another line of duty he would not be diverted from his purpose. He would not be parted from

Faithful Elijah, caught up to heaven in a chariot of fire, represents those who will be translated without seeing death.

© P.P.P.A.   JOHN STEEL, ARTIST

his master, so long as opportunity remained for gaining a further fitting up for service. Unknown to Elijah, the revelation that he was to be translated had been made known to his disciples in the schools of the prophets, and in particular to Elisha. And now the tried servant of the man of God kept close beside him. As often as the invitation to turn back was given, his answer was, "As the Lord liveth, and as thy soul liveth, I will not leave thee."

"And they two went on. . . . And they two stood by Jordan. And Elijah took his mantle, and wrapped it together, and smote the waters, and they were divided hither and thither, so that they two went over on dry ground. And it came to pass, when they were gone over, that Elijah said unto Elisha, Ask what I shall do for thee, before I be taken away from thee."

Elisha asked not for worldly honor, or for a high place among the great men of earth. That which he craved was a large measure of the Spirit that God had bestowed so freely upon the one about to be honored with translation. He knew that nothing but the Spirit which had rested upon Elijah could fit him to fill the place in Israel to which God had called him, and so he asked, "I pray thee, let a double portion of thy Spirit be upon me."

In response to this request, Elijah said, "Thou hast asked a hard thing: nevertheless, if thou see me when I am taken from thee, it shall be so unto thee; but if not, it shall not be so. And it came to pass, as they still went on, and talked, that, behold, there appeared a chariot of fire, and horses of fire, and parted them both asunder; and Elijah went up by a whirlwind into heaven." See 2 Kings 2:1-11.

Elijah was a type of the saints who will be living on the earth at the time of the second advent of Christ and who will be "changed, in a moment, in the twinkling of an eye, at the last trump," without tasting of death. 1 Corinthians 15:51, 52. It was as a representative of those who shall be thus translated that Elijah, near the close of Christ's earthly ministry, was permitted to stand with Moses by the side of the Saviour on the mount of transfiguration. In these glorified ones, the disciples saw in miniature a representation of the kingdom of the redeemed. They beheld Jesus clothed with the light of heaven; they heard the "voice out of the cloud" (Luke 9:35), acknowledging Him as the Son of God; they saw Moses, representing those who will be raised from the dead at the time of the second advent; and there also stood Elijah, representing those who at the close of earth's history will be changed from mortal to immortal and be translated to heaven without seeing death.

In the desert, in loneliness and discouragement, Elijah had said that he had had enough of life and had prayed that he might die. But the Lord in His mercy had not taken him at his word. There was yet a great work for Elijah to do; and when his work was done, he was not to perish in discouragement and solitude. Not for him the descent into the tomb, but the ascent with God's angels to the presence of His glory.

"And Elisha saw it, and he cried, My father, my father, the chariot of Israel, and the horsemen thereof. And he saw him no more: and he took hold of his own clothes, and rent them in two pieces. He took up also the mantle of Elijah that fell from him, and went back, and stood by the bank of Jordan; and he took the mantle of Elijah that fell from him, and smote the waters, and said, Where is the Lord God of Elijah? and when he also had smitten the waters, they parted hither and thither: and Elisha went over. And when the sons of the prophets which were to view at Jericho saw him, they said, The Spirit of Elijah doth rest on Elisha. And they came to meet him, and bowed themselves to the ground before him." 2 Kings 2:12-15.

When the Lord in His providence sees fit to remove from His work those to whom He has given wisdom, He helps and strengthens their successors, if they will look to Him for aid and will walk in His ways. They may be even wiser than their predecessors; for they may profit by their experience and learn wisdom from their mistakes.

Henceforth Elisha stood in Elijah's place. He who had been faithful in that which was least was to prove himself faithful also in much.

chapter 18

The Healing of the Waters

IN PATRIARCHAL times the Jordan Valley was "well watered everywhere, . . . even as the garden of the Lord." It was in this fair valley that Lot chose to make his home when he "pitched his tent toward Sodom." Genesis 13:10, 12. At the time that the cities of the plain were destroyed, the region round about became a desolate waste, and it has since formed a part of the wilderness of Judea.

A portion of the beautiful valley remained, with its life-giving springs and streams, to gladden the heart of man. In this valley, rich with fields of grain and forests of date palms and other fruit-bearing trees, the hosts of Israel had encamped after crossing the Jordan and had first partaken of the fruits of the Promised Land. Before them had stood the walls of Jericho, a heathen stronghold, the center of the worship of Ashtoreth, vilest and most degrading of all Canaanitish forms of idolatry. Soon its walls were thrown down and its inhabitants slain, and at the time of its fall the solemn declaration was made, in the presence of all Israel: "Cursed be the man before the Lord, that riseth up and buildeth this city Jericho: he shall lay the foundation thereof in his first-born, and in his youngest son shall he set up the gates of it." Joshua 6:26.

Five centuries passed. The spot lay desolate, accursed of God. Even the springs that had made residence in this portion of the valley so desirable suffered the blighting effects of the curse. But in the days of Ahab's apostasy, when through Jezebel's influence the worship of Ashtoreth was revived, Jericho, the ancient seat of this worship, was rebuilt, though at a fearful cost to the builder. Hiel the Bethelite "laid the foundation thereof in Abiram his first-born, and set up the gates thereof in his youngest son Segub, according to the word of the Lord." 1 Kings 16:34.

Not far from Jericho, in the midst of fruitful groves, was one of the schools of the prophets, and thither, after the ascension of Elijah, Elisha went. During his sojourn among them the men of the city came to the prophet and said, "Behold, I pray thee, the situation of this city is pleasant, as my lord seeth: but the water is nought, and the ground barren." The spring that in former years had been pure and life-giving, and had contributed largely to the water supply of the city and the surrounding district, was now unfit for use.

In response to the plea of the men of Jericho, Elisha said, "Bring me a new cruse, and put salt therein." Having received this, "he went forth unto the spring of the waters, and cast the salt in there, and said, Thus saith the Lord, I have healed these waters; there shall not be from thence any more death or barren land." 2 Kings 2:19-21.

The healing of the waters of Jericho was accomplished, not by any wisdom of man, but by the miraculous interposition of God. Those who had rebuilt the city were undeserving of the favor of Heaven; yet He who "maketh His sun to rise on the evil and on the good, and sendeth rain on the just and on the unjust," saw fit in this instance to reveal, through this token of compassion, His willingness to heal Israel of their spiritual maladies. Matthew 5:45.

The restoration was permanent; "the waters were healed unto this day, according to the saying of Elisha which he spake." 2 Kings 2:22. From age to age the waters have flowed on, making that portion of the valley an oasis of beauty.

Many are the spiritual lessons to be gathered from the story of the healing of the waters. The new cruse, the salt, the spring—all are highly symbolic.

In casting salt into the bitter spring, Elisha taught the same spiritual lesson imparted centuries later by the Saviour to His disciples when He declared, "Ye are the salt of the earth." Matthew 5:13. The salt mingling with the polluted spring purified its waters and brought life and blessing where before had been blighting and death. When God compares His children to salt, He would teach them that His purpose in making them the subjects of His grace is that they may become agents in saving others. The object of God in choosing a people before all the world was not only that He might adopt them as His sons and daughters, but that through them the world might receive the grace that bringeth salvation. When the Lord chose Abraham, it was not simply to be the special friend of God, but to be a medium of the peculiar privileges the Lord desired to bestow upon the nations.

The world needs evidences of sincere Christianity. The poison of sin is at work at the heart of society. Cities and towns are steeped in sin and moral corruption. The world is full of sickness, suffering, and iniquity. Nigh and afar off are souls in poverty and distress, weighed down with a sense of guilt and perishing for want of a saving influence. The gospel of truth is kept ever before them, yet they perish because the example of those who should be a savor of life to them is a savor of death. Their souls drink in bitterness because the springs are poisoned, when they should be like a well of water springing up unto everlasting life.

Salt must be mingled with the substance to which it is added; it must penetrate, infuse it, that it may be preserved. So it is through personal contact and association that men are reached by the saving power of the gospel. They are not saved as masses, but as individuals. Personal influence is a power. It is to work with the influence of Christ, to lift where Christ lifts, to impart correct principles, and to stay the progress of the world's corruption. It is to diffuse that grace which Christ alone can impart. It is to uplift, to sweeten the lives and characters of others by the power of a pure example united with earnest faith and love.

Of the hitherto polluted spring at Jericho, the Lord declared, "I have healed these waters; there shall not be from thence any more death or barren land." The polluted stream represents the soul that is separate from God. Sin not only shuts away from God, but destroys in the human soul both the desire and the capacity for knowing Him. Through sin, the whole human organism is deranged, the mind is perverted, the imagination corrupted; the faculties of the soul are degraded. There is an absence of pure religion, of heart holiness. The converting power of God has not wrought in transforming the character. The soul is weak, and for want of moral force to overcome, is polluted and debased.

To the heart that has become purified, all is changed. Transformation of character is the testimony to the world of an indwelling Christ. The Spirit of God produces a new life in the soul, bringing the thoughts and desires into obedience to the will of Christ; and the inward man is renewed in the image of God. Weak and erring men and women show to the world that the redeeming power of grace can cause the faulty character to develop into symmetry and abundant fruitfulness.

The heart that receives the word of God is not as a pool that evaporates, not like a broken cistern that loses its treasure. It is like the mountain stream, fed by unfailing springs, whose cool, sparkling waters leap from rock to rock, refreshing the weary, the thirsty, the heavy-laden. It is like a river constantly flowing and, as it advances, becoming deeper and wider, until its life-giving waters are spread over all the earth. The stream that goes singing on its way leaves behind its gift of verdure and fruitfulness. The grass on its banks is a fresher green, the trees have a richer verdure, the flowers are more abundant. When the earth lies bare and brown under the summer's scorching heat, a line of verdure marks the river's course.

So it is with the true child of God. The religion of Christ reveals itself as a vitalizing, pervading principle, a living, working, spiritual energy. When the heart is opened to the heavenly influence of truth and love, these principles will flow forth again like streams in the desert, causing fruitfulness to appear where now are barrenness and dearth.

As those who have been cleansed and sanctified through a knowledge of Bible truth engage heartily in the work of soulsaving, they will become indeed a savor of life unto life. And as daily they drink of the inexhaustible fountain of grace and knowledge, they will find that their own hearts are filled to overflowing with the Spirit of their Master, and that through their unselfish ministry many are benefited physically, mentally, and spiritually. The weary are refreshed, the sick restored to health, and the sin-burdened relieved. In far-off countries thanksgiving is heard from the lips of those whose hearts are turned from the service of sin unto righteousness.

"Give, and it shall be given unto you;" for the word of God is "a fountain of gardens, a well of living waters, and streams from Lebanon." Luke 6:38; Song of Solomon 4:15.

chapter 19

This chapter is based on 2 Kings 4.

A Prophet of Peace

THE work of Elisha as a prophet was in some respects very different from that of Elijah. To Elijah had been committed messages of condemnation and judgment; his was the voice of fearless reproof, calling king and people to turn from their evil ways. Elisha's was a more peaceful mission; his it was to build up and strengthen the work that Elijah had begun; to teach the people the way of the Lord. Inspiration pictures him as coming into personal touch with the people, surrounded by the sons of the prophets, bringing by his miracles and his ministry healing and rejoicing.

Elisha was a man of mild and kindly spirit; but that he could also be stern is shown by his course when, on the way to Bethel, he was mocked by ungodly youth who had come out of the city. These youth had heard of Elijah's ascension, and they made this solemn event the subject of their jeers, saying to Elisha, "Go up, thou bald head; go up, thou bald

When ungodly youth mocked the prophet, "there came forth two she-bears out of the wood and tare forty and two" of them.

head." At the sound of their mocking words the prophet turned back, and under the inspiration of the Almighty he pronounced a curse upon them. The awful judgment that followed was of God. "There came forth two she-bears out of the wood, and tare forty and two" of them. 2 Kings 2:23, 24.

Had Elisha allowed the mockery to pass unnoticed, he would have continued to be ridiculed and reviled by the rabble, and his mission to instruct and save in a time of grave national peril might have been defeated. This one instance of terrible severity was sufficient to command respect throughout his life. For fifty years he went in and out of the gate of Bethel, and to and fro in the land, from city to city, passing through crowds of idle, rude, dissolute youth; but none mocked him or made light of his qualifications as the prophet of the Most High.

Even kindness should have its limits. Authority must be maintained by a firm severity, or it will be received by many with mockery and contempt. The so-called tenderness, the coaxing and indulgence, used toward youth by parents and guardians, is one of the worst evils which can come upon them. In every family, firmness, decision, positive requirements, are essential.

Reverence, in which the youth who mocked Elisha were so lacking, is a grace that should be carefully cherished. Every child should be taught to show true reverence for God. Never should His name be spoken lightly or thoughtlessly. Angels, as they speak it, veil their faces. With what reverence should we, who are fallen and sinful, take it upon our lips!

Reverence should be shown for God's representatives—for ministers, teachers, and parents, who are called to speak and act in His stead. In the respect shown them, God is honored.

Courtesy, also, is one of the graces of the Spirit and should be cultivated by all. It has power to soften natures which without it would grow hard and rough. Those who profess to be followers of Christ, and are at the same time rough, unkind, and uncourteous, have not learned of Jesus. Their sincerity may not be doubted, their uprightness may not be questioned; but sincerity and uprightness will not atone for a lack of kindness and courtesy.

The kindly spirit that enabled Elisha to exert a powerful influence over the lives of many in Israel, is revealed in the story of his friendly relations with a family dwelling at Shunem. In his journeyings to and fro throughout the kingdom "it fell on a day, that Elisha passed to Shunem, where was a great woman; and she constrained him to eat bread. And so it was, that as oft as he passed by, he turned in thither to eat bread." The mistress of the house perceived that Elisha was "an holy man of God," and she said to her husband: "Let us make a little chamber, I pray thee, on the wall; and let us set for him there a bed, and a table, and a stool, and a candlestick: and it shall be, when he cometh to us, that he shall turn in thither." To this retreat Elisha often came, thankful for its quiet peace. Nor was God unmindful of the woman's kindness. Her home had been childless; and now the Lord rewarded her hospitality by the gift of a son.

Years passed. The child was old enough to be out in the field with the reapers. One day he was stricken down by the heat, "and he said unto his father, My head, my head." The father bade a lad carry the child to his mother; "and when he had taken him, and brought him to his mother, he sat on

[237-238] 225

her knees till noon, and then died. And she went up, and laid him on the bed of the man of God, and shut the door upon him, and went out."

In her distress, the Shunammite determined to go to Elisha for help. The prophet was then at Mount Carmel, and the woman, accompanied by her servant, set forth immediately. "And it came to pass, when the man of God saw her afar off, that he said to Gehazi his servant, Behold, yonder is that Shunammite: run now, I pray thee, to meet her, and say unto her, Is it well with thee? is it well with thy husband? is it well with the child?" The servant did as he was bidden, but not till she had reached Elisha did the stricken mother reveal the cause of her sorrow. Upon hearing of her loss, Elisha bade Gehazi: "Gird up thy loins, and take my staff in thine hand, and go thy way: if thou meet any man, salute him not; and if any salute thee, answer him not again: and lay my staff upon the face of the child."

But the mother would not be satisfied till Elisha himself came with her. "As the Lord liveth, and as thy soul liveth, I will not leave thee," she declared. "And he arose, and followed her. And Gehazi passed on before them, and laid the staff upon the face of the child; but there was neither voice, nor hearing. Wherefore he went again to meet him, and told him, saying, The child is not awaked."

When they reached the house, Elisha went into the room where the dead child lay, "and shut the door upon them twain, and prayed unto the Lord. And he went up, and lay upon the child, and put his mouth upon his mouth, and his eyes upon his eyes, and his hands upon his hands: and he stretched himself upon the child; and the flesh of the child waxed warm. Then he returned, and walked in the house to and fro; and went up, and stretched himself upon him: and the child sneezed seven times, and the child opened his eyes."

Calling Gehazi, Elisha bade him send the mother to him. "And when she was come in unto him, he said, Take up thy son. Then she went in, and fell at his feet, and bowed herself to the ground, and took up her son, and went out."

So was the faith of this woman rewarded. Christ, the great Life-giver, restored her son to her. In like manner will His faithful ones be rewarded, when, at His coming, death loses its sting and the grave is robbed of the victory it has claimed. Then will He restore to His servants the children that have been taken from them by death. "Thus saith the Lord; A voice was heard in Ramah, lamentation, and bitter weeping; Rachel weeping for her children refused to be comforted for her children, because they were not. Thus saith the Lord; Refrain thy voice from weeping, and thine eyes from tears: for thy work shall be rewarded, . . . and they shall come again from the land of the enemy. And there is hope in thine end, saith the Lord, that thy children shall come again to their own border." Jeremiah 31:15-17.

Jesus comforts our sorrow for the dead with a message of infinite hope: "I will ransom them from the power of the grave; I will redeem them from death: O death, I will be thy plagues; O grave, I will be thy destruction." Hosea 13:14. "I am He that liveth, and was dead; and, behold, I am alive for evermore, . . . and have the keys of hell and of death." Revelation 1:18. "The Lord Himself shall descend from heaven with a shout, with the voice of the Archangel, and

with the trump of God: and the dead in Christ shall rise first: then we which are alive and remain shall be caught up together with them in the clouds, to meet the Lord in the air: and so shall we ever be with the Lord." 1 Thessalonians 4:16, 17.

Like the Saviour of mankind, of whom he was a type, Elisha in his ministry among men combined the work of healing with that of teaching. Faithfully, untiringly, throughout his long and effective labors, Elisha endeavored to foster and advance the important educational work carried on by the schools of the prophets. In the providence of God his words of instruction to the earnest groups of young men assembled were confirmed by the deep movings of the Holy Spirit, and at times by other unmistakable evidences of his authority as a servant of Jehovah.

It was on the occasion of one of his visits to the school established at Gilgal that he healed the poisoned pottage. "There was a dearth in the land; and the sons of the prophets were sitting before him: and he said unto his servant, Set on the great pot, and seethe pottage for the sons of the prophets. And one went out into the field to gather herbs, and found a wild vine, and gathered thereof wild gourds his lap full, and came and shred them into the pot of pottage: for they knew them not. So they poured out for the men to eat. And it came to pass, as they were eating of the pottage, that they cried out, and said, O thou man of God, there is death in the pot. And they could not eat thereof. But he said, Then bring meal. And he cast it into the pot; and he said, Pour out for the people, that they may eat. And there was no harm in the pot."

When Elisha called the Shunammite woman to his chamber, she rejoiced to see her son alive again and thanked God.

© P.P.P.A.   JOHN STEEL, ARTIST

At Gilgal, also, while the dearth was still in the land, Elisha fed one hundred men with the present brought to him by "a man from Baalshalisha," "bread of the first fruits, twenty loaves of barley, and full ears of corn in the husk thereof." There were those with him who were sorely in need of food. When the offering came, he said to his servant, "Give unto the people, that they may eat. And his servitor said, What, should I set this before an hundred men? He said again, Give the people, that they may eat: for thus saith the Lord, They shall eat, and shall leave thereof. So he set it before them, and they did eat, and left thereof, according to the word of the Lord."

What condescension it was on the part of Christ, through His messenger, to work this miracle to satisfy hunger! Again and again since that time, though not always in so marked and perceptible a manner, has the Lord Jesus worked to supply human need. If we had clearer spiritual discernment we would recognize more readily than we do God's compassionate dealing with the children of men.

It is the grace of God on the small portion that makes it all-sufficient. God's hand can multiply it a hundredfold. From His resources He can spread a table in the wilderness. By the touch of His hand He can increase the scanty provision and make it sufficient for all. It was His power that increased the loaves and corn in the hands of the sons of the prophets.

In the days of Christ's earthly ministry, when He performed a similar miracle in feeding the multitudes, the same unbelief was manifested as was shown by those associated with the prophet of old. "What!" said Elisha's servant; "should I set this before an hundred men?" And when Jesus bade His disciples give the multitude to eat, they answered, "We have no more but five loaves and two fishes; except we should go and buy meat for all this people." Luke 9:13. What is that among so many?

The lesson is for God's children in every age. When the Lord gives a work to be done, let not men stop to inquire into the reasonableness of the command or the probable result of their efforts to obey. The supply in their hands may seem to fall short of the need to be filled; but in the hands of the Lord it will prove more than sufficient. The servitor "set it before them, and they did eat, and left thereof, according to the word of the Lord."

A fuller sense of God's relationship to those whom He has purchased with the gift of His Son, a greater faith in the onward progress of His cause in the earth—this is the great need of the church today. Let none waste time in deploring the scantiness of their visible resources. The outward appearance may be unpromising, but energy and trust in God will develop resources. The gift brought to Him with thanksgiving and with prayer for His blessing, He will multiply as He multiplied the food given to the sons of the prophets and to the weary multitude.

chapter 20

This chapter is based on 2 Kings 5.

Naaman

"NOW Naaman, captain of the host of the king of Syria, was a great man with his master, and honorable, because by him the Lord had given deliverance unto Syria: he was also a mighty man in valor, but he was a leper."

Ben-hadad, king of Syria, had defeated the armies of Israel in the battle which resulted in the death of Ahab. Since that time the Syrians had maintained against Israel a constant border warfare, and in one of their raids they had carried away a little maid who, in the land of her captivity, "waited on Naaman's wife." A slave, far from her home, this little maid was nevertheless one of God's witnesses, unconsciously fulfilling the purpose for which God had chosen Israel as His people. As she ministered in that heathen home, her sympathies were aroused in behalf of her master; and, remembering the wonderful miracles of healing wrought through Elisha, she said to her mistress, "Would God my lord were with

As the captive maid from Israel saw her mistress, the wife of Naaman, grieving, she told her about Elisha's miracles.

the prophet that is in Samaria! for he would recover him of his leprosy." She knew that the power of Heaven was with Elisha, and she believed that by this power Naaman could be healed.

The conduct of the captive maid, the way that she bore herself in that heathen home, is a strong witness to the power of early home training. There is no higher trust than that committed to fathers and mothers in the care and training of their children. Parents have to do with the very foundations of habit and character. By their example and teaching the future of their children is largely decided.

Happy are the parents whose lives are a true reflection of the divine, so that the promises and commands of God awaken in the child gratitude and reverence; the parents whose tenderness and justice and long-suffering interpret to the child the love and justice and long-suffering of God, and who by teaching the child to love and trust and obey them, are teaching him to love and trust and obey his Father in heaven. Parents who impart to the child such a gift have endowed him with a treasure more precious than the wealth of all the ages, a treasure as enduring as eternity.

We know not in what line our children may be called to serve. They may spend their lives within the circle of the home; they may engage in life's common vocations, or go as teachers of the gospel to heathen lands; but all are alike called to be missionaries for God, ministers of mercy to the world. They are to obtain an education that will help them to stand by the side of Christ in unselfish service.

The parents of that Hebrew maid, as they taught her of God, did not know the destiny that would be hers. But they were faithful to their trust; and in the home of the captain of the Syrian host, their child bore witness to the God whom she had learned to honor.

Naaman heard of the words that the maid had spoken to her mistress; and, obtaining permission from the king, he went forth to seek healing, taking with him "ten talents of silver, and six thousand pieces of gold, and ten changes of raiment." He also carried a letter from the king of Syria to the king of Israel, in which was written the message, "Behold, I have . . . sent Naaman my servant to thee, that thou mayest recover him of his leprosy." When the king of Israel read the letter, "he rent his clothes, and said, Am I God, to kill and to make alive, that this man doth send unto me to recover a man of his leprosy? wherefore consider, I pray you, and see how he seeketh a quarrel against me."

Tidings of the matter reached Elisha, and he sent word to the king, saying, "Wherefore hast thou rent thy clothes? let him come now to me, and he shall know that there is a prophet in Israel."

"So Naaman came with his horses and with his chariot, and stood at the door of the house of Elisha." Through a messenger the prophet bade him, "Go and wash in Jordan seven times, and thy flesh shall come again to thee, and thou shalt be clean."

Naaman had expected to see some wonderful manifestation of power from heaven. "I thought," he said, "he will surely come out to me, and stand, and call on the name of the Lord his God, and strike his hand over the place, and recover the leper." When told to wash in the Jordan, his pride was touched, and in mortification and disappointment he

exclaimed, "Are not Abana and Pharpar, rivers of Damascus, better than all the waters of Israel? may I not wash in them, and be clean?" "So he turned and went away in a rage."

The proud spirit of Naaman rebelled against following the course outlined by Elisha. The rivers mentioned by the Syrian captain were beautified by surrounding groves, and many flocked to the banks of these pleasant streams to worship their idol gods. It would have cost Naaman no great humiliation of soul to descend into one of those streams. But it was only through following the specific directions of the prophet that he could find healing. Willing obedience alone would bring the desired result.

Naaman's servants entreated him to carry out Elisha's directions: "If the prophet had bid thee do some great thing," they urged, "wouldest thou not have done it? how much rather then, when he saith to thee, Wash, and be clean?" The faith of Naaman was being tested, while pride struggled for the mastery. But faith conquered, and the haughty Syrian yielded his pride of heart and bowed in submission to the revealed will of Jehovah. Seven times he dipped himself in Jordan, "according to the saying of the man of God." And his faith was honored; "his flesh came again like unto the flesh of a little child, and he was clean."

Gratefully "he returned to the man of God, he and all his company," with the acknowledgment, "Behold, now I know that there is no God in all the earth, but in Israel."

In accordance with the custom of the times, Naaman now asked Elisha to accept a costly present. But the prophet refused. It was not for him to take payment for a blessing that God had in mercy bestowed. "As the Lord liveth," he said,

Naaman at first spurned Elisha's bidding
that he bathe in the Jordan River, but
he finally obeyed and came forth healed.
© P.P.P.A.   AMADO GONZALEZ, ARTIST

"I will receive none." The Syrian "urged him to take it; but he refused.

"And Naaman said, Shall there not then, I pray thee, be given to thy servant two mules' burden of earth? for thy servant will henceforth offer neither burnt offering nor sacrifice unto other gods, but unto the Lord. In this thing the Lord pardon thy servant, that when my master goeth into the house of Rimmon to worship there, and he leaneth on my hand, and I bow myself in the house of Rimmon: when I bow down myself in the house of Rimmon, the Lord pardon thy servant in this thing.

"And he said unto him, Go in peace. So he departed from him a little way."

Gehazi, Elisha's servant, had had opportunity during the years to develop the spirit of self-denial characterizing his master's lifework. It had been his privilege to become a noble standard-bearer in the army of the Lord. The best gifts of Heaven had long been within his reach; yet, turning from these, he had coveted instead the base alloy of worldly wealth. And now the hidden longings of his avaricious spirit led him to yield to an overmastering temptation. "Behold," he reasoned within himself, "my master hath spared Naaman this Syrian, in not receiving at his hands that which he brought: but . . . I will run after him, and take somewhat of him." And thus it came about that in secrecy "Gehazi followed after Naaman."

"When Naaman saw him running after him, he lighted down from the chariot to meet him, and said, Is all well? And he said, All is well." Then Gehazi uttered a deliberate lie. "My master," he said, "hath sent me, saying, Behold, even now there be come to me from Mount Ephraim two young men of the sons of the prophets: give them, I pray thee, a talent of silver, and two changes of garments." To the request Naaman gladly acceded, pressing upon Gehazi two talents of silver instead of one, "with two changes of garments," and commissioning servants to bear the treasure back.

As Gehazi neared Elisha's home, he dismissed the servants and placed the silver and the garments in hiding. This accomplished, "he went in, and stood before his master;" and, to shield himself from censure, he uttered a second lie. In response to the inquiry of the prophet, "Whence comest thou?" Gehazi answered, "Thy servant went no whither."

Then came the stern denunciation, showing that Elisha knew all. "Went not mine heart with thee," he asked, "when the man turned again from his chariot to meet thee? Is it a time to receive money, and to receive garments, and olive yards, and vineyards, and sheep, and oxen, and menservants, and maidservants? The leprosy therefore of Naaman shall cleave unto thee, and unto thy seed forever." Swift was the retribution that overtook the guilty man. He went out from Elisha's presence "a leper as white as snow."

Solemn are the lessons taught by this experience of one to whom had been given high and holy privileges. The course of Gehazi was such as to place a stumbling block in the pathway of Naaman, upon whose mind had broken a wonderful light, and who was favorably disposed toward the service of the living God. For the deception practiced by Gehazi there could be pleaded no excuse. To the day of his death he remained a leper, cursed of God and shunned by his fellow men.

"A false witness shall not be unpunished, and he that

speaketh lies shall not escape." Proverbs 19:5. Men may think to hide their evil deeds from human eyes, but they cannot deceive God. "All things are naked and opened unto the eyes of Him with whom we have to do." Hebrews 4:13. Gehazi thought to deceive Elisha, but God revealed to His prophet the words that Gehazi had spoken to Naaman, and every detail of the scene between the two men.

Truth is of God; deception in all its myriad forms is of Satan, and whoever in any way departs from the straight line of truth is betraying himself into the power of the wicked one. Those who have learned of Christ will "have no fellowship with the unfruitful works of darkness." Ephesians 5:11. In speech, as in life, they will be simple, straightforward, and true, for they are preparing for the fellowship of those holy ones in whose mouth is found no guile. See Revelation 14:5.

Centuries after Naaman returned to his Syrian home, healed in body and converted in spirit, his wonderful faith was referred to and commended by the Saviour as an object lesson for all who claim to serve God. "Many lepers were in Israel in the time of Eliseus the prophet," the Saviour declared; "and none of them was cleansed, saving Naaman the Syrian." Luke 4:27. God passed over the many lepers in Israel because their unbelief closed the door of good to them. A heathen nobleman who had been true to his convictions of right, and who felt his need of help, was in the sight of God more worthy of His blessing than were the afflicted in Israel, who had slighted and despised their God-given privileges. God works for those who appreciate His favors and respond to the light given them from heaven.

Today in every land there are those who are honest in heart, and upon these the light of heaven is shining. If they continue faithful in following that which they understand to be duty, they will be given increased light, until, like Naaman of old, they will be constrained to acknowledge that "there is no God in all the earth," save the living God, the Creator.

To every sincere soul "that walketh in darkness, and hath no light," is given the invitation, "Let him trust in the name of the Lord, and stay upon his God." "For since the beginning of the world men have not heard, nor perceived by the ear, neither hath the eye seen, O God, beside Thee, what He hath prepared for him that waiteth for Him. Thou meetest him that rejoiceth and worketh righteousness, those that remember Thee in Thy ways." Isaiah 50:10; 64:4, 5.

chapter 21

Elisha's Closing Ministry

CALLED to the prophetic office while Ahab was still reigning, Elisha had lived to see many changes take place in the kingdom of Israel. Judgment upon judgment had befallen the Israelites during the reign of Hazael the Syrian, who had been anointed to be the scourge of the apostate nation. The stern measures of reform instituted by Jehu had resulted in the slaying of all the house of Ahab. In continued wars with the Syrians, Jehoahaz, Jehu's successor, had lost some of the cities lying east of the Jordan. For a time it had seemed as if the Syrians might gain control of the entire kingdom. But the reformation begun by Elijah and carried forward by Elisha had led many to inquire after God. The altars of Baal were being forsaken, and slowly yet surely God's purpose was being fulfilled in the lives of those who chose to serve Him with all the heart.

It was because of His love for erring Israel that God permitted the Syrians to scourge them. It was because of His

Intending to take Elisha captive, the Syrians camped outside the city could not see the angelic hosts protecting him.

compassion for those whose moral power was weak that He raised up Jehu to slay wicked Jezebel and all the house of Ahab. Once more, through a merciful providence, the priests of Baal and of Ashtoreth were set aside and their heathen altars thrown down. God in His wisdom foresaw that if temptation were removed, some would forsake heathenism and turn their faces heavenward, and this is why He permitted calamity after calamity to befall them. His judgments were tempered with mercy; and when His purpose was accomplished, He turned the tide in favor of those who had learned to inquire after Him.

While influences for good and for evil were striving for the ascendancy, and Satan was doing all in his power to complete the ruin he had wrought during the reign of Ahab and Jezebel, Elisha continued to bear his testimony. He met with opposition, yet none could gainsay his words. Throughout the kingdom he was honored and venerated. Many came to him for counsel. While Jezebel was still living, Joram, the king of Israel, sought his advice; and once, when in Damascus, he was visited by messengers from Benhadad, king of Syria, who desired to learn whether a sickness then upon him would result in death. To all the prophet bore faithful witness in a time when, on every hand, truth was being perverted and the great majority of the people were in open rebellion against Heaven.

And God never forsook His chosen messenger. On one occasion, during a Syrian invasion, the king of Syria sought to destroy Elisha because of his activity in apprising the king of Israel of the plans of the enemy. The Syrian king had taken counsel with his servants, saying, "In such and such a place shall be my camp." This plan was revealed by the Lord to Elisha, who "sent unto the king of Israel, saying, Beware that thou pass not such a place; for thither the Syrians are come down. And the king of Israel sent to the place which the man of God told him and warned him of, and saved himself there, not once nor twice.

"Therefore the heart of the king of Syria was sore troubled for this thing; and he called his servants, and said unto them, Will ye not show me which of us is for the king of Israel? And one of his servants said, None, my lord, O king: but Elisha, the prophet that is in Israel, telleth the king of Israel the words that thou speakest in thy bedchamber."

Determined to make away with the prophet, the Syrian king commanded, "Go and spy where he is, that I may send and fetch him." The prophet was in Dothan; and, learning this, the king sent thither "horses, and chariots, and a great host: and they came by night, and compassed the city about. And when the servant of the man of God was risen early, and gone forth, behold, an host compassed the city both with horses and chariots."

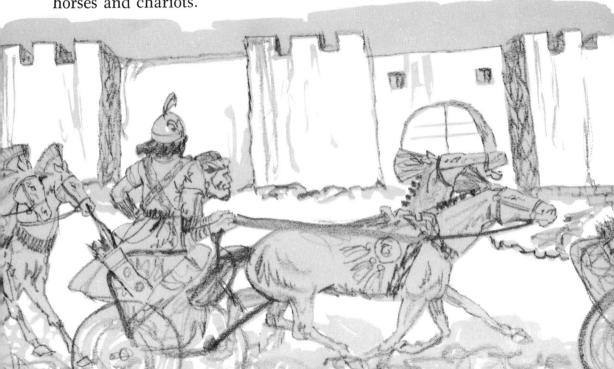

In terror Elisha's servant sought him with the tidings. "Alas, my master!" he said, "how shall we do?"

"Fear not," was the answer of the prophet; "for they that be with us are more than they that be with them." And then, that the servant might know this for himself, "Elisha prayed, and said, Lord, I pray Thee, open his eyes, that he may see." "The Lord opened the eyes of the young man; and he saw: and behold, the mountain was full of horses and chariots of fire round about Elisha." Between the servant of God and the hosts of armed foemen was an encircling band of heavenly angels. They had come down in mighty power, not to destroy, not to exact homage, but to encamp round about and minister to the Lord's weak and helpless ones.

When the people of God are brought into strait places, and apparently there is no escape for them, the Lord alone must be their dependence.

As the company of Syrian soldiers boldly advanced, ignorant of the unseen hosts of heaven, "Elisha prayed unto the Lord, and said, Smite this people, I pray Thee, with blindness. And He smote them with blindness according to the word of Elisha. And Elisha said unto them, This is not the way, neither is this the city: follow me, and I will bring you to the man whom ye seek. But he led them to Samaria.

"And it came to pass, when they were come into Samaria, that Elisha said, Lord, open the eyes of these men, that they may see. And the Lord opened their eyes, and they saw; and, behold, they were in the midst of Samaria. And the king of Israel said unto Elisha, when he saw them, My father, shall I smite them? shall I smite them? And he answered, Thou shalt not smite them: wouldest thou smite those whom thou hast taken captive with thy sword and with thy bow? set bread and water before them, that they may eat and drink, and go to their master. And he prepared great provision for them: and when they had eaten and drunk, he sent them away, and they went to their master." See 2 Kings 6.

For a time after this, Israel was free from the attacks of the Syrians. But later, under the energetic direction of a determined king, Hazael, the Syrian hosts surrounded Samaria and besieged it. Never had Israel been brought into so great a strait as during this siege. The sins of the fathers were indeed being visited upon the children and the children's children. The horrors of prolonged famine were driving the king of Israel to desperate measures, when Elisha predicted deliverance the following day.

As the next morning was about to dawn, the Lord "made the host of the Syrians to hear a noise of chariots, and a noise of horses, even the noise of a great host;" and they, seized with fear, "arose and fled in the twilight," leaving "their tents, and their horses, and their asses, even the camp as it was," with rich stores of food. They "fled for their life," not tarrying until after the Jordan had been crossed.

During the night of the flight, four leprous men at the gate of the city, made desperate by hunger, had proposed to visit the Syrian camp and throw themselves upon the mercy of the besiegers, hoping thereby to arouse sympathy and obtain food. What was their astonishment when, entering the camp, they found "no man there." With none to molest or forbid, "they went into one tent, and did eat and drink, and carried thence silver, and gold, and raiment, and went and hid it; and came again, and entered into another tent, and carried thence also, and went and hid it. Then they said one to another, We do not well: this day is a day of good tidings, and we hold our peace." Quickly they returned to the city with the glad news.

Great was the spoil; so abundant were the supplies that on that day "a measure of fine flour was sold for a shekel, and two measures of barley for a shekel," as had been foretold by Elisha the day before. Once more the name of God was exalted before the heathen "according to the word of the Lord" through His prophet in Israel. See 2 Kings 7:5-16.

Thus the man of God continued to labor from year to year, drawing close to the people in faithful ministry, and in times of crisis standing by the side of kings as a wise counselor. The long years of idolatrous backsliding on the part of rulers and people had wrought their baleful work; the dark shadow of apostasy was still everywhere apparent, yet here and there were those who had steadfastly refused to bow the knee to Baal. As Elisha continued his work of reform, many were reclaimed from heathenism, and these learned to rejoice in the service of the true God. The prophet was cheered by these miracles of divine grace, and he was inspired with a great longing to reach all who were honest in heart. Wherever he was he endeavored to be a teacher of righteousness.

From a human point of view the outlook for the spiritual regeneration of the nation was as hopeless as is the outlook today before God's servants who are laboring in the dark places of the earth. But the church of Christ is God's agency for the proclamation of truth; she is empowered by Him to do a special work; and if she is loyal to God, obedient to His commandments, there will dwell within her the excellency of divine power. If she will be true to her allegiance, there is no power that can stand against her. The forces of the enemy will be no more able to overwhelm her than is the chaff to resist the whirlwind.

There is before the church the dawn of a bright, glorious day, if she will put on the robe of Christ's righteousness, withdrawing from all allegiance to the world.

God calls upon His faithful ones, who believe in Him, to talk courage to those who are unbelieving and hopeless. Turn to the Lord, ye prisoners of hope. Seek strength from God, the living God. Show an unwavering, humble faith in His power and His willingness to save. When in faith we take hold of His strength, He will change, wonderfully change, the most hopeless, discouraging outlook. He will do this for the glory of His name.

So long as Elisha was able to journey from place to place throughout the kingdom of Israel, he continued to take an active interest in the upbuilding of the schools of the prophets. Wherever he was, God was with him, giving him words to speak and power to work miracles. On one occasion "the sons of the prophets said unto Elisha, Behold now, the place where we dwell with thee is too strait for us. Let us go, we pray thee, unto Jordan, and take thence every man a beam, and let us make us a place there, where we may dwell." 2 Kings 6:1, 2. Elisha went with them to Jordan, encouraging them by his presence, giving them instruction, and even performing a miracle to aid them in their work. "As one was felling a beam, the axhead fell into the water: and he cried, and said, Alas, master! for it was borrowed. And the man of God said, Where fell it? And he showed him the place. And he cut down a stick, and cast it in thither; and the iron did swim. Therefore said he, Take it up to thee. And he put out his hand, and took it." Verses 5-7.

So effectual had been his ministry and so widespread his influence that, as he lay upon his deathbed, even the youthful King Joash, an idolater with but little respect for God, recognized in the prophet a father in Israel, and acknowledged that his presence among them was of more value in time of trouble than the possession of an army of horses and chariots. The record reads: "Now Elisha was fallen sick of his sickness whereof he died. And Joash the king of Israel came down unto him, and wept over his face, and said, O my father, my father, the chariot of Israel, and the horsemen thereof." 2 Kings 13:14.

To many a troubled soul in need of help the prophet had acted the part of a wise, sympathetic father. And in this instance he turned not from the godless youth before him, so unworthy of the position of trust he was occupying, and yet so greatly in need of counsel. God in His providence was bringing to the king an opportunity to redeem the failures of the past and to place his kingdom on vantage ground. The Syrian foe, now occupying the territory east of the Jordan, was to be repulsed. Once more the power of God was to be manifested in behalf of erring Israel.

The dying prophet bade the king, "Take bow and arrows." Joash obeyed. Then the prophet said, "Put thine hand upon the bow." Joash "put his hand upon it: and Elisha put his hands upon the king's hands. And he said, Open the window eastward"—toward the cities beyond the Jordan in possession of the Syrians. The king having opened the latticed window, Elisha bade him shoot. As the arrow sped on its way, the prophet was inspired to say, "The arrow of the Lord's deliverance, and the arrow of deliverance from Syria: for thou shalt smite the Syrians in Aphek, till thou have consumed them."

And now the prophet tested the faith of the king. Bidding Joash take up the arrows, he said, "Smite upon the ground." Thrice the king smote the ground, and then he stayed his hand. "Thou shouldest have smitten five or six times," Elisha exclaimed in dismay; "then hadst thou smitten Syria till thou hadst consumed it: whereas now thou shalt smite Syria but thrice." 2 Kings 13:15-19.

The lesson is for all in positions of trust. When God opens the way for the accomplishment of a certain work and gives assurance of success, the chosen instrumentality must do all in his power to bring about the promised result. In proportion to the enthusiasm and perseverance with which the work is carried forward will be the success given. God can work miracles for His people only as they act their part with untiring energy. He calls for men of devotion to His work, men of moral courage, with ardent love for souls, and with a zeal that never flags. Such workers will find no task too arduous, no prospect too hopeless; they will labor on, undaunted, until apparent defeat is turned into glorious victory. Not even prison walls nor the martyr's stake beyond, will cause them to swerve from their purpose of laboring together with God for the upbuilding of His kingdom.

With the counsel and encouragement given Joash, the work of Elisha closed. He upon whom had fallen in full measure the Spirit resting upon Elijah, had proved faithful to the end. Never had he wavered. Never had he lost his trust in the power of Omnipotence. Always, when the way before him seemed utterly closed, he had still advanced by faith, and God had honored his confidence and opened the way before him.

It was not given Elisha to follow his master in a fiery chariot. Upon him the Lord permitted to come a lingering illness. During the long hours of human weakness and suffering his faith laid fast hold on the promises of God, and he beheld ever about him heavenly messengers of comfort and peace. As on the heights of Dothan he had seen the encircling hosts of heaven, the fiery chariots of Israel and the horsemen thereof, so now he was conscious of the presence of sympathizing angels, and he was sustained. Throughout his life he had exercised strong faith, and as he had advanced in a knowledge of God's providences and of His merciful kindness, faith had ripened into an abiding trust in his God, and when death called him he was ready to rest from his labors.

"Precious in the sight of the Lord is the death of His saints." Psalm 116:15. "The righteous hath hope in his death." Proverbs 14:32. With the psalmist, Elisha could say in all confidence, "God will redeem my soul from the power of the grave: for He shall receive me." Psalm 49:15. And with rejoicing he could testify, "I know that my Redeemer liveth, and that He shall stand at the latter day upon the earth." Job 19:25. "As for me, I will behold Thy face in righteousness: I shall be satisfied, when I awake, with Thy likeness." Psalm 17:15.

chapter 22

"Nineveh, That Great City"

AMONG the cities of the ancient world in the days of divided Israel one of the greatest was Nineveh, the capital of the Assyrian realm. Founded on the fertile bank of the Tigris, soon after the dispersion from the tower of Babel, it had flourished through the centuries until it had become "an exceeding great city of three days' journey." Jonah 3:3.

In the time of its temporal prosperity Nineveh was a center of crime and wickedness. Inspiration has characterized it as "the bloody city, . . . full of lies and robbery." In figurative language the prophet Nahum compared the Ninevites to a cruel, ravenous lion. "Upon whom," he inquired, "hath not thy wickedness passed continually?" Nahum 3:1, 19.

Yet Nineveh, wicked though it had become, was not wholly given over to evil. He who "beholdeth all the sons of men" (Psalm 33:13) and "seeth every precious thing" (Job 28:10) perceived in that city many who were reaching out after something better and higher, and who, if granted opportunity

The sailors took Jonah up and tossed him overboard into the tempestuous sea, where a "great fish" swallowed him.
© P.P.P.A.   JOHN STEEL, ARTIST

18—P.A.K.

to learn of the living God, would put away their evil deeds and worship Him. And so in His wisdom God revealed Himself to them in an unmistakable manner, to lead them, if possible, to repentance.

The instrument chosen for this work was the prophet Jonah, the son of Amittai. To him came the word of the Lord, "Arise, go to Nineveh, that great city, and cry against it; for their wickedness is come up before Me." Jonah 1:1, 2.

As the prophet thought of the difficulties and seeming impossibilities of this commission, he was tempted to question the wisdom of the call. From a human viewpoint it seemed as if nothing could be gained by proclaiming such a message in that proud city. He forgot for the moment that the God whom he served was all-wise and all-powerful. While he hesitated, still doubting, Satan overwhelmed him with discouragement. The prophet was seized with a great dread, and he "rose up to flee unto Tarshish." Going to Joppa, and finding there a ship ready to sail, "he paid the fare thereof and went down into it, to go with them." Verse 3.

In the charge given him, Jonah had been entrusted with a heavy responsibility; yet He who had bidden him go was able to sustain His servant and grant him success. Had the prophet obeyed unquestioningly, he would have been spared many bitter experiences, and would have been blessed abundantly. Yet in the hour of Jonah's despair the Lord did not desert him. Through a series of trials and strange providences, the prophet's confidence in God and in His infinite power to save was to be revived.

If, when the call first came to him, Jonah had stopped to consider calmly, he might have known how foolish would be any effort on his part to escape the responsibility placed upon him. But not for long was he permitted to go on undisturbed in his mad flight. "The Lord sent out a great wind into the sea, and there was a mighty tempest in the sea, so that the ship was like to be broken. Then the mariners were afraid, and cried every man unto his god, and cast forth the wares that were in the ship into the sea, to lighten it of them. But Jonah was gone down into the sides of the ship; and he lay, and was fast asleep." Verses 4, 5.

As the mariners were beseeching their heathen gods for help, the master of the ship, distressed beyond measure, sought out Jonah and said, "What meanest thou, O sleeper? arise, call upon thy God, if so be that God will think upon us, that we perish not." Verse 6.

But the prayers of the man who had turned aside from the path of duty brought no help. The mariners, impressed with the thought that the strange violence of the storm betokened the anger of their gods, proposed as a last resort the casting of lots, "that we may know," they said, "for whose cause this evil is upon us. So they cast lots, and the lot fell upon Jonah. Then said they unto him, Tell us, we pray thee, for whose cause this evil is upon us; what is thine occupation? and whence comest thou? what is thy country? and of what people art thou?

"And he said unto them, I am an Hebrew; and I fear the Lord, the God of heaven, which hath made the sea and the dry land.

"Then were the men exceedingly afraid, and said unto him, Why hast thou done this? For the men knew that he fled from the presence of the Lord, because he had told them.

"Then said they unto him, What shall we do unto thee, that the sea may be calm unto us? for the sea wrought, and was tempestuous. And he said unto them, Take me up, and cast me forth into the sea; so shall the sea be calm unto you: for I know that for my sake this great tempest is upon you.

"Nevertheless the men rowed hard to bring it to the land; but they could not: for the sea wrought, and was tempestuous against them. Wherefore they cried unto the Lord, and said, We beseech Thee, O Lord, we beseech Thee, let us not perish for this man's life, and lay not upon us innocent blood: for Thou, O Lord, hast done as it pleased Thee. So they took up Jonah, and cast him forth into the sea: and the sea ceased from her raging. Then the men feared the Lord exceedingly, and offered a sacrifice unto the Lord, and made vows.

"Now the Lord had prepared a great fish to swallow up Jonah. And Jonah was in the belly of the fish three days and three nights.

"Then Jonah prayed unto the Lord his God out of the fish's belly, and said:

"I cried by reason of mine affliction unto the Lord,
    And He heard me;
Out of the belly of hell cried I,
    And Thou heardest my voice.

"For Thou hadst cast me into the deep,
    In the midst of the seas;
And the floods compassed me about:
    All Thy billows and Thy waves passed over me.

"Then I said, I am cast out of Thy sight;
    Yet I will look again toward Thy holy temple.
The waters compassed me about,
    Even to the soul:

"The depth closed me round about,
    The weeds were wrapped about my head.
I went down to the bottoms of the mountains;
    The earth with her bars was about me forever:

"Yet hast Thou brought up my life from corruption, O
    Lord my God.
    When my soul fainted within me I remembered the
    Lord:
And my prayer came in unto Thee,
    Into Thine holy temple.

"They that observe lying vanities forsake their own mercy.
But I will sacrifice unto Thee with the voice of
    thanksgiving;
I will pay that that I have vowed.
    Salvation is of the Lord."
                    Jonah 1:7 to 2:9.

At last Jonah had learned that "salvation belongeth unto the Lord." Psalm 3:8. With penitence and a recognition of the saving grace of God, came deliverance. Jonah was released from the perils of the mighty deep and was cast upon the dry land.

Once more the servant of God was commissioned to warn Nineveh. "The word of the Lord came unto Jonah the second time, saying, Arise, go unto Nineveh, that great city, and preach unto it the preaching that I bid thee." This time he did not stop to question or doubt, but obeyed unhesitatingly. He "arose, and went unto Nineveh, according to the word of the Lord." Jonah 3:1-3.

As Jonah entered the city, he began at once to "cry against" it the message, "Yet forty days, and Nineveh shall be overthrown." Verse 4. From street to street he went, sounding the note of warning.

The message was not in vain. The cry that rang through the streets of the godless city was passed from lip to lip until all the inhabitants had heard the startling announcement. The Spirit of God pressed the message home to every heart and caused multitudes to tremble because of their sins and to repent in deep humiliation.

"The people of Nineveh believed God, and proclaimed a fast, and put on sackcloth, from the greatest of them even to the least of them. For word came unto the king of Nineveh, and he arose from his throne, and he laid his robe from him, and covered him with sackcloth, and sat in ashes. And he caused it to be proclaimed and published through Nineveh by the decree of the king and his nobles, saying, Let neither man nor beast, herd nor flock, taste anything: let them not feed, nor drink water: but let man and beast be covered with sackcloth, and cry mightily unto God: yea, let them turn everyone from his evil way, and from the violence that is in their hands. Who can tell if God will turn and repent, and turn away from His fierce anger, that we perish not?" Verses 5-9.

As king and nobles, with the common people, the high and the low, "repented at the preaching of Jonas" (Matthew 12:41) and united in crying to the God of heaven, His mercy was granted them. He "saw their works, that they turned from their evil way; and God repented of the evil, that He had said that He would do unto them; and He did it not." Jonah 3:10. Their doom was averted, the God of Israel was exalted and honored throughout the heathen world, and His law was revered. Not until many years later was Nineveh to fall a prey to the surrounding nations through forgetfulness of God and through boastful pride. [For an account of the downfall of Assyria, see chapter 30.]

When Jonah learned of God's purpose to spare the city that, notwithstanding its wickedness, had been led to repent in sackcloth and ashes, he should have been the first to rejoice because of God's amazing grace; but instead he allowed his mind to dwell upon the possibility of his being regarded as a false prophet. Jealous of his reputation, he lost sight of the infinitely greater value of the souls in that wretched city. The compassion shown by God toward the repentant Ninevites "displeased Jonah exceedingly, and he was very angry." "Was not this my saying," he inquired of the Lord, "when I was yet in my country? Therefore I fled before unto Tarshish: for I knew that Thou art a gracious God, and merciful, slow to anger, and of great kindness, and repentest Thee of the evil." Jonah 4:1, 2.

Once more he yielded to his inclination to question and doubt, and once more he was overwhelmed with discouragement. Losing sight of the interests of others, and feeling as if he would rather die than live to see the city spared, in his dissatisfaction he exclaimed, "Now, O Lord, take, I beseech Thee, my life from me; for it is better for me to die than to live."

"Doest thou well to be angry?" the Lord inquired. "So Jonah went out of the city, and sat on the east side of the city, and there made him a booth, and sat under it in the shadow, till he might see what would become of the city. And the Lord God prepared a gourd, and made it to come up over Jonah, that it might be a shadow over his head, to deliver him from his grief. So Jonah was exceeding glad of the gourd." Verses 3-6.

Then the Lord gave Jonah an object lesson. He "prepared a worm when the morning rose the next day, and it smote the gourd that it withered. And it came to pass, when the sun did arise, that God prepared a vehement east wind; and the sun beat upon the head of Jonah, that he fainted, and wished in himself to die, and said, It is better for me to die than to live."

Again God spoke to His prophet, "Doest thou well to be angry for the gourd?" And he said, "I do well to be angry, even unto death."

"Then said the Lord, Thou hast had pity on the gourd, for the which thou hast not labored, neither madest it grow; which came up in a night, and perished in a night: and should not I spare Nineveh, that great city, wherein are more than sixscore thousand persons that cannot discern between their right hand and their left hand; and also much cattle?" Verses 7-11.

Confused, humiliated, and unable to understand God's purpose in sparing Nineveh, Jonah nevertheless had fulfilled the commission given him to warn that great city; and though the event predicted did not come to pass, yet the message of warning was nonetheless from God. And it accomplished the purpose God designed it should. The glory of His grace was revealed among the heathen. Those who had long been sitting "in darkness and in the shadow of death, being bound in affliction and iron," "cried unto the Lord in their trouble," and "He saved them out of their distresses. He brought them out of darkness and the shadow of death, and brake their bands in sunder." "He sent His word, and healed them, and delivered them from their destructions." Psalm 107:10, 13, 14, 20.

Christ during His earthly ministry referred to the good wrought by the preaching of Jonah in Nineveh, and compared the inhabitants of that heathen center with the professed people of God in His day. "The men of Nineveh," He declared, "shall rise in judgment with this generation, and shall condemn it: because they repented at the preaching of Jonas; and, behold, a greater than Jonas is here." Matthew 12:40, 41. Into the busy world, filled with the din of commerce and the altercation of trade, where men were trying to get all they could for self, Christ had come; and above the confusion His voice, like the trump of God, was heard: "What shall it profit a man, if he shall gain the whole world, and lose his own soul? or what shall a man give in exchange for his soul?" Mark 8:36, 37.

As the preaching of Jonah was a sign to the Ninevites, so Christ's preaching was a sign to His generation. But what a contrast in the reception of the word! Yet in the face of indifference and scorn the Saviour labored on and on, until He had accomplished His mission.

The lesson is for God's messengers today, when the cities of the nations are as verily in need of a knowledge of the attributes and purposes of the true God as were the Ninevites of old. Christ's ambassadors are to point men to the nobler world, which has largely been lost sight of. According to the teaching of the Holy Scriptures, the only city that will endure is the city whose builder and maker is God. With the eye of faith man may behold the threshold of heaven, flushed with God's living glory. Through His ministering servants the Lord Jesus is calling upon men to strive with sanctified ambition to secure the immortal inheritance. He urges them to lay up treasure beside the throne of God.

There is coming rapidly and surely an almost universal guilt upon the inhabitants of the cities, because of the steady increase of determined wickedness. The corruption that prevails is beyond the power of the human pen to describe. Every day brings fresh revelations of strife, bribery, and fraud; every day brings its heart-sickening record of violence and lawlessness, of indifference to human suffering, of brutal, fiendish destruction of human life. Every day testifies to the increase of insanity, murder, and suicide.

From age to age Satan has sought to keep men in ignorance of the beneficent designs of Jehovah. He has endeavored to remove from their sight the great things of God's law—the principles of justice, mercy, and love therein set forth. Men boast of the wonderful progress and enlightenment of the age in which we are now living; but God sees the earth filled with iniquity and violence. Men declare that the law of God has been abrogated, that the Bible is not authentic; and as a result, a tide of evil, such as has not been seen since the days of Noah and of apostate Israel, is sweeping over the world. Nobility of soul, gentleness, piety, are bartered away to gratify the lust for forbidden things. The black record of crime committed for the sake of gain is enough to chill the blood and fill the soul with horror.

Our God is a God of mercy. With long-sufferance and tender compassion He deals with the transgressors of His law. And yet, in this our day, when men and women have so many opportunities for becoming familiar with the divine law as revealed in Holy Writ, the great Ruler of the universe cannot behold with any satisfaction the wicked cities, where reign violence and crime. The end of God's forbearance with those who persist in disobedience is approaching rapidly.

Ought men to be surprised over a sudden and unexpected change in the dealings of the Supreme Ruler with the inhabitants of a fallen world? Ought they to be surprised when punishment follows transgression and increasing crime? Ought they to be surprised that God should bring destruction and death upon those whose ill-gotten gains have been obtained through deception and fraud? Notwithstanding the fact that increasing light regarding God's requirements has been shining on their pathway, many have refused to recognize Jehovah's rulership, and have chosen to remain under the black banner of the originator of all rebellion against the government of heaven.

The forbearance of God has been very great—so great that when we consider the continuous insult to His holy commandments, we marvel. The Omnipotent One has been exerting a restraining power over His own attributes. But He will certainly arise to punish the wicked, who so boldly defy the just claims of the Decalogue.

God allows men a period of probation; but there is a point beyond which divine patience is exhausted, and the judgments of God are sure to follow. The Lord bears long with men, and with cities, mercifully giving warnings to save them from divine wrath; but a time will come when pleadings for mercy will no longer be heard, and the rebellious element that continues to reject the light of truth will be blotted out, in mercy to themselves and to those who would otherwise be influenced by their example.

The time is at hand when there will be sorrow in the world that no human balm can heal. The Spirit of God is being withdrawn. Disasters by sea and by land follow one another in quick succession. How frequently we hear of earthquakes and tornadoes, of destruction by fire and flood, with great loss of life and property! Apparently these calamities are capricious outbreaks of disorganized, unregulated forces of nature, wholly beyond the control of man; but in them all, God's purpose may be read. They are among the agencies by which He seeks to arouse men and women to a sense of their danger.

God's messengers in the great cities are not to become discouraged over the wickedness, the injustice, the depravity, which they are called upon to face while endeavoring to proclaim the glad tidings of salvation. The Lord would cheer every such worker with the same message that He gave to the apostle Paul in wicked Corinth: "Be not afraid, but speak, and hold not thy peace: for I am with thee, and no man shall set on thee to hurt thee: for I have much people in this city." Acts 18:9, 10. Let those engaged in soul-saving ministry remember that while there are many who will not heed the counsel of God in His word, the whole world will not turn from light and truth, from the invitations of a patient, forbearing Saviour. In every city, filled though it may be with violence and crime, there are many who with proper teaching may learn to become followers of Jesus. Thousands may thus be reached with saving truth and be led to receive Christ as a personal Saviour.

God's message for the inhabitants of earth today is, "Be ye also ready: for in such an hour as ye think not the Son of man cometh." Matthew 24:44. The conditions prevailing in society, and especially in the great cities of the nations, proclaim in thunder tones that the hour of God's judgment is come and that the end of all things earthly is at hand. We are standing on the threshold of the crisis of the ages. In quick succession the judgments of God will follow one another—fire, and flood, and earthquake, with war and bloodshed. We are not to be surprised at this time by events both great and decisive; for the angel of mercy cannot remain much longer to shelter the impenitent.

"Behold, the Lord cometh out of His place to punish the inhabitants of the earth for their iniquity: the earth also shall disclose her blood, and shall no more cover her slain." Isaiah 26:21. The storm of God's wrath is gathering; and those only will stand who respond to the invitations of mercy, as did the inhabitants of Nineveh under the preaching of Jonah, and become sanctified through obedience to the laws of the divine Ruler. The righteous alone shall be hid with Christ in God till the desolation be overpast. Let the language of the soul be:

> "Other refuge have I none,
> Hangs my helpless soul on Thee;
> Leave, O, leave me not alone!
> Still support and comfort me.

> "Hide me, O my Saviour, hide!
> Till the storm of life is past;
> Safe into the haven guide,
> O receive my soul at last!"

chapter 23

The Assyrian Captivity

THE closing years of the ill-fated kingdom of Israel were marked with violence and bloodshed such as had never been witnessed even in the worst periods of strife and unrest under the house of Ahab. For two centuries and more the rulers of the ten tribes had been sowing the wind; now they were reaping the whirlwind. King after king was assassinated to make way for others ambitious to rule. "They have set up kings," the Lord declared of these godless usurpers, "but not by Me: they have made princes, and I knew it not." Hosea 8:4. Every principle of justice was set aside; those who should have stood before the nations of earth as the depositaries of divine grace, "dealt treacherously against the Lord" and with one another. Hosea 5:7.

With the severest reproofs, God sought to arouse the impenitent nation to a realization of its imminent danger of utter destruction. Through Hosea and Amos He sent the ten tribes message after message, urging full and complete repentance, and threatening disaster as the result of continued transgression. "Ye have plowed wickedness," declared Hosea,

"ye have reaped iniquity; ye have eaten the fruit of lies: because thou didst trust in thy way, in the multitude of thy mighty men. Therefore shall a tumult arise among thy people, and all thy fortresses shall be spoiled. . . . In a morning shall the king of Israel utterly be cut off." Hosea 10:13-15.

Of Ephraim the prophet testified, "Strangers have devoured his strength, and he knoweth it not: yea, gray hairs are here and there upon him, yet he knoweth not." [The prophet Hosea often referred to Ephraim, a leader in apostasy among the tribes of Israel, as a symbol of the apostate nation.] "Israel hath cast off the thing that is good." "Broken in judgment," unable to discern the disastrous outcome of their evil course, the ten tribes were soon to be "wanderers among the nations." Hosea 7:9; 8:3; 5:11; 9:17.

Some of the leaders in Israel felt keenly their loss of prestige and wished that this might be regained. But instead of turning away from those practices which had brought weakness to the kingdom, they continued in iniquity, flattering themselves that when occasion arose, they would attain to the political power they desired by allying themselves with the heathen. "When Ephraim saw his sickness, and Judah saw his wound, then went Ephraim to the Assyrian." "Ephraim also is like a silly dove without heart: they call to Egypt, they go to Assyria." "They do make a covenant with the Assyrians." Hosea 5:13; 7:11; 12:1.

Through the man of God that had appeared before the altar at Bethel, through Elijah and Elisha, through Amos and Hosea, the Lord had repeatedly set before the ten tribes the evils of disobedience. But notwithstanding reproof and entreaty, Israel had sunk lower and still lower in apostasy. "Israel

Following two centuries of apostasy and rejection of divine reproof, Israel was taken captive by the Assyrians.

© P.P.P.A.   JOHN STEEL, ARTIST

slideth back as a backsliding heifer," the Lord declared; "My people are bent to backsliding from Me." Hosea 4:16; 11:7.

There were times when the judgments of Heaven fell very heavily on the rebellious people. "I hewed them by the prophets," God declared; "I have slain them by the words of My mouth: and thy judgments are as the light that goeth forth. For I desired mercy, and not sacrifice; and the knowledge of God more than burnt offerings. But they like men have transgressed the covenant: there have they dealt treacherously against Me." Hosea 6:5-7.

"Hear the word of the Lord, ye children of Israel," was the message that finally came to them: "Seeing thou hast forgotten the law of thy God, I will also forget thy children. As they were increased, so they sinned against Me: therefore will I change their glory into shame. . . . I will punish them for their ways, and reward them their doings." Hosea 4:1, 6-9.

The iniquity in Israel during the last half century before the Assyrian captivity was like that of the days of Noah, and of every other age when men have rejected God and have given themselves wholly to evil-doing. The exaltation of nature above the God of nature, the worship of the creature instead of the Creator, has always resulted in the grossest of evils. Thus when the people of Israel, in their worship of Baal and Ashtoreth, paid supreme homage to the forces of nature, they severed their connection with all that is uplifting and ennobling, and fell an easy prey to temptation. With the defenses of the soul broken down, the misguided worshipers had no barrier against sin and yielded themselves to the evil passions of the human heart.

Against the marked oppression, the flagrant injustice, the

unwonted luxury and extravagance, the shameless feasting and drunkenness, the gross licentiousness and debauchery, of their age, the prophets lifted their voices; but in vain were their protests, in vain their denunciation of sin. "Him that rebuketh in the gate," declared Amos, "they hate, . . . and they abhor him that speaketh uprightly." "They afflict the just, they take a bribe, and they turn aside the poor in the gate from their right." Amos 5:10, 12.

Such were some of the results that had followed the setting up of the two calves of gold by Jeroboam. The first departure from established forms of worship had led to the introduction of grosser forms of idolatry, until finally nearly all the inhabitants of the land had given themselves over to the alluring practices of nature worship. Forgetting their Maker, Israel "deeply corrupted themselves." Hosea 9:9.

The prophets continued to protest against these evils and to plead for rightdoing. "Sow to yourselves in righteousness, reap in mercy," Hosea urged; "break up your fallow ground: for it is time to seek the Lord, till He come and rain righteousness upon you." "Turn thou to thy God: keep mercy and judgment, and wait on thy God continually." "O Israel, return unto the Lord thy God; for thou hast fallen by thine iniquity: . . . say unto Him, Take away all iniquity, and receive us graciously." Hosea 10:12; 12:6; 14:1, 2.

The transgressors were given many opportunities to repent. In their hour of deepest apostasy and greatest need, God's message to them was one of forgiveness and hope. "O Israel," He declared, "thou hast destroyed thyself; but in Me is thine help. I will be thy King: where is any other that may save thee?" Hosea 13:9, 10.

"Come, and let us return unto the Lord," the prophet entreated; "for He hath torn, and He will heal us; He hath smitten, and He will bind us up. After two days will He revive us: in the third day He will raise us up, and we shall live in His sight. Then shall we know, if we follow on to know the Lord: His going forth is prepared as the morning; and He shall come unto us as the rain, as the latter and former rain unto the earth." Hosea 6:1-3.

To those who had lost sight of the plan of the ages for the deliverance of sinners ensnared by the power of Satan, the Lord offered restoration and peace. "I will heal their backsliding, I will love them freely," He declared: "for Mine anger is turned away from him. I will be as the dew unto Israel: he shall grow as the lily, and cast forth his roots as Lebanon. His branches shall spread, and his beauty shall be as the olive tree, and his smell as Lebanon. They that dwell under His shadow shall return; they shall revive as the corn, and grow as the vine: the scent thereof shall be as the wine of Lebanon. Ephraim shall say, What have I to do any more with idols? I have heard him, and observed him: I am like a green fir tree. From Me is thy fruit found.

> "Who is wise, and he shall understand these things?
>   Prudent, and he shall know them?
> For the ways of the Lord are right,
>   And the just shall walk in them:
> But the transgressors shall fall therein."
>
> Hosea 14:4-9.

The benefits of seeking God were strongly urged. "Seek ye Me," the Lord invited, "and ye shall live: but seek not Bethel, nor enter into Gilgal, and pass not to Beersheba: for Gilgal shall surely go into captivity, and Bethel shall come to nought."

"Seek good, and not evil, that ye may live: and so the Lord, the God of hosts, shall be with you, as ye have spoken. Hate the evil, and love the good, and establish judgment in the gate: it may be that the Lord God of hosts will be gracious unto the remnant of Joseph." Amos 5:4, 5, 14, 15.

By far the greater number of those who heard these invitations refused to profit by them. So contrary to the evil desires of the impenitent were the words of God's messengers, that the idolatrous priest at Bethel sent to the ruler in Israel, saying, "Amos hath conspired against thee in the midst of the house of Israel: the land is not able to bear all his words." Amos 7:10.

Through Hosea the Lord declared, "When I would have healed Israel, then the iniquity of Ephraim was discovered, and the wickedness of Samaria." "The pride of Israel testifieth to his face: and they do not return to the Lord their God, nor seek Him for all this." Hosea 7:1, 10.

From generation to generation the Lord had borne with His wayward children, and even now, in the face of defiant rebellion, He still longed to reveal Himself to them as willing to save. "O Ephraim," He cried, "what shall I do unto thee? O Judah, what shall I do unto thee? for your goodness is as a morning cloud, and as the early dew it goeth away." Hosea 6:4.

The evils that had overspread the land had become incurable; and upon Israel was pronounced the dread sentence: "Ephraim is joined to idols: let him alone." "The days of visitation are come, the days of recompense are come; Israel shall know it." Hosea 4:17; 9:7.

The ten tribes of Israel were now to reap the fruitage of the apostasy that had taken form with the setting up of the strange altars at Bethel and at Dan. God's message to them was: "Thy calf, O Samaria, hath cast thee off; Mine anger is kindled against them: how long will it be ere they attain to innocency? For from Israel was it also: the workman made it; therefore it is not God: but the calf of Samaria shall be broken in pieces." "The inhabitants of Samaria shall fear because of the calves of Beth-aven: for the people thereof shall mourn over it, and the priests thereof that rejoiced on it. . . . It shall be also carried unto Assyria for a present to King Jareb" (Sennacherib). Hosea 8:5, 6; 10:5, 6.

"Behold, the eyes of the Lord God are upon the sinful kingdom, and I will destroy it from off the face of the earth; saying that I will not utterly destroy the house of Jacob, saith the Lord. For, lo, I will command, and I will sift the house of Israel among all nations, like as corn is sifted in a sieve, yet shall not the least grain fall upon the earth. All the sinners of My people shall die by the sword, which say, The evil shall not overtake nor prevent us."

"The houses of ivory shall perish, and the great houses shall have an end, saith the Lord." "The Lord God of hosts is He that toucheth the land, and it shall melt, and all that dwell therein shall mourn." "Thy sons and thy daughters shall fall by the sword, and thy land shall be divided by line; and thou shalt die in a polluted land: and Israel shall surely go into captivity forth of his land." "Because I will do this unto thee, prepare to meet thy God, O Israel." Amos 9:8-10; 3:15; 9:5; 7:17; 4:12.

For a season these predicted judgments were stayed, and

Had Israel heeded the messages sent to them through the prophets, they could have escaped the judgments of God.

during the long reign of Jeroboam II the armies of Israel gained signal victories; but this time of apparent prosperity wrought no change in the hearts of the impenitent, and it was finally decreed, "Jeroboam shall die by the sword, and Israel shall surely be led away captive out of their own land." Amos 7:11.

The boldness of this utterance was lost on king and people, so far had they gone in impenitence. Amaziah, a leader among the idolatrous priests at Bethel, stirred by the plain words spoken by the prophet against the nation and their king, said to Amos, "O thou seer, go, flee thee away into the land of Judah, and there eat bread, and prophesy there: but prophesy not again any more at Bethel: for it is the king's chapel, and it is the king's court." Verses 12, 13.

To this the prophet firmly responded: "Thus saith the Lord, . . . Israel shall surely go into captivity." Verse 17.

The words spoken against the apostate tribes were literally fulfilled; yet the destruction of the kingdom came gradually. In judgment the Lord remembered mercy, and at first, when "Pul the king of Assyria came against the land," Menahem, then king of Israel, was not taken captive, but was permitted to remain on the throne as a vassal of the Assyrian realm. "Menahem gave Pul a thousand talents of silver, that his hand might be with him to confirm the kingdom in his hand. And Menahem exacted the money of Israel, even of all the mighty men of wealth, of each man fifty shekels of silver, to give to the king of Assyria." 2 Kings 15:19, 20. The Assyrians, having humbled the ten tribes, returned for a season to their own land.

Menahem, far from repenting of the evil that had wrought

ruin in his kingdom, continued in "the sins of Jeroboam the son of Nebat, who made Israel to sin." Pekahiah and Pekah, his successors, also "did that which was evil in the sight of the Lord." Verses 18, 24, 28. "In the days of Pekah," who reigned twenty years, Tiglath-pileser, king of Assyria, invaded Israel and carried away with him a multitude of captives from among the tribes living in Galilee and east of the Jordan. "The Reubenites, and the Gadites, and the half tribe of Manasseh," with others of the inhabitants of "Gilead, and Galilee, all the land of Naphtali" (1 Chronicles 5:26; 2 Kings 15:29), were scattered among the heathen in lands far removed from Palestine.

From this terrible blow the northern kingdom never recovered. The feeble remnant continued the forms of government, though no longer possessed of power. Only one more ruler, Hoshea, was to follow Pekah. Soon the kingdom was to be swept away forever. But in that time of sorrow and distress God still remembered mercy, and gave the people another opportunity to turn from idolatry. In the third year of Hoshea's reign, good King Hezekiah began to rule in Judah and as speedily as possible instituted important reforms in the temple service at Jerusalem. A Passover celebration was arranged for, and to this feast were invited not only the tribes of Judah and Benjamin, over which Hezekiah had been anointed king, but all the northern tribes as well. A proclamation was sounded "throughout all Israel, from Beersheba even to Dan, that they should come to keep the Passover unto the Lord God of Israel at Jerusalem: for they had not done it of a long time in such sort as it was written.

"So the posts went with the letters from the king and his

princes throughout all Israel and Judah," with the pressing invitation, "Ye children of Israel, turn again unto the Lord God of Abraham, Isaac, and Israel, and He will return to the remnant of you, that are escaped out of the hand of the kings of Assyria. . . . Be ye not stiff-necked, as your fathers were, but yield yourselves unto the Lord, and enter into His sanctuary, which He hath sanctified forever: and serve the Lord your God, that the fierceness of His wrath may turn away from you. For if ye turn again unto the Lord, your brethren and your children shall find compassion before them that lead them captive, so that they shall come again into this land: for the Lord your God is gracious and merciful, and will not turn away His face from you, if ye return unto Him." 2 Chronicles 30:5-9.

"From city to city through the country of Ephraim and Manasseh even unto Zebulun," the couriers sent out by Hezekiah carried the message. Israel should have recognized in this invitation an appeal to repent and turn to God. But the remnant of the ten tribes still dwelling within the territory of the once-flourishing northern kingdom treated the royal messengers from Judah with indifference and even with contempt. "They laughed them to scorn, and mocked them." There were a few, however, who gladly responded. "Divers of Asher and Manasseh and of Zebulun humbled themselves, and came to Jerusalem, . . . to keep the feast of unleavened bread." Verses 10-13.

About two years later, Samaria was invested by the hosts of Assyria under Shalmaneser; and in the siege that followed, multitudes perished miserably of hunger and disease as well as by the sword. The city and nation fell, and the broken

Messengers sent by King Hezekiah and his princes called Israel and Judah to repent and come to the Passover.

© P.P.P.A.   JOHN STEEL, ARTIST

remnant of the ten tribes were carried away captive and scattered in the provinces of the Assyrian realm.

The destruction that befell the northern kingdom was a direct judgment from Heaven. The Assyrians were merely the instruments that God used to carry out His purpose. Through Isaiah, who began to prophesy shortly before the fall of Samaria, the Lord referred to the Assyrian hosts as "the rod of Mine anger." "The staff in their hand," He said, "is Mine indignation." Isaiah 10:5.

Grievously had the children of Israel "sinned against the Lord their God, . . . and wrought wicked things." "They would not hear, but . . . rejected His statutes, and His covenant that He made with their fathers, and His testimonies which He testified against them." It was because they had "left all the commandments of the Lord their God, and made them molten images, even two calves, and made a grove, and worshiped all the host of heaven, and served Baal," and refused steadfastly to repent, that the Lord "afflicted them, and delivered them into the hand of spoilers, until He had cast them out of His sight," in harmony with the plain warnings He had sent them "by all His servants the prophets."

"So was Israel carried away out of their own land to Assyria," "because they obeyed not the voice of the Lord their God, but transgressed His covenant, and all that Moses the servant of the Lord commanded." 2 Kings 17:7, 11, 14-16, 20, 23; 18:12.

In the terrible judgments brought upon the ten tribes the Lord had a wise and merciful purpose. That which He could no longer do through them in the land of their fathers He would seek to accomplish by scattering them among the heathen. His plan for the salvation of all who should choose to avail themselves of pardon through the Saviour of the human race must yet be fulfilled; and in the afflictions brought upon Israel, He was preparing the way for His glory to be revealed to the nations of earth. Not all who were carried captive were impenitent. Among them were some who had remained true to God, and others who had humbled themselves before Him. Through these, "the sons of the living God" (Hosea 1:10), He would bring multitudes in the Assyrian realm to a knowledge of the attributes of His character and the beneficense of His law.

chapter 24

"Destroyed for Lack of Knowledge"

GOD'S favor toward Israel had always been conditional on their obedience. At the foot of Sinai they had entered into covenant relationship with Him as His "peculiar treasure . . . above all people." Solemnly they had promised to follow in the path of obedience. "All that the Lord hath spoken we will do," they had said. Exodus 19:5, 8. And when, a few days afterward, God's law was spoken from Sinai, and additional instruction in the form of statutes and judgments was communicated through Moses, the Israelites with one voice had again promised, "All the words which the Lord hath said will we do." At the ratification of the covenant, the people had once more united in declaring, "All that the Lord hath said will we do, and be obedient." Exodus 24:3, 7. God had chosen Israel as His people, and they had chosen Him as their King.

Near the close of the wilderness wandering the conditions of the covenant had been repeated. At Baalpeor, on the very borders of the Promised Land, where many fell a prey to subtle temptation, those who remained faithful renewed their vows of allegiance. Through Moses they were warned against the temptations that would assail them in the future; and they were earnestly exhorted to remain separate from the surrounding nations and to worship God alone.

"Now therefore hearken," Moses had instructed Israel, "unto the statutes and unto the judgments, which I teach you, for to do them, that ye may live, and go in and possess the land which the Lord God of your fathers giveth you. Ye shall not add unto the word which I command you, neither shall ye diminish aught from it, that ye may keep the commandments of the Lord your God which I command you. . . . Keep therefore and do them; for this is your wisdom and your understanding in the sight of the nations, which shall hear all these statutes, and say, Surely this great nation is a wise and understanding people." Deuteronomy 4:1-6.

The Israelites had been specially charged not to lose sight of the commandments of God, in obedience to which they would find strength and blessing. "Take heed to thyself, and keep thy soul diligently," had been the word of the Lord to them through Moses, "lest thou forget the things which thine eyes have seen, and lest they depart from thy heart all the days of thy life: but teach them thy sons, and thy sons' sons." Verse 9. The awe-inspiring scenes connected with the giving of the law at Sinai were never to be forgotten. Plain and decided were the warnings that had been given Israel against the idolatrous customs prevailing among the neighboring nations. "Take ye . . . good heed unto yourselves," was the counsel given; "lest ye corrupt yourselves, and make you a graven image, the similitude of any figure," "and lest thou lift up thine eyes unto heaven, and when thou seest the sun, and the moon, and the stars, even all the host of heaven, shouldest be driven to worship them, and serve them, which the Lord thy God hath divided unto all nations under the whole heaven." "Take heed unto yourselves, lest ye forget the covenant of the Lord your God, which He made with you, and make you a graven image, or the likeness of anything, which the Lord thy God hath forbidden thee." Verses 15, 16, 19, 23.

Moses traced the evils that would result from a departure from the statutes of Jehovah. Calling heaven and earth to witness, he declared that if, after having dwelt long in the Land of Promise, the people should introduce corrupt forms of worship and bow down to graven images and should refuse to return to the worship of the true God, the anger of the Lord would be aroused, and they would be carried away captive and scattered among the heathen. "Ye shall soon utterly perish from off the land whereunto ye go over Jordan to possess it," he warned them; "ye shall not prolong your days upon it, but shall utterly be destroyed. And the Lord shall scatter you among the nations, and ye shall be left few in number among the heathen, whither the Lord shall lead you. And there ye shall serve gods, the work of men's hands, wood and stone, which neither see, nor hear, nor eat, nor smell." Verses 26-28.

This prophecy, fulfilled in part in the time of the judges, met a more complete and literal fulfillment in the captivity of Israel in Assyria and of Judah in Babylon.

The apostasy of Israel had developed gradually. From generation to generation, Satan had made repeated attempts to cause the chosen nation to forget "the commandments, the statutes, and the judgments" that they had promised to keep forever. Deuteronomy 6:1. He knew that if he could only lead Israel to forget God, and to "walk after other gods, and serve them, and worship them," they would "surely perish." Deuteronomy 8:19.

The enemy of God's church upon the earth had not, however, taken fully into account the compassionate nature of Him who "will by no means clear the guilty," yet whose glory it is to be "merciful and gracious, long-suffering, and abundant in goodness and truth, keeping mercy for thousands, forgiving iniquity and transgression and sin." Exodus 34:6, 7. Despite the efforts of Satan to thwart God's purpose for Israel, nevertheless even in some of the darkest hours of their history, when it seemed as if the forces of evil were about to gain the victory, the Lord graciously revealed Himself. He spread before Israel the things that were for the welfare of the nation. "I have written to him the great things of My law," He declared through Hosea, "but they were counted as a strange thing." "I taught Ephraim also to go, taking them by their arms; but they knew not that I healed them." Hosea 8:12; 11:3. Tenderly had the Lord dealt with them, instructing them by His prophets line upon line, precept upon precept.

Had Israel heeded the messages of the prophets, they would have been spared the humiliation that followed. It was because they had persisted in turning aside from His law that God was compelled to let them go into captivity. "My people are destroyed for lack of knowledge," was His

[296-297] 287

message to them through Hosea. "Because thou hast rejected knowledge, I will also reject thee: . . . seeing thou hast forgotten the law of thy God." Hosea 4:6.

In every age, transgression of God's law has been followed by the same result. In the days of Noah, when every principle of rightdoing was violated, and iniquity became so deep and widespread that God could no longer bear with it, the decree went forth, "I will destroy man whom I have created from the face of the earth." Genesis 6:7. In Abraham's day the people of Sodom openly defied God and His law; and there followed the same wickedness, the same corruption, the same unbridled indulgence, that had marked the antediluvian world. The inhabitants of Sodom passed the limits of divine forbearance, and there was kindled against them the fire of God's vengeance.

The time preceding the captivity of the ten tribes of Israel was one of similar disobedience and of similar wickedness. God's law was counted as a thing of nought, and this opened the floodgates of iniquity upon Israel. "The Lord hath a controversy with the inhabitants of the land," Hosea declared, "because there is no truth, nor mercy, nor knowledge of God in the land. By swearing, and lying, and killing, and stealing, and committing adultery, they break out, and blood toucheth blood." Hosea 4:1, 2.

The prophecies of judgment delivered by Amos and Hosea were accompanied by predictions of future glory. To the ten tribes, long rebellious and impenitent, was given no promise of complete restoration to their former power in Palestine. Until the end of time, they were to be "wanderers among the nations." But through Hosea was given a prophecy that set before them the privilege of having a part in the final restoration that is to be made to the people of God at the close of earth's history, when Christ shall appear as King of kings and Lord of lords. "Many days," the prophet declared, the ten tribes were to abide "without a king, and without a prince, and without a sacrifice, and without an image, and without an ephod, and without teraphim." "Afterward," the prophet continued, "shall the children of Israel return, and seek the Lord their God, and David their king; and shall fear the Lord and His goodness in the latter days." Hosea 3:4, 5.

In symbolic language Hosea set before the ten tribes God's plan of restoring to every penitent soul who would unite with His church on earth, the blessings granted Israel in the days of their loyalty to Him in the Promised Land. Referring to Israel as one to whom He longed to show mercy, the Lord declared, "I will allure her, and bring her into the wilderness, and speak comfortably unto her. And I will give her her vineyards from thence, and the valley of Achor for a door of hope:

and she shall sing there, as in the days of her youth, and as in the day when she came up out of the land of Egypt. And it shall be at that day, saith the Lord, that thou shalt call Me Ishi ["My husband," margin]; and shalt call Me no more Baali ["My lord," margin]. For I will take away the names of Baalim out of her mouth, and they shall no more be remembered by their name." Hosea 2:14-17.

In the last days of this earth's history, God's covenant with His commandment-keeping people is to be renewed. "In that day will I make a covenant for them with the beasts of the field, and with the fowls of heaven, and with the creeping things of the ground: and I will break the bow and the sword and the battle out of the earth, and will make them to lie down safely. And I will betroth thee unto Me forever; yea, I will betroth thee unto Me in righteousness, and in judgment, and in loving-kindness, and in mercies. I will even betroth thee unto Me in faithfulness: and thou shalt know the Lord.

"And it shall come to pass in that day, I will hear, saith the Lord, I will hear the heavens, and they shall hear the earth; and the earth shall hear the corn, and the wine, and the oil; and they shall hear Jezreel. And I will sow her unto Me in the earth; and I will have mercy upon her that had not obtained mercy; and I will say to them which were not My people, Thou art My people; and they shall say, Thou art my God." Verses 18-23.

"In that day" "the remnant of Israel, and such as are escaped of the house of Jacob, . . . shall stay upon the Lord, the Holy One of Israel, in truth." Isaiah 10:20. From "every nation, and kindred, and tongue, and people" there will be some who will gladly respond to the message, "Fear God, and give glory to Him; for the hour of His judgment is come." They will turn from every idol that binds them to earth, and will "worship Him that made heaven, and earth, and the sea, and the fountains of waters." They will free themselves from every entanglement and will stand before the world as monuments of God's mercy. Obedient to the divine requirements, they will be recognized by angels and by men as those that have kept "the commandments of God, and the faith of Jesus." Revelation 14:6, 7, 12.

"Behold, the days come, saith the Lord, that the plowman shall overtake the reaper, and the treader of grapes him that soweth seed; and the mountains shall drop sweet wine, and all the hills shall melt. And I will bring again the captivity of My people of Israel, and they shall build the waste cities, and inhabit them; and they shall plant vineyards, and drink the wine thereof; they shall also make gardens, and eat the fruit of them. And I will plant them upon their land, and they shall no more be pulled up out of their land which I have given them, saith the Lord thy God." Amos 9:13-15.

chapter 25

The Call of Isaiah

THE long reign of Uzziah [also known as Azariah] in the land of Judah and Benjamin was characterized by a prosperity greater than that of any other ruler since the death of Solomon, nearly two centuries before. For many years the king ruled with discretion. Under the blessing of Heaven his armies regained some of the territory that had been lost in former years. Cities were rebuilt and fortified, and the position of the nation among the surrounding peoples was greatly strengthened. Commerce revived, and the riches of the nations flowed into Jerusalem. Uzziah's name "spread far abroad; for he was marvelously helped, till he was strong." 2 Chronicles 26:15.

This outward prosperity, however, was not accompanied by a corresponding revival of spiritual power. The temple services were continued as in former years, and multitudes assembled to worship the living God; but pride and formality

As the prophet Isaiah worshiped in the temple, he saw a vision of God's glory, and he was ready to do the Lord's will.

gradually took the place of humility and sincerity. Of Uzziah himself it is written: "When he was strong, his heart was lifted up to his destruction: for he transgressed against the Lord his God." Verse 16.

The sin that resulted so disastrously to Uzziah was one of presumption. In violation of a plain command of Jehovah, that none but the descendants of Aaron should officiate as priests, the king entered the sanctuary "to burn incense upon the altar." Azariah the high priest and his associates remonstrated, and pleaded with him to turn from his purpose. "Thou hast trespassed," they urged; "neither shall it be for thine honor." Verses 16, 18.

Uzziah was filled with wrath that he, the king, should be thus rebuked. But he was not permitted to profane the sanctuary against the united protest of those in authority. While standing there, in wrathful rebellion, he was suddenly smitten with a divine judgment. Leprosy appeared on his forehead. In dismay he fled, never again to enter the temple courts. Unto the day of his death, some years later, Uzziah remained a leper—a living example of the folly of departing from a plain "Thus saith the Lord." Neither his exalted position nor his long life of service could be pleaded as an excuse for the presumptuous sin by which he marred the closing years of his reign, and brought upon himself the judgment of Heaven.

God is no respecter of persons. "The soul that doeth aught presumptuously, whether he be born in the land, or a stranger, the same reproacheth the Lord; and that soul shall be cut off from among his people." Numbers 15:30.

The judgment that befell Uzziah seemed to have a restraining influence on his son. Jotham bore heavy responsibilities during the later years of his father's reign and succeeded to the throne after Uzziah's death. Of Jotham it is written: "He did that which was right in the sight of the Lord: he did according to all that his father Uzziah had done. Howbeit the high places were not removed: the people sacrificed and burned incense still in the high places." 2 Kings 15:34, 35.

The reign of Uzziah was drawing to a close, and Jotham was already bearing many of the burdens of state, when Isaiah, of the royal line, was called, while yet a young man, to the prophetic mission. The times in which Isaiah was to labor were fraught with peculiar peril to the people of God. The prophet was to witness the invasion of Judah by the combined armies of northern Israel and of Syria; he was to behold the Assyrian hosts encamped before the chief cities of the kingdom. During his lifetime, Samaria was to fall, and the ten tribes of Israel were to be scattered among the nations. Judah was again and again to be invaded by the Assyrian armies, and Jerusalem was to suffer a siege that would have resulted in her downfall had not God miraculously interposed. Already grave perils were threatening the peace of the southern kingdom. The divine protection was being removed, and the Assyrian forces were about to overspread the land of Judah.

But the dangers from without, overwhelming though they seemed, were not so serious as the dangers from within. It was the perversity of his people that brought to the Lord's servant the greatest perplexity and the deepest depression. By their apostasy and rebellion those who should have been standing as light bearers among the nations were inviting the judgments of God. Many of the evils which were hastening the swift destruction of the northern kingdom, and which had recently been denounced in unmistakable terms by Hosea and Amos, were fast corrupting the kingdom of Judah.

The outlook was particularly discouraging as regards the social conditions of the people. In their desire for gain, men were adding house to house and field to field. See Isaiah 5:8. Justice was perverted, and no pity was shown the poor. Of these evils God declared, "The spoil of the poor is in your houses." "Ye beat My people to pieces, and grind the faces of the poor." Isaiah 3:14, 15. Even the magistrates, whose duty it was to protect the helpless, turned a deaf ear to the cries of the poor and needy, the widows and the fatherless. See Isaiah 10:1, 2.

With oppression and wealth came pride and love of display, gross drunkenness, and a spirit of revelry. See Isaiah 2:11, 12; 3:16, 18-23; 5:22, 11, 12. And in Isaiah's day idolatry itself no longer provoked surprise. See Isaiah 2:8, 9. Iniquitous practices had become so prevalent among all classes that the few who remained true to God were often tempted to lose heart and to give way to discouragement and despair. It seemed as if God's purpose for Israel were about to fail and that the rebellious nation was to suffer a fate similar to that of Sodom and Gomorrah.

In the face of such conditions it is not surprising that when, during the last year of Uzziah's reign, Isaiah was called to bear to Judah God's messages of warning and reproof, he shrank from the responsibility. He well knew that he would encounter obstinate resistance. As he realized his own inability to meet the situation and thought of the stubbornness and unbelief of the people for whom he was to labor, his task seemed hopeless. Should he in despair relinquish his mission and leave Judah undisturbed to their idolatry? Were the gods of Nineveh to rule the earth in defiance of the God of heaven?

Such thoughts as these were crowding through Isaiah's mind as he stood under the portico of the temple. Suddenly the gate and the inner veil of the temple seemed to be uplifted or withdrawn, and he was permitted to gaze within, upon the holy of holies, where even the prophet's feet might not enter. There rose up before him a vision of Jehovah sitting upon a throne high and lifted up, while the train of His glory filled the temple. On each side of the throne hovered the seraphim, their faces veiled in adoration, as they ministered before their Maker and united in the solemn invocation, "Holy, holy, holy, is the Lord of hosts: the whole earth is full of His glory," until post and pillar and cedar gate seemed shaken with the sound, and the house was filled with their tribute of praise. Isaiah 6:3.

As Isaiah beheld this revelation of the glory and majesty of his Lord, he was overwhelmed with a sense of the purity and holiness of God. How sharp the contrast between the matchless perfection of his Creator, and the sinful course of those who, with himself, had long been numbered among the chosen people of Israel and Judah! "Woe is me!" he cried; "for I am undone; because I am a man of unclean lips, and I dwell in the midst of a people of unclean lips: for mine eyes have seen the King, the Lord of hosts." Verse 5. Standing, as it were, in the full light of the divine presence within the inner sanctuary, he realized that if left to his own imperfection and inefficiency, he would be utterly unable to accomplish the mission to which he had been called. But a seraph was sent to relieve him of his distress and to fit him for his great mission. A living coal from the altar was laid upon his lips, with the words, "Lo, this hath touched thy lips; and thine iniquity is taken away, and thy sin purged." Then the voice of God was heard saying, "Whom shall I send, and who will go for Us?" and Isaiah responded, "Here am I; send me." Verses 7, 8.

The heavenly visitant bade the waiting messenger, "Go, and tell this people,

> "Hear ye indeed, but understand not;
> And see ye indeed, but perceive not.
> Make the heart of this people fat,
> And make their ears heavy, and shut
>   their eyes;
> Lest they see with their eyes, and hear
>   with their ears,
> And understand with their heart,
> And convert, and be healed."
> Verses 9, 10.

The prophet's duty was plain; he was to lift his voice in protest against the prevailing evils. But he dreaded to undertake the work without some assurance of hope. "Lord, how long?" he inquired. Verse 11. Are none of Thy chosen people ever to understand and repent and be healed?

His burden of soul in behalf of erring Judah was not to be borne in vain. His mission was not to be wholly fruitless. Yet the evils that had been multiplying for many generations could not be removed in his day. Throughout his lifetime he must be a patient, courageous teacher—a prophet of hope as well as of doom. The divine purpose finally accomplished, the full fruitage of his efforts, and of the labors of all God's faithful messengers, would appear. A remnant should be saved. That this might be brought about, the messages of warning and entreaty were to be delivered to the rebellious nation, the Lord declared:

"Until the cities be wasted without inhabitant,
And the houses without man,
And the land be utterly desolate,
And the Lord have removed men far away,
And there be a great forsaking in the midst of the land."
Verses 11, 12.

The heavy judgments that were to befall the impenitent, —war, exile, oppression, the loss of power and prestige among the nations,—all these were to come in order that those who would recognize in them the hand of an offended God might be led to repent. The ten tribes of the northern kingdom were soon to be scattered among the nations and their cities left desolate; the destroying armies of hostile nations were to sweep over their land again and again; even Jerusalem was finally to fall, and Judah was to be carried away captive; yet the Promised Land was not to remain wholly forsaken forever. The assurance of the heavenly visitant to Isaiah was:

"In it shall be a tenth,
And it shall return, and shall be eaten:
As a teil tree, and as an oak,
Whose substance is in them, when they cast their leaves:
So the holy seed shall be the substance thereof."
Verse 13.

This assurance of the final fulfillment of God's purpose brought courage to the heart of Isaiah. What though earthly powers array themselves against Judah? What though the

Lord's messenger meet with opposition and resistance? Isaiah had seen the King, the Lord of hosts; he had heard the song of the seraphim, "The whole earth is full of His glory;" he had the promise that the messages of Jehovah to backsliding Judah would be accompanied by the convicting power of the Holy Spirit; and the prophet was nerved for the work before him. Verse 3. Throughout his long and arduous mission he carried with him the memory of this vision. For sixty years or more he stood before the children of Judah as a prophet of hope, waxing bolder and still bolder in his predictions of the future triumph of the church.

chapter 26

"Behold Your God!"

IN ISAIAH'S day the spiritual understanding of mankind was dark through misapprehension of God. Long had Satan sought to lead men to look upon their Creator as the author of sin and suffering and death. Those whom he had thus deceived, imagined that God was hard and exacting. They regarded Him as watching to denounce and condemn, unwilling to receive the sinner so long as there was a legal excuse for not helping him. The law of love by which heaven is ruled had been misrepresented by the archdeceiver as a restriction upon men's happiness, a burdensome yoke from which they should be glad to escape. He declared that its precepts could not be obeyed and that the penalties of transgression were bestowed arbitrarily.

In losing sight of the true character of Jehovah, the Israelites were without excuse. Often had God revealed Himself to them as one "full of compassion, and gracious, long-suffering, and plenteous in mercy and truth." Psalm 86:15. "When Israel was a child," He testified, "then I loved him, and called My son out of Egypt." Hosea 11:1.

Tenderly had the Lord dealt with Israel in their deliverance from Egyptian bondage and in their journey to the Promised Land. "In all their affliction He was afflicted, and the angel of His presence saved them: in His love and in His pity He redeemed them; and He bare them, and carried them all the days of old." Isaiah 63:9.

"My presence shall go with thee," was the promise given during the journey through the wilderness. Exodus 33:14. This assurance was accompanied by a marvelous revelation of Jehovah's character, which enabled Moses to proclaim to all Israel the goodness of God, and to instruct them fully concerning the attributes of their invisible King. "The Lord passed by before him, and proclaimed, The Lord, The Lord God, merciful and gracious, long-suffering, and abundant in goodness and truth, keeping mercy for thousands, forgiving iniquity and transgression and sin, and that will by no means clear the guilty." Exodus 34:6, 7.

It was upon his knowledge of the long-sufferance of Jehovah and of His infinite love and mercy, that Moses based his wonderful plea for the life of Israel when, on the borders of the Promised Land, they refused to advance in obedience to the command of God. At the height of their rebellion the Lord had declared, "I will smite them with the pestilence, and disinherit them;" and He had proposed to make of the descendants of Moses "a greater nation and mightier than they." Numbers 14:12. But the prophet pleaded the marvelous providences and promises of God in behalf of the chosen nation. And then, as the strongest of all pleas, he urged the love of God for fallen man. See verses 17-19.

Graciously the Lord responded, "I have pardoned according to thy word." And then He imparted to Moses, in the form of a prophecy, a knowledge of His purpose concerning the final triumph of Israel. "As truly as I live," He declared, "all the earth shall be filled with the glory of the Lord." Verses 20, 21. God's glory, His character, His merciful kindness and tender love—that which Moses had pleaded in behalf of Israel—were to be revealed to all mankind. And this promise of Jehovah was made doubly sure; it was confirmed by an oath. As surely as God lives and reigns, His glory should be declared "among the heathen, His wonders among all people." Psalm 96:3.

It was concerning the future fulfillment of this prophecy that Isaiah had heard the shining seraphim singing before the throne, "The whole earth is full of His glory." Isaiah 6:3. The prophet, confident of the certainty of these words, himself afterward boldly declared of those who were bowing down to images of wood and stone, "They shall see the glory of the Lord, and the excellency of our God." Isaiah 35:2.

Today this prophecy is meeting rapid fulfillment. The missionary activities of the church of God on earth are bearing rich fruitage, and soon the gospel message will have been proclaimed to all nations. "To the praise of the glory of His grace," men and women from every kindred, tongue, and people are being made "accepted in the Beloved," "that in the ages to come He might show the exceeding riches of His grace in His kindness toward us through Christ Jesus." Ephesians 1:6; 2:7. "Blessed be the Lord God, the God of Israel, who only doeth wondrous things. And blessed be His glorious name forever: and let the whole earth be filled with His glory." Psalm 72:18, 19.

In the vision that came to Isaiah in the temple court, he was given a clear view of the character of the God of Israel. "The high and lofty One that inhabiteth eternity, whose name is Holy," had appeared before him in great majesty; yet the prophet was made to understand the compassionate nature of his Lord. He who dwells "in the high and holy place" dwells "with him also that is of a contrite and humble spirit, to revive the spirit of the humble, and to revive the heart of the contrite ones." Isaiah 57:15. The angel commissioned to touch Isaiah's lips had brought to him the message, "Thine iniquity is taken away, and thy sin purged." Isaiah 6:7.

In beholding his God, the prophet, like Saul of Tarsus at the gate of Damascus, had not only been given a view of his own unworthiness; there had come to his humbled heart the assurance of forgiveness, full and free; and he had arisen a changed man. He had seen his Lord. He had caught a glimpse of the loveliness of the divine character. He could testify of the transformation wrought through beholding Infinite Love. Henceforth he was inspired with longing desire to see erring Israel set free from the burden and penalty of sin. "Why should ye be stricken any more?" the prophet inquired. "Come now, and let us reason together, saith the Lord: though your sins be as scarlet, they shall be as white as snow; though they be red like crimson, they shall be as wool." "Wash you, make you clean; put away the evil of your doings from before Mine eyes; cease to do evil; learn to do well." Isaiah 1:5, 18, 16, 17.

The God whom they had been claiming to serve, but whose character they had misunderstood, was set before them as the great Healer of spiritual disease. What though the whole head was sick and the whole heart faint? what though from the sole of the foot even unto the crown of the head there was no soundness, but wounds, and bruises, and putrefying sores? See Isaiah 1:6. He who had been walking frowardly in the way of his heart might find healing by turning to the Lord. "I have seen his ways," the Lord declared, "and will heal him: I will lead him also, and restore comforts unto him. . . . Peace, peace to him that is far off, and to him that is near, saith the Lord; and I will heal him." Isaiah 57:18, 19.

The prophet exalted God as Creator of all. His message to the cities of Judah was, "Behold your God!" Isaiah 40:9. "Thus saith God the Lord, He that created the heavens, and stretched them out; He that spread forth the earth, and that which cometh out of it;" "I am the Lord that maketh all things;" "I form the light, and create darkness;" "I have made the earth, and created man upon it: I, even My hands, have stretched out the heavens, and all their host have I commanded." Isaiah 42:5; 44:24; 45:7, 12. "To whom then will ye liken Me, or shall I be equal? saith the Holy One. Lift up your eyes on high, and behold who hath created these things, that bringeth out their host by number: He calleth them all by names by the greatness of His might, for that He is strong in power; not one faileth." Isaiah 40:25, 26.

To those who feared they would not be received if they should return to God, the prophet declared:

"Why sayest thou, O Jacob, and speakest, O Israel, My way is hid from the Lord, and my judgment is passed over from my God? Hast thou not known? hast thou not heard, that the everlasting God, the Lord, the Creator of the ends of the earth, fainteth not, neither is weary? there is no searching of His understanding. He giveth power to the faint; and to them that have no might He increaseth strength. Even the youths shall faint and be weary, and the young men shall utterly fall: but they that wait upon the Lord shall renew their strength; they shall mount up with wings as eagles; they shall run, and not be weary; and they shall walk, and not faint." Verses 27-31.

The heart of Infinite Love yearns after those who feel powerless to free themselves from the snares of Satan; and He graciously offers to strengthen them to live for Him. "Fear thou not," He bids them; "for I am with thee: be not dismayed; for I am thy God: I will strengthen thee; yea, I will help thee; yea, I will uphold thee with the right hand of My righteousness." "I the Lord thy God will hold thy right hand, saying unto thee, Fear not; I will help thee. Fear not, thou worm Jacob, and ye men of Israel; I will help thee, saith the Lord, and thy Redeemer, the Holy One of Israel." Isaiah 41:10, 13, 14.

The inhabitants of Judah were all undeserving, yet God would not give them up. By them His name was to be exalted among the heathen. Many who were wholly unacquainted with His attributes were yet to behold the glory of the divine character. It was for the purpose of making plain His merciful designs that He kept sending His servants the prophets with the message, "Turn ye again now everyone from his evil way." Jeremiah 25:5. "For My name's sake," He declared through Isaiah, "will I defer Mine anger, and for My praise will I refrain for thee, that I cut thee not off." "For Mine own sake, even for Mine own sake, will I do it: for how should

My name be polluted? and I will not give My glory unto another." Isaiah 48:9, 11.

The call to repentance was sounded with unmistakable clearness, and all were invited to return. "Seek ye the Lord while He may be found," the prophet pleaded; "call ye upon Him while He is near: let the wicked forsake his way, and the unrighteous man his thoughts: and let him return unto the Lord, and He will have mercy upon him; and to our God, for He will abundantly pardon." Isaiah 55:6, 7.

Have you, reader, chosen your own way? Have you wandered far from God? Have you sought to feast upon the fruits of transgression, only to find them turn to ashes upon your lips? And now, your life plans thwarted and your hopes dead, do you sit alone and desolate? That voice which has long been speaking to your heart, but to which you would not listen, comes to you distinct and clear, "Arise ye, and depart; for this is not your rest: because it is polluted, it shall destroy you, even with a sore destruction." Micah 2:10. Return to your Father's house. He invites you, saying, "Return unto Me; for I have redeemed thee." "Come unto Me: hear, and your soul shall live; and I will make an everlasting covenant with you, even the sure mercies of David." Isaiah 44:22; 55:3.

Do not listen to the enemy's suggestion to stay away from Christ until you have made yourself better, until you are good enough to come to God. If you wait until then you will never come. When Satan points to your filthy garments, repeat the promise of the Saviour, "Him that cometh to Me I will in no wise cast out." John 6:37. Tell the enemy that the blood of Jesus Christ cleanses from all sin. Make the prayer of David your own: "Purge me with hyssop, and I shall be clean:

wash me, and I shall be whiter than snow." Psalm 51:7.

The exhortations of the prophet to Judah to behold the living God, and to accept His gracious offers, were not in vain. There were some who gave earnest heed, and who turned from their idols to the worship of Jehovah. They learned to see in their Maker love and mercy and tender compassion. And in the dark days that were to come in the history of Judah, when only a remnant were to be left in the land, the prophet's words were to continue bearing fruit in decided reformation. "At that day," declared Isaiah, "shall a man look to his Maker, and his eyes shall have respect to the Holy One of Israel. And he shall not look to the altars, the work of his hands, neither shall respect that which his fingers have made, either the groves, or the images." Isaiah 17:7, 8.

Many were to behold the One altogether lovely, the chiefest among ten thousand. "Thine eyes shall see the King in His beauty," was the gracious promise made them. Isaiah 33:17. Their sins were to be forgiven, and they were to make their boast in God alone. In that glad day of redemption from idolatry they would exclaim, "The glorious Lord will be unto us a place of broad rivers and streams. . . . The Lord is our judge, the Lord is our lawgiver, the Lord is our king; He will save us." Verses 21, 22.

The messages borne by Isaiah to those who chose to turn from their evil ways were full of comfort and encouragement. Hear the word of the Lord through His prophet:

> "Remember these, O Jacob and Israel;
> For thou art My servant:
> I have formed thee; thou art My servant:

O Israel, thou shalt not be forgotten of Me.
I have blotted out, as a thick cloud, thy transgressions,
And, as a cloud, thy sins:
Return unto Me; for I have redeemed thee."
Isaiah 44:21, 22.

"In that day thou shalt say,
O Lord, I will praise Thee:
Though Thou wast angry with me,
Thine anger is turned away, and Thou comfortedst me.

"Behold, God is my salvation;
I will trust, and not be afraid:
For the Lord Jehovah is my strength and my song;
He also is become my salvation. . . .

"Sing unto the Lord; for He hath done excellent things:
This is known in all the earth.
Cry out and shout, thou inhabitant of Zion:
For great is the Holy One of Israel in the midst of thee."
Isaiah 12.

chapter 27

Ahaz

THE accession of Ahaz to the throne brought Isaiah and his associates face to face with conditions more appalling than any that had hitherto existed in the realm of Judah. Many who had formerly withstood the seductive influence of idolatrous practices were now being persuaded to take part in the worship of heathen deities. Princes in Israel were proving untrue to their trust; false prophets were arising with messages to lead astray; even some of the priests were teaching for hire. Yet the leaders in apostasy still kept up the forms of divine worship and claimed to be numbered among the people of God.

The prophet Micah, who bore his testimony during those troublous times, declared that sinners in Zion, while claiming to "lean upon the Lord," and blasphemously boasting, "Is not the Lord among us? none evil can come upon us," continued to "build up Zion with blood, and Jerusalem with iniquity." Micah 3:11, 10. Against these evils the prophet Isaiah lifted

Near the end of Ahaz's wicked reign the temple at Jerusalem was closed by regal decree and heathenism seemed to triumph.

his voice in stern rebuke: "Hear the word of the Lord, ye rulers of Sodom; give ear unto the law of our God, ye people of Gomorrah. To what purpose is the multitude of your sacrifices unto Me? saith the Lord. . . . When ye come to appear before Me, who hath required this at your hand, to tread My courts?" Isaiah 1:10-12.

Inspiration declares, "The sacrifice of the wicked is abomination: how much more, when he bringeth it with a wicked mind?" Proverbs 21:27. The God of heaven is "of purer eyes than to behold evil," and cannot "look on iniquity." Habakkuk 1:13. It is not because He is unwilling to forgive that He turns from the transgressor; it is because the sinner refuses to make use of the abundant provisions of grace, that God is unable to deliver from sin. "The Lord's hand is not shortened, that it cannot save; neither His ear heavy, that it cannot hear: but your iniquities have separated between you and your God, and your sins have hid His face from you, that He will not hear." Isaiah 59:1, 2.

Solomon had written, "Woe to thee, O land, when thy king is a child!" Ecclesiastes 10:16. Thus it was with the land of Judah. Through continued transgression her rulers had become as children. Isaiah called the attention of the people to the weakness of their position among the nations of earth, and he showed that this was the result of wickedness in high places. "Behold," he said, "the Lord, the Lord of hosts, doth take away from Jerusalem and from Judah the stay and the staff, the whole stay of bread, and the whole stay of water, the mighty man, and the man of war, the judge, and the prophet, and the prudent, and the ancient, the captain of fifty, and the honorable man, and the counselor, and the cunning artificer, and the eloquent orator. And I will give children to be their princes, and babes shall rule over them." "For Jerusalem is ruined, and Judah is fallen: because their tongue and their doings are against the Lord." Isaiah 3:1-4, 8.

"They which lead thee," the prophet continued, "cause thee to err, and destroy the way of thy paths." Verse 12. During the reign of Ahaz this was literally true; for of him it is written: "He walked in the ways of the kings of Israel, and made also molten images for Baalim. Moreover he burnt incense in the valley of the son of Hinnom" (2 Chronicles 28: 2, 3); "yea, and made his son to pass through the fire, according to the abominations of the heathen, whom the Lord cast out from before the children of Israel." 2 Kings 16:3.

This was indeed a time of great peril for the chosen nation. Only a few short years, and the ten tribes of the kingdom of Israel were to be scattered among the nations of heathendom. And in the kingdom of Judah also the outlook was dark. The forces for good were rapidly diminishing, the forces for evil multiplying. The prophet Micah, viewing the situation, was constrained to exclaim: "The good man is perished out of the earth: and there is none upright among men." "The best of them is as a brier: the most upright is sharper than a thorn hedge." Micah 7:2, 4. "Except the Lord of hosts had left unto us a very small remnant," declared Isaiah, "we should have been as Sodom, and . . . Gomorrah." Isaiah 1:9.

In every age, for the sake of those who have remained true, as well as because of His infinite love for the erring, God has borne long with the rebellious, and has urged them to forsake their course of evil and return to Him. "Precept upon precept; line upon line, . . . here a little, and there a little," through men of His appointment, He has taught transgressors the way of righteousness. Isaiah 28:10.

And thus it was during the reign of Ahaz. Invitation upon invitation was sent to erring Israel to return to their allegiance to Jehovah. Tender were the pleadings of the prophets; and as they stood before the people, earnestly exhorting to repentance and reformation, their words bore fruit to the glory of God.

Through Micah came the wonderful appeal, "Hear ye now what the Lord saith; Arise, contend thou before the mountains, and let the hills hear thy voice. Hear ye, O mountains, the Lord's controversy, and ye strong foundations of the earth: for the Lord hath a controversy with His people, and He will plead with Israel.

"O My people, what have I done unto thee? and wherein have I wearied thee? testify against Me. For I brought thee up out of the land of Egypt, and redeemed thee out of the house of servants; and I sent before thee Moses, Aaron, and Miriam.

"O My people, remember now what Balak king of Moab consulted, and what Balaam the son of Beor answered him from Shittim unto Gilgal; that ye may know the righteousness of the Lord." Micah 6:1-5.

The God whom we serve is long-suffering; "His compassions fail not." Lamentations 3:22. Throughout the period of probationary time His Spirit is entreating men to accept the gift of life. "As I live, saith the Lord God, I have no pleasure in the death of the wicked; but that the wicked turn from his way and live: turn ye, turn ye from your evil ways; for why will ye die?" Ezekiel 33:11. It is Satan's special device to lead man into sin and then leave him there, helpless and hopeless, fearing to seek for pardon. But God invites, "Let him take hold of My strength, that he may make peace with Me; and he shall make peace with Me." Isaiah 27:5. In Christ every provision has been made, every encouragement offered.

In the days of apostasy in Judah and Israel, many were inquiring: "Wherewith shall I come before the Lord, and bow myself before the high God? shall I come before Him with burnt offerings, with calves of a year old? will the Lord be pleased with thousands of rams, or with ten thousands of rivers of oil?" The answer is plain and positive: "He hath showed thee, O man, what is good; and what doth the Lord require of thee, but to do justly, and to love mercy, and to walk humbly with thy God?" Micah 6:6-8.

In urging the value of practical godliness, the prophet was only repeating the counsel given Israel centuries before. Through Moses, as they were about to enter the Promised Land, the word of the Lord had been: "And now, Israel, what doth the Lord thy God require of thee, but to fear the Lord thy God, to walk in all His ways, and to love Him, and to serve the Lord thy God with all thy heart and with all thy soul, to keep the commandments of the Lord, and His statutes, which I command thee this day for thy good?" Deuteronomy 10:12, 13. From age to age these counsels were repeated by the servants of Jehovah to those who were in danger of falling into habits of formalism and of forgetting to show mercy. When Christ Himself, during His earthly ministry, was approached by a lawyer with the question, "Master, which is the great commandment in the law?" Jesus said to him, "Thou shalt love the Lord thy God with all thy heart, and with all thy soul, and with all thy mind. This is the first and great commandment. And the second is like unto it, Thou shalt love thy neighbor as thyself. On these two commandments hang all the law and the prophets." Matthew 22:36-40.

These plain utterances of the prophets and of the Master Himself, should be received by us as the voice of God to every soul. We should lose no opportunity of performing deeds of mercy, of tender forethought and Christian courtesy, for the burdened and the oppressed. If we can do no more, we may speak words of courage and hope to those who are unacquainted with God, and who can be approached most easily by the avenue of sympathy and love.

Rich and abundant are the promises made to those who are watchful of opportunities to bring joy and blessing into the lives of others. "If thou draw out thy soul to the hungry, and satisfy the afflicted soul; then shall thy light rise in obscurity, and thy darkness be as the noonday: and the Lord shall guide thee continually, and satisfy thy soul in drought, and make fat thy bones: and thou shalt be like a watered garden, and like a spring of water, whose waters fail not." Isaiah 58:10, 11.

The idolatrous course of Ahaz, in the face of the earnest appeals of the prophets, could have but one result. "The wrath of the Lord was upon Judah and Jerusalem, and He . . . delivered them to trouble, to astonishment, and to hissing." 2 Chronicles 29:8. The kingdom suffered a rapid decline, and its very existence was soon imperiled by invading armies. "Rezin king of Syria and Pekah son of Remaliah king of Israel came up to Jerusalem to war: and they besieged Ahaz." 2 Kings 16:5.

Had Ahaz and the chief men of his realm been true servants of the Most High, they would have had no fear of so unnatural an alliance as had been formed against them. But repeated transgression had shorn them of strength. Stricken with a nameless dread of the retributive judgments of an offended God, the heart of the king "was moved, and the heart of his people, as the trees of the wood are moved with the wind." Isaiah 7:2. In this crisis the word of the Lord came to Isaiah, bidding him meet the trembling king and say:

"Take heed, and be quiet; fear not, neither be fainthearted. . . . Because Syria, Ephraim, and the son of Remaliah, have taken evil counsel against thee, saying, Let us go up against Judah, and vex it, and let us make a breach therein for us, and set a king in the midst of it: . . . thus saith the Lord God, It shall not stand, neither shall it come to pass." The prophet declared that the kingdom of Israel, and Syria as well, would soon come to an end. "If ye will not believe," he concluded, "surely ye shall not be established." Verses 4-7, 9.

Well would it have been for the kingdom of Judah had

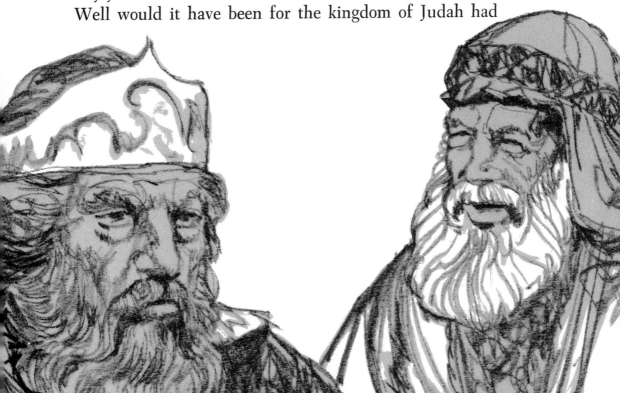

Ahaz received this message as from heaven. But choosing to lean on the arm of flesh, he sought help from the heathen. In desperation he sent word to Tiglath-pileser, king of Assyria: "I am thy servant and thy son: come up, and save me out of the hand of the king of Syria, and out of the hand of the king of Israel, which rise up against me." 2 Kings 16:7. The request was accompanied by a rich present from the king's treasure and from the temple storehouse.

The help asked for was sent, and King Ahaz was given temporary relief, but at what a cost to Judah! The tribute offered aroused the cupidity of Assyria, and that treacherous nation soon threatened to overflow and spoil Judah. Ahaz and his unhappy subjects were now harassed by the fear of falling completely into the hands of the cruel Assyrians.

"The Lord brought Judah low" because of continued transgression. In this time of chastisement Ahaz, instead of repenting, trespassed "yet more against the Lord: . . . for he sacrificed unto the gods of Damascus." "Because the gods of the kings of Syria help them," he said, "therefore will I sacrifice to them, that they may help me." 2 Chronicles 28:19, 22, 23.

As the apostate king neared the end of his reign, he caused the doors of the temple to be closed. The sacred services were interrupted. No longer were the candlesticks kept burning before the altar. No longer were offerings made for the sins of the people. No longer did sweet incense ascend on high at the time of the morning and the evening sacrifice. Deserting the courts of the house of God and locking fast its doors, the inhabitants of the godless city boldly set up altars for the worship of heathen deities on the street corners throughout

Jerusalem. Heathenism had seemingly triumphed; the powers of darkness had well-nigh prevailed.

But in Judah there dwelt some who maintained their allegiance to Jehovah, steadfastly refusing to be led into idolatry. It was to these that Isaiah and Micah and their associates looked in hope as they surveyed the ruin wrought during the last years of Ahaz. Their sanctuary was closed, but the faithful ones were assured: "God is with us." "Sanctify the Lord of hosts Himself; and let Him be your fear, and let Him be your dread. And He shall be for a sanctuary." Isaiah 8:10, 13, 14.

chapter 28

Hezekiah

IN SHARP contrast with the reckless rule
of Ahaz was the reformation wrought dur-
ing the prosperous reign of his son. Hezekiah came to the
throne determined to do all in his power to save Judah from
the fate that was overtaking the northern kingdom. The messages of the prophets offered no encouragement to halfway
measures. Only by most decided reformation could the threatened judgments be averted.

In the crisis, Hezekiah proved to be a man of opportunity.
No sooner had he ascended the throne than he began to plan
and to execute. He first turned his attention to the restoration
of the temple services, so long neglected; and in this work he
earnestly solicited the co-operation of a band of priests and
Levites who had remained true to their sacred calling. Confident of their loyal support, he spoke with them freely concerning his desire to institute immediate and far-reaching
reforms. "Our fathers have trespassed," he confessed, "and
done that which was evil in the eyes of the Lord our God, and

have forsaken Him, and have turned away their faces from the habitation of the Lord." "Now it is in mine heart to make a covenant with the Lord God of Israel, that His fierce wrath may turn away from us." 2 Chronicles 29:6, 10.

In a few well-chosen words the king reviewed the situation they were facing—the closed temple and the cessation of all services within its precincts; the flagrant idolatry practiced in the streets of the city and throughout the kingdom; the apostasy of multitudes who might have remained true to God had the leaders in Judah set before them a right example; and the decline of the kingdom and loss of prestige in the estimation of surrounding nations. The northern kingdom was rapidly crumbling to pieces; many were perishing by the sword; a multitude had already been carried away captive; soon Israel would fall completely into the hands of the Assyrians, and be utterly ruined; and this fate would surely befall Judah as well, unless God should work mightily through chosen representatives.

Hezekiah appealed directly to the priests to unite with him in bringing about the necessary reforms. "Be not now negligent," he exhorted them; "for the Lord hath chosen you to stand before Him, to serve Him, and that ye should minister unto Him, and burn incense." "Sanctify now yourselves, and sanctify the house of the Lord God of your fathers." Verses 11, 5.

It was a time for quick action. The priests began at once. Enlisting the co-operation of others of their number who had not been present during this conference, they engaged heartily in the work of cleansing and sanctifying the temple. Because of the years of desecration and neglect, this was attended with many difficulties; but the priests and the Levites labored untiringly, and within a remarkably short time they were able to report their task completed. The temple doors had been repaired and thrown open; the sacred vessels had been assembled and put into place; and all was in readiness for the reestablishment of the sanctuary services.

In the first service held, the rulers of the city united with King Hezekiah and with the priests and Levites in seeking forgiveness for the sins of the nation. Upon the altar were placed sin offerings "to make an atonement for all Israel." "And when they had made an end of offering, the king and all that were present with him bowed themselves, and worshiped." Once more the temple courts resounded with words of praise and adoration. The songs of David and of Asaph were sung with joy, as the worshipers realized that they were being delivered from the bondage of sin and apostasy. "Hezekiah rejoiced, and all the people, that God had prepared the people: for the thing was done suddenly." Verses 24, 29, 36.

God had indeed prepared the hearts of the chief men of Judah to lead out in a decided reformatory movement, that the tide of apostasy might be stayed. Through His prophets He had sent to His chosen people message after message of earnest entreaty—messages that had been despised and rejected by the ten tribes of the kingdom of Israel, now given over to the enemy. But in Judah there remained a goodly remnant, and to these the prophets continued to appeal. Hear Isaiah urging, "Turn ye unto Him from whom the children of Israel have deeply revolted." Isaiah 31:6. Hear Micah declaring with confidence: "I will look unto the Lord; I will wait for the God of my salvation: my God will hear me. Rejoice not against me, O mine enemy: when I fall, I shall arise; when I sit in darkness, the Lord shall be a light unto me. I will bear the indignation of the Lord, because I have sinned against Him, until He plead my cause, and execute judgment for me: He will bring me forth to the light, and I shall behold His righteousness." Micah 7:7-9.

These and other like messages revealing the willingness of God to forgive and accept those who turned to Him with full purpose of heart, had brought hope to many a fainting soul in the dark years when the temple doors remained closed; and now, as the leaders began to institute a reform, a multitude of the people, weary of the thralldom of sin, were ready to respond.

Those who entered the temple courts to seek forgiveness and to renew their vows of allegiance to Jehovah, had wonderful encouragement offered them in the prophetic portions of Scripture. The solemn warnings against idolatry, spoken through Moses in the hearing of all Israel, had been accompanied by prophecies of God's willingness to hear and forgive those who in times of apostasy should seek Him with all the heart. "If thou turn to the Lord thy God," Moses had said, "and shalt be obedient unto His voice; (for the Lord thy God is a merciful God;) He will not forsake thee, neither destroy thee, nor forget the covenant of thy fathers which He sware unto them." Deuteronomy 4:30, 31.

And in the prophetic prayer offered at the dedication of the temple whose services Hezekiah and his associates were now restoring, Solomon had prayed, "When Thy people Israel be smitten down before the enemy, because they have sinned against Thee, and shall turn again to Thee, and confess Thy name, and pray, and make supplication unto Thee in this house: then hear Thou in heaven, and forgive the sin of Thy people Israel." 1 Kings 8:33, 34. The seal of divine approval had been placed upon this prayer; for at its close fire had come down from heaven to consume the burnt offering and the sacrifices, and the glory of the Lord had filled the temple. See 2 Chronicles 7:1. And by night the Lord had appeared to Solomon to tell him that his prayer had been heard, and that mercy would be shown those who should worship there. The gracious assurance was given: "If My people, which are called by My name, shall humble themselves, and pray, and seek My face, and turn from their wicked ways; then will I hear from heaven, and will forgive their sin, and will heal their land." Verse 14.

These promises met abundant fulfillment during the reformation under Hezekiah.

The good beginning made at the time of the purification of the temple was followed by a broader movement, in which Israel as well as Judah participated. In his zeal to make the temple services a real blessing to the people, Hezekiah determined to revive the ancient custom of gathering the Israelites together for the celebration of the Passover feast.

For many years the Passover had not been observed as a national festival. The division of the kingdom after the close of Solomon's reign had made this seem impracticable. But the terrible judgments befalling the ten tribes were awakening in the hearts of some a desire for better things; and the stirring messages of the prophets were having their effect. By royal couriers the invitation to the Passover at Jerusalem was heralded far and wide, "from city to city through the country of Ephraim and Manasseh even unto Zebulun." The bearers of the gracious invitation were usually repulsed. The impenitent turned lightly aside; nevertheless some, eager to seek God for a clearer knowledge of His will, "humbled themselves, and came to Jerusalem." 2 Chronicles 30:10, 11.

In the land of Judah the response was very general; for upon them was "the hand of God," "to give them one heart to do the commandment of the king and of the princes"—a command in accord with the will of God as revealed through His prophets. Verses 22, 21.

The occasion was one of the greatest profit to the multitudes assembled. The desecrated streets of the city were cleared of the idolatrous shrines placed there during the reign of Ahaz. On the appointed day the Passover was observed, and the week was spent by the people in offering peace offerings and in learning what God would have them do. Daily the Levites "taught the good knowledge of the Lord;" and those who had prepared their hearts to seek God, found pardon. A great gladness took possession of the worshiping multitude; "the Levites and the priests praised the Lord day by day, singing with loud instruments;" all were united in their desire to praise Him who had proved so gracious and merciful. Verse 12.

The seven days usually allotted to the Passover feast passed all too quickly, and the worshipers determined to spend another seven days in learning more fully the way of the Lord. The teaching priests continued their work of instruction from the book of the law; daily the people assembled at the temple to offer their tribute of praise and thanksgiving; and as the great meeting drew to a close, it was evident that God had wrought

marvelously in the conversion of backsliding Judah and in stemming the tide of idolatry which threatened to sweep all before it. The solemn warnings of the prophets had not been uttered in vain. "There was great joy in Jerusalem: for since the time of Solomon the son of David king of Israel there was not the like in Jerusalem." Verse 26.

The time had come for the return of the worshipers to their homes. "The priests the Levites arose and blessed the people: and their voice was heard, and their prayer came up to His holy dwelling place, even unto heaven." Verse 27. God had accepted those who with broken hearts had confessed their sins and with resolute purpose had turned to Him for forgiveness and help.

There now remained an important work in which those who were returning to their homes must take an active part, and the accomplishment of this work bore evidence to the genuineness of the reformation wrought. The record reads: "All Israel that were present went out to the cities of Judah, and brake the images in pieces, and cut down the groves, and threw down the high places and the altars out of all Judah and Benjamin, in Ephraim also and Manasseh, until they had utterly destroyed them all. Then all the children of Israel returned, every man to his possession, into their own cities." 2 Chronicles 31:1.

Hezekiah and his associates instituted various reforms for the upbuilding of the spiritual and temporal interests of the kingdom. "Throughout all Judah" the king "wrought that which was good and right and truth before the Lord his God. And in every work that he began, . . . he did it with all his heart, and prospered." "He trusted in the Lord God of Israel,

During the revival wrought by Hezekiah the people destroyed the images and cut down groves dedicated to false worship.

. . . and departed not from following Him, but kept His commandments, which the Lord commanded Moses. And the Lord was with him; and he prospered." Verses 20, 21; 2 Kings 18:5-7.

The reign of Hezekiah was characterized by a series of remarkable providences which revealed to the surrounding nations that the God of Israel was with His people. The success of the Assyrians in capturing Samaria and in scattering the shattered remnant of the ten tribes among the nations, during the earlier portion of his reign, was leading many to question the power of the God of the Hebrews. Emboldened by their successes, the Ninevites had long since set aside the message of Jonah and had become defiant in their opposition to the purposes of Heaven. A few years after the fall of Samaria the victorious armies reappeared in Palestine, this time directing their forces against the fenced cities of Judah, with some measure of success; but they withdrew for a season because of difficulties arising in other portions of their realm. Not until some years later, toward the close of Hezekiah's reign, was it to be demonstrated before the nations of the world whether the gods of the heathen were finally to prevail.

chapter 29

The Ambassadors From Babylon

IN THE midst of his prosperous reign King Hezekiah was suddenly stricken with a fatal malady. "Sick unto death," his case was beyond the power of man to help. And the last vestige of hope seemed removed when the prophet Isaiah appeared before him with the message. "Thus saith the Lord, Set thine house in order: for thou shalt die, and not live." Isaiah 38:1.

The outlook seemed utterly dark; yet the king could still pray to the One who had hitherto been his "refuge and strength, a very present help in trouble." Psalm 46:1. And so "he turned his face to the wall, and prayed unto the Lord, saying, I beseech Thee, O Lord, remember now how I have walked before Thee in truth and with a perfect heart, and have done that which is good in Thy sight. And Hezekiah wept sore." 2 Kings 20:2, 3.

Since the days of David there had reigned no king who had wrought so mightily for the upbuilding of the kingdom of God in a time of apostasy and discouragement as had Hezekiah. The dying ruler had served his God faithfully, and had strengthened the confidence of the people in Jehovah as their Supreme Ruler. And, like David, he could now plead:

> "Let my prayer come before Thee:
> Incline Thine ear unto my cry;
> For my soul is full of troubles:
> And my life draweth nigh unto the grave."
>
> Psalm 88:2, 3.

> "Thou art my hope, O Lord God:
> Thou art my trust from my youth.
> By Thee have I been holden up."
> "Forsake me not when my strength faileth."
> "O God, be not far from me:
> O my God, make haste for my help."
> "O God, forsake me not;
> Until I have showed Thy strength unto this generation,
> And Thy power to everyone that is to come."
>
> Psalm 71:5, 6, 9, 12, 18.

He whose "compassions fail not," heard the prayer of His servant. Lamentations 3:22. "It came to pass, afore Isaiah was gone out into the middle court, that the word of the Lord came to him, saying, Turn again, and tell Hezekiah the captain of My people, Thus saith the Lord, the God of David thy father, I have heard thy prayer, I have seen thy tears: behold, I will heal thee: on the third day thou shalt go up unto the house of the Lord. And I will add unto thy days fifteen years; and I will deliver thee and this city out of the hand of the king of Assyria; and I will defend this city for Mine own sake, and for My servant David's sake." 2 Kings 20:4-6.

Gladly the prophet returned with the words of assurance and hope. Directing that a lump of figs be laid upon the diseased part, Isaiah delivered to the king the message of God's mercy and protecting care.

Like Moses in the land of Midian, like Gideon in the presence of the heavenly messenger, like Elisha just before the ascension of his master, Hezekiah pleaded for some sign that the message was from heaven. "What shall be the sign," he inquired of the prophet, "that the Lord will heal me, and that I shall go up into the house of the Lord the third day?"

"This sign shalt thou have of the Lord," the prophet answered, "that the Lord will do the thing that He hath spoken: shall the shadow go forward ten degrees, or go back ten degrees?" "It is a light thing," Hezekiah replied, "for the shadow to go down ten degrees: nay, but let the shadow return backward ten degrees."

Only by the direct interposition of God could the shadow on the sundial be made to turn back ten degrees; and this was to be the sign to Hezekiah that the Lord had heard his prayer. Accordingly, "the prophet cried unto the Lord: and He brought the shadow ten degrees backward, by which it had gone down in the dial of Ahaz." Verses 8-11.

Restored to his wonted strength, the king of Judah acknowledged in words of song the mercies of Jehovah, and vowed to spend his remaining days in willing service to the King of kings. His grateful recognition of God's compassionate dealing with him is an inspiration to all who desire to spend their years to the glory of their Maker.

> "I said
> In the cutting off of my days,
> I shall go to the gates of the grave:
> I am deprived of the residue of my years.

"I said,
I shall not see the Lord, even the Lord, in the land of
the living:
I shall behold man no more with the inhabitants of the world.

"Mine age is departed,
And is removed from me as a shepherd's tent:

"I have cut off like a weaver my life:
He will cut me off with pining sickness:

"From day even to night wilt Thou make an end of me.
I reckoned till morning, that,
As a lion, so will He break all my bones:

"From day even to night wilt Thou make an end of me.
Like a crane or a swallow, so did I chatter:
I did mourn as a dove:
Mine eyes fail with looking upward:
O Lord, I am oppressed; undertake for me.

"What shall I say?
He hath both spoken unto me,
And Himself hath done it:
I shall go softly all my years in the bitterness of my soul.

"O Lord, by these things men live,
And in all these things is the life of my spirit:
So wilt Thou recover me, and make me to live.

"Behold, for peace I had great bitterness:
But Thou hast in love to my soul delivered it from the
pit of corruption:
For Thou hast cast all my sins behind Thy back.

"For the grave cannot praise Thee,
Death cannot celebrate Thee:
They that go down into the pit cannot hope for Thy truth.

"The living, the living, he shall praise Thee,
  As I do this day:
  The father to the children shall make known Thy truth.

"The Lord was ready to save me:
  Therefore we will sing my songs to the stringed instruments
  All the days of our life in the house of the Lord."
                                    Isaiah 38:10-20.

In the fertile valleys of the Tigris and the Euphrates there
dwelt an ancient race which, though at that time subject to
Assyria, was destined to rule the world. Among its people
were wise men who gave much attention to the study of
astronomy; and when they noticed that the shadow on the
sundial had been turned back ten degrees, they marveled
greatly. Their king, Merodachbaladan, upon learning that
this miracle had been wrought as a sign to the king of Judah
that the God of heaven had granted him a new lease of life,
sent ambassadors to Hezekiah to congratulate him on his
recovery and to learn, if possible, more of the God who was
able to perform so great a wonder.

The visit of these messengers from the ruler of a faraway
land gave Hezekiah an opportunity to extol the living God.
How easy it would have been for him to tell them of God, the
upholder of all created things, through whose favor his own
life had been spared when all other hope had fled! What
momentous transformations might have taken place had these
seekers after truth from the plains of Chaldea been led to
acknowledge the supreme sovereignty of the living God!

But pride and vanity took possession of Hezekiah's heart,
and in self-exaltation he laid open to covetous eyes the treasures with which God had enriched His people. The king

"showed them the house of his precious things, the silver, and the gold, and the spices, and the precious ointment, and all the house of his armor, and all that was found in his treasures: there was nothing in his house, nor in all his dominion, that Hezekiah showed them not." Isaiah 39:2. Not to glorify God did he do this, but to exalt himself in the eyes of the foreign princes. He did not stop to consider that these men were representatives of a powerful nation that had not the fear nor the love of God in their hearts, and that it was imprudent to make them his confidants concerning the temporal riches of the nation.

The visit of the ambassadors to Hezekiah was a test of his gratitude and devotion. The record says, "Howbeit in the business of the ambassadors of the princes of Babylon, who sent unto him to inquire of the wonder that was done in the land, God left him, to try him, that He might know all that was in his heart." 2 Chronicles 32:31. Had Hezekiah improved the opportunity given him to bear witness to the power, the goodness, the compassion, of the God of Israel, the report of the ambassadors would have been as light piercing darkness. But he magnified himself above the Lord of hosts. He "rendered not again according to the benefit done unto him; for his heart was lifted up." Verse 25.

How disastrous the results which were to follow! To Isaiah it was revealed that the returning ambassadors were carrying with them a report of the riches they had seen, and that the king of Babylon and his counselors would plan to enrich their own country with the treasures of Jerusalem. Hezekiah had grievously sinned; "therefore there was wrath upon him, and upon Judah and Jerusalem." Verse 25.

Hezekiah gave the envoys from Babylon
a royal welcome, and he proudly showed
them all the treasures of his kingdom.
© P.P.P.A.   JOHN STEEL, ARTIST

"Then came Isaiah the prophet unto King Hezekiah, and said unto him, What said these men? and from whence came they unto thee? And Hezekiah said, They are come from a far country unto me, even from Babylon. Then said he, What have they seen in thine house? And Hezekiah answered, All that is in mine house have they seen: there is nothing among my treasures that I have not showed them.

"Then said Isaiah to Hezekiah, Hear the word of the Lord of hosts: Behold, the days come, that all that is in thine house, and that which thy fathers have laid up in store until this day, shall be carried to Babylon: nothing shall be left, saith the Lord. And of thy sons that shall issue from thee, which thou shalt beget, shall they take away; and they shall be eunuchs in the palace of the king of Babylon.

"Then said Hezekiah to Isaiah, Good is the word of the Lord which thou hast spoken." Isaiah 39:3-8.

Filled with remorse, "Hezekiah humbled himself for the pride of his heart, both he and the inhabitants of Jerusalem, so that the wrath of the Lord came not upon them in the days of Hezekiah." 2 Chronicles 32:26. But the evil seed had been sown and in time was to spring up and yield a harvest of desolation and woe. During his remaining years the king of Judah was to have much prosperity because of his steadfast purpose to redeem the past and to bring honor to the name of the God whom he served; yet his faith was to be severely tried, and he was to learn that only by putting his trust fully in Jehovah could he hope to triumph over the powers of darkness that were plotting his ruin and the utter destruction of his people.

The story of Hezekiah's failure to prove true to his trust

at the time of the visit of the ambassadors is fraught with an important lesson for all. Far more than we do, we need to speak of the precious chapters in our experience, of the mercy and loving-kindness of God, of the matchless depths of the Saviour's love. When mind and heart are filled with the love of God, it will not be difficult to impart that which enters into the spiritual life. Great thoughts, noble aspirations, clear perceptions of truth, unselfish purposes, yearnings for piety and holiness, will find expression in words that reveal the character of the heart treasure.

Those with whom we associate day by day need our help, our guidance. They may be in such a condition of mind that a word spoken in season will be as a nail in a sure place. Tomorrow some of these souls may be where we can never reach them again. What is our influence over these fellow travelers?

Every day of life is freighted with responsibilities which we must bear. Every day, our words and acts are making impressions upon those with whom we associate. How great the need that we set a watch upon our lips and guard carefully our steps! One reckless movement, one imprudent step, and the surging waves of some strong temptation may sweep a soul into the downward path. We cannot gather up the thoughts we have planted in human minds. If they have been evil, we may have set in motion a train of circumstances, a tide of evil, which we are powerless to stay.

On the other hand, if by our example we aid others in the development of good principles, we give them power to do good. In their turn they exert the same beneficial influence over others. Thus hundreds and thousands are helped by our unconscious influence. The true follower of Christ strengthens the good purposes of all with whom he comes in contact. Before an unbelieving, sin-loving world he reveals the power of God's grace and the perfection of His character.

chapter 30

Deliverance From Assyria

IN A time of grave national peril, when the hosts of Assyria were invading the land of Judah and it seemed as if nothing could save Jerusalem from utter destruction, Hezekiah rallied the forces of his realm to resist with unfailing courage their heathen oppressors and to trust in the power of Jehovah to deliver. "Be strong and courageous, be not afraid nor dismayed for the king of Assyria, nor for all the multitude that is with him," Hezekiah exhorted the men of Judah; "for there be more with us than with him: with him is an arm of flesh; but with us is the Lord our God to help us, and to fight our battles." 2 Chronicles 32:7, 8.

It was not without reason that Hezekiah could speak with certainty of the outcome. The boastful Assyrian, while used by God for a season as the rod of His anger for the punishment of the nations, was not always to prevail. See Isaiah 10:5. "Be not afraid of the Assyrian," had been the message of the Lord through Isaiah some years before to those that dwelt in Zion; "for yet a very little while, . . . and the Lord of hosts shall stir up a scourge for him according to the slaughter of Midian at the rock of Oreb: and as His rod was upon the sea, so shall He lift it up after the manner of Egypt. And it shall come to pass in that day, that his burden shall be taken away from off thy shoulder, and his yoke from off thy neck, and the yoke shall be destroyed because of the anointing." Verses 24-27.

In another prophetic message, given "in the year that King Ahaz died," the prophet had declared: "The Lord of hosts hath sworn, saying, Surely as I have thought, so shall it come to pass; and as I have purposed, so shall it stand: that I will break the Assyrian in My land, and upon My mountains tread him underfoot: then shall his yoke depart from off them, and his burden depart from off their shoulders. This is the purpose that is purposed upon the whole earth: and this is the hand that is stretched out upon all the nations. For the Lord of hosts hath purposed, and who shall disannul it? and His hand is stretched out, and who shall turn it back?" Isaiah 14:28, 24-27.

The power of the oppressor was to be broken. Yet Hezekiah, in the earlier years of his reign, had continued to pay tribute to Assyria, in harmony with the agreement entered into by Ahaz. Meanwhile the king had taken "counsel with his princes and his mighty men," and had done everything possible for the defense of his kingdom. He had made sure of a bountiful supply of water within the walls of Jerusalem, while without the city there should be a scarcity. "Also he strengthened himself, and built up all the wall that was broken, and raised it up to the towers, and another wall without, and repaired Millo in the city of David, and made darts and shields in abundance. And he set captains of war over the people." 2 Chronicles 32:3, 5, 6. Nothing had been left undone that could be done in preparation for a siege.

At the time of Hezekiah's accession to the throne of Judah, the Assyrians had already carried captive a large number of the children of Israel from the northern kingdom; and a few years after he had begun to reign, and while he was still strengthening the defenses of Jerusalem, the Assyrians besieged and captured Samaria and scattered the ten tribes among the many provinces of the Assyrian realm. The borders of Judah were only a few miles distant, with Jerusalem less than fifty miles away; and the rich spoils to be found within the temple would tempt the enemy to return.

But the king of Judah had determined to do his part in preparing to resist the enemy; and, having accomplished all that human ingenuity and energy could do, he had assembled his forces and had exhorted them to be of good courage. "Great is the Holy One of Israel in the midst of thee" had been the message of the prophet Isaiah to Judah; and the king with unwavering faith now declared, "With us is the Lord our God to help us, and to fight our battles." Isaiah 12:6; 2 Chronicles 32:8.

Nothing more quickly inspires faith than the exercise of faith. The king of Judah had prepared for the coming storm; and now, confident that the prophecy against the Assyrians would be fulfilled, he stayed his soul upon God. "And the people rested themselves upon the words of Hezekiah." 2 Chronicles 32:8. What though the armies of Assyria, fresh from the conquest of the greatest nations of earth, and triumphant over Samaria in Israel, should now turn their forces against Judah? What though they should boast, "As my hand hath found the kingdoms of the idols, and whose graven images did excel them of Jerusalem and of Samaria; shall I not, as I have done unto Samaria and her idols, so do to Jerusalem and her idols?" Isaiah 10:10, 11. Judah had nothing to fear; for their trust was in Jehovah.

The long-expected crisis finally came. The forces of Assyria, advancing from triumph to triumph, appeared in Judea. Confident of victory, the leaders divided their forces into two armies, one of which was to meet the Egyptian army to the southward, while the other was to besiege Jerusalem.

Judah's only hope was now in God. All possible help from Egypt had been cut off, and no other nations were near to lend a friendly hand.

The Assyrian officers, sure of the strength of their disciplined forces, arranged for a conference with the chief men of Judah, during which they insolently demanded the surrender of the city. This demand was accompanied by blasphemous revilings against the God of the Hebrews. Because of the weakness and apostasy of Israel and Judah, the name of God was no longer feared among the nations, but had become a subject for continual reproach. See Isaiah 52:5.

"Speak ye now to Hezekiah," said Rabshakeh, one of Sennacherib's chief officers, "Thus saith the great king, the king of Assyria, What confidence is this wherein thou trustest? Thou sayest, (but they are but vain words,) I have counsel and strength for the war. Now on whom dost thou trust, that thou rebellest against me?" 2 Kings 18:19, 20.

The officers were conferring outside the gates of the city, but within the hearing of the sentries on the wall; and as the

Rabshakeh, a chief officer of the invaders from Assyria, taunted the people of Jerusalem for trusting God to save them.
© P.P.P.A.   JOHN STEEL, ARTIST

representatives of the Assyrian king loudly urged their proposals upon the chief men of Judah, they were requested to speak in the Syrian rather than the Jewish language, in order that those upon the wall might not have knowledge of the proceedings of the conference. Rabshakeh, scorning this suggestion, lifted his voice still higher, and, continuing to speak in the Jewish language, said:

"Hear ye the words of the great king, the king of Assyria. Thus saith the king, Let not Hezekiah deceive you: for he shall not be able to deliver you. Neither let Hezekiah make you trust in the Lord, saying, The Lord will surely deliver us: this city shall not be delivered into the hand of the king of Assyria.

"Hearken not to Hezekiah: for thus saith the king of Assyria, Make an agreement with me by a present, and come out to me: and eat ye everyone of his vine, and everyone of his fig tree, and drink ye everyone the waters of his own cistern; until I come and take you away to a land like your own land, a land of corn and wine, a land of bread and vineyards.

"Beware lest Hezekiah persuade you, saying, The Lord will deliver us. Hath any of the gods of the nations delivered his land out of the hand of the king of Assyria? Where are the gods of Hamath and Arphad? where are the gods of Sepharvaim? and have they delivered Samaria out of my hand? Who are they among all the gods of these lands, that have delivered their land out of my hand, that the Lord should deliver Jerusalem out of my hand?" Isaiah 36:13-20.

To these taunts the children of Judah "answered him not a word." The conference was at an end. The Jewish representatives returned to Hezekiah "with their clothes rent, and told him the words of Rabshakeh." Verses 21, 22. The king, upon learning of the blasphemous challenge, "rent his clothes, and covered himself with sackcloth, and went into the house of the Lord." 2 Kings 19:1.

A messenger was dispatched to Isaiah to inform him of the outcome of the conference. "This day is a day of trouble, and of rebuke, and blasphemy," was the word the king sent. "It may be the Lord thy God will hear all the words of Rabshakeh, whom the king of Assyria his master hath sent to reproach the living God; and will reprove the words which the Lord thy God hath heard: wherefore lift up thy prayer for the remnant that are left." Verses 3, 4.

"For this cause Hezekiah the king, and the prophet Isaiah the son of Amoz, prayed and cried to Heaven." 2 Chronicles 32:20.

God answered the prayers of His servants. To Isaiah was given the message for Hezekiah: "Thus saith the Lord, Be not afraid of the words which thou hast heard, with which the servants of the king of Assyria have blasphemed Me. Behold, I will send a blast upon him, and he shall hear a rumor, and shall return to his own land; and I will cause him to fall by the sword in his own land." 2 Kings 19:6, 7.

The Assyrian representatives, after taking leave of the chief men of Judah, communicated direct with their king, who was with the division of his army guarding the approach from Egypt. Upon hearing the report, Sennacherib wrote "letters to rail on the Lord God of Israel, and to speak against Him, saying, As the gods of the nations of other lands have not delivered their people out of mine hand, so shall not the

God of Hezekiah deliver His people out of mine hand." 2 Chronicles 32:17.

The boastful threat was accompanied by the message: "Let not thy God in whom thou trustest deceive thee, saying, Jerusalem shall not be delivered into the hand of the king of Assyria. Behold, thou hast heard what the kings of Assyria have done to all lands, by destroying them utterly: and shalt thou be delivered? Have the gods of the nations delivered them which my fathers have destroyed; as Gozan, and Haran, and Rezeph, and the children of Eden which were in Thelasar? Where is the king of Hamath, and the king of Arpad, and the king of the city of Sepharvaim, of Hena, and Ivah?" 2 Kings 19:10-13.

When the king of Judah received the taunting letter, he took it into the temple and "spread it before the Lord" and prayed with strong faith for help from heaven, that the nations of earth might know that the God of the Hebrews still lived and reigned. Verse 14. The honor of Jehovah was at stake; He alone could bring deliverance.

"O Lord God of Israel, which dwellest between the cherubims," Hezekiah pleaded, "Thou art the God, even Thou alone, of all the kingdoms of the earth; Thou hast made heaven and earth. Lord, bow down Thine ear, and hear: open, Lord, Thine eyes, and see: and hear the words of Sennacherib, which hath sent him to reproach the living God. Of a truth, Lord, the kings of Assyria have destroyed the nations and their lands, and have cast their gods into the fire: for they were no gods, but the work of men's hands, wood and stone: therefore they have destroyed them. Now therefore, O Lord our God, I beseech Thee, save Thou us out of his

When King Hezekiah received the taunting letter from Sennacherib, he spread it before the Lord and prayed for deliverance.
© P.P.P.A.   AMADO GONZALEZ, ARTIST

hand, that all the kingdoms of the earth may know that Thou art the Lord God, even Thou only." 2 Kings 19:15-19.

"Give ear, O Shepherd of Israel,
Thou that leadest Joseph like a flock;
Thou that dwellest between the cherubims, shine forth.
Before Ephraim and Benjamin and Manasseh stir up Thy
    strength,
And come and save us.
Turn us again, O God,
And cause Thy face to shine; and we shall be saved.

"O Lord God of hosts,
How long wilt Thou be angry against the prayer of Thy
    people?
Thou feedest them with the bread of tears;
And givest them tears to drink in great measure.
Thou makest us a strife unto our neighbors:
And our enemies laugh among themselves.
Turn us again, O God of hosts,
And cause Thy face to shine; and we shall be saved.

"Thou hast brought a vine out of Egypt:
Thou hast cast out the heathen, and planted it.
Thou preparedst room before it,
And didst cause it to take deep root, and it filled the land.
The hills were covered with the shadow of it,
And the boughs thereof were like the goodly cedars.
She sent out her boughs unto the sea,
And her branches unto the river.

"Why hast Thou then broken down her hedges,
So that all they which pass by the way do pluck her?
The boar out of the wood doth waste it,
And the wild beast of the field doth devour it.
Return, we beseech Thee, O God of hosts:
Look down from heaven, and behold, and visit this vine;

And the vineyard which Thy right hand hath planted,
And the branch that Thou madest strong for Thyself. . . .

"Quicken us, and we will call upon Thy name.
Turn us again, O Lord God of hosts,
Cause Thy face to shine; and we shall be saved." Psalm 80.

Hezekiah's pleadings in behalf of Judah and of the honor of their Supreme Ruler were in harmony with the mind of God. Solomon, in his benediction at the dedication of the temple, had prayed the Lord to maintain "the cause of His people Israel at all times, as the matter shall require: that all the people of the earth may know that the Lord is God, and that there is none else." 1 Kings 8:59, 60. Especially was the Lord to show favor when, in times of war or of oppression by an army, the chief men of Israel should enter the house of prayer and plead for deliverance. Verses 33, 34.

Hezekiah was not left without hope. Isaiah sent to him, saying, "Thus saith the Lord God of Israel, That which thou hast prayed to Me against Sennacherib king of Assyria I have heard. This is the word that the Lord hath spoken concerning him:

"The virgin the daughter of Zion hath despised thee, and laughed thee to scorn; the daughter of Jerusalem hath shaken her head at thee.

"Whom hast thou reproached and blasphemed? and against whom hast thou exalted thy voice, and lifted up thine eyes on high? even against the Holy One of Israel. By thy messengers thou hast reproached the Lord, and hast said, With the multitude of my chariots I am come up to the height of the mountains, to the sides of Lebanon, and will cut down the tall cedar trees thereof, and the choice fir trees thereof:

and I will enter into the lodgings of his borders, and into the forest of his Carmel. I have digged and drunk strange waters, and with the sole of my feet have I dried up all the rivers of besieged places.

"Hast thou not heard long ago how I have done it, and of ancient times that I have formed it? now have I brought it to pass, that thou shouldest be to lay waste fenced cities into ruinous heaps. Therefore their inhabitants were of small power, they were dismayed and confounded; they were as the grass of the field, and as the green herb, as the grass on the housetops, and as corn blasted before it be grown up.

"But I know thy abode, and thy going out, and thy coming in, and thy rage against Me. Because thy rage against Me and thy tumult is come up into Mine ears, therefore I will put My hook in thy nose, and My bridle in thy lips, and I will turn thee back by the way by which thou camest." 2 Kings 19:20-28.

The land of Judah had been laid waste by the army of occupation, but God had promised to provide miraculously for the needs of the people. To Hezekiah came the message: "This shall be a sign unto thee, Ye shall eat this year such things as grow of themselves, and in the second year that which springeth of the same; and in the third year sow ye, and reap, and plant vineyards, and eat the fruits thereof. And the remnant that is escaped of the house of Judah shall yet again take root downward, and bear fruit upward. For out of Jerusalem shall go forth a remnant, and they that escape out of Mount Zion: the zeal of the Lord of hosts shall do this.

"Therefore thus saith the Lord concerning the king of Assyria, He shall not come into this city, nor shoot an arrow there, nor come before it with shield, nor cast a bank against it. By the way that he came, by the same shall he return, and shall not come into this city, saith the Lord. For I will defend this city, to save it, for Mine own sake, and for My servant David's sake." Verses 29-34.

That very night deliverance came. "The angel of the Lord went out, and smote in the camp of the Assyrians an hundred fourscore and five thousand." Verse 35. "All the mighty men of valor, and the leaders and captains in the camp of the king of Assyria," were slain. 2 Chronicles 32:21.

Tidings of this terrible judgment upon the army that had been sent to take Jerusalem, soon reached Sennacherib, who was still guarding the approach to Judea from Egypt. Stricken with fear, the Assyrian king hasted to depart and "returned with shame of face to his own land." Verse 21. But he had not long to reign. In harmony with the prophecy that had been uttered concerning his sudden end, he was assassinated by those of his own home, "and Esarhaddon his son reigned in his stead." Isaiah 37:38.

The God of the Hebrews had prevailed over the proud

Assyrian. The honor of Jehovah was vindicated in the eyes of the surrounding nations. In Jerusalem the hearts of the people were filled with holy joy. Their earnest entreaties for deliverance had been mingled with confession of sin and with many tears. In their great need they had trusted wholly in the power of God to save, and He had not failed them. Now the temple courts resounded with songs of solemn praise.

"In Judah is God known:
His name is great in Israel.
In Salem also is His tabernacle,
And His dwelling place in Zion.
There brake He the arrows of the bow,
The shield, and the sword, and the battle.

"Thou art more glorious and excellent
Than the mountains of prey.
The stouthearted are spoiled, they have slept their sleep:
And none of the men of might have found their hands.
At Thy rebuke, O God of Jacob,
Both the chariot and horse are cast into a dead sleep.

"Thou, even Thou, art to be feared:
And who may stand in Thy sight when once Thou art angry?
Thou didst cause judgment to be heard from heaven;
The earth feared, and was still,
When God arose to judgment,
To save all the meek of the earth.

"Surely the wrath of man shall praise Thee:
The remainder of wrath shalt Thou restrain.
Vow, and pay unto the Lord your God:
Let all that be round about Him bring presents unto Him
    that ought to be feared.
He shall cut off the spirit of princes:
He is terrible to the kings of the earth."

Psalm 76.

The rise and fall of the Assyrian Empire is rich in lessons for the nations of earth today. Inspiration has likened the glory of Assyria at the height of her prosperity to a noble tree in the garden of God, towering above the surrounding trees.

"The Assyrian was a cedar in Lebanon with fair branches, and with a shadowing shroud, and of an high stature; and his top was among the thick boughs. . . . Under his shadow dwelt all great nations. Thus was he fair in his greatness, in the length of his branches: for his root was by great waters. The cedars in the garden of God could not hide him: the fir trees were not like his boughs, and the chestnut trees were not like his branches; nor any tree in the garden of God was like unto him in his beauty. . . . All the trees of Eden, that were in the garden of God, envied him." Ezekiel 31:3-9.

But the rulers of Assyria, instead of using their unusual blessings for the benefit of mankind, became the scourge of many lands. Merciless, with no thought of God or their fellow men, they pursued the fixed policy of causing all nations to acknowledge the supremacy of the gods of Nineveh, whom they exalted above the Most High. God had sent Jonah to them with a message of warning, and for a season they humbled themselves before the Lord of hosts and sought forgiveness. But soon they turned again to idol worship and to the conquest of the world.

The prophet Nahum, in his arraignment of the evildoers in Nineveh, exclaimed:

"Woe to the bloody city!
It is all full of lies and robbery;
The prey departeth not;

"The noise of a whip, and the noise of the rattling
of the wheels,
And of the prancing horses, and of the jumping chariots.
The horseman lifteth up both the bright sword and the
glittering spear:
And there is a multitude of slain. . . .

"Behold, I am against thee,
Saith the Lord of hosts."
Nahum 3:1-5.

With unerring accuracy the Infinite One still keeps account with the nations. While His mercy is tendered, with calls to repentance, this account remains open; but when the figures reach a certain amount which God has fixed, the ministry of His wrath begins. The account is closed. Divine patience ceases. Mercy no longer pleads in their behalf.

"The Lord is slow to anger, and great in power, and will not at all acquit the wicked: the Lord hath His way in the whirlwind and in the storm, and the clouds are the dust of His feet. He rebuketh the sea, and maketh it dry, and drieth up all the rivers: Bashan languisheth, and Carmel, and the flower of Lebanon languisheth. The mountains quake at Him, and the hills melt, and the earth is burned at His presence, yea, the world, and all that dwell therein. Who can stand before His indignation? and who can abide in the fierceness of His anger? His fury is poured out like fire, and the rocks are thrown down by Him." Nahum 1:3-6.

It was thus that Nineveh, "the rejoicing city that dwelt carelessly, that said in her heart, I am, and there is none beside me," became a desolation, "empty, and void, and waste," "the dwelling of the lions, and the feeding place of the young lions, where the lion, even the old lion, walked, and the lion's whelp, and none made them afraid." Zephaniah 2:15; Nahum 2:10, 11.

Looking forward to the time when the pride of Assyria should be brought low, Zephaniah prophesied of Nineveh: "Flocks shall lie down in the midst of her, all the beasts of the nations: both the cormorant and the bittern shall lodge in the upper lintels of it; their voice shall sing in the windows; desolation shall be in the thresholds: for He shall uncover the cedar work." Zephaniah 2:14.

Great was the glory of the Assyrian realm; great was its downfall. The prophet Ezekiel, carrying farther the figure of a noble cedar tree, plainly foretold the fall of Assyria because of its pride and cruelty. He declared:

"Thus saith the Lord God; . . . He hath shot up his top

among the thick boughs, and his heart is lifted up in his height; I have therefore delivered him into the hand of the mighty one of the heathen; he shall surely deal with him: I have driven him out for his wickedness. And strangers, the terrible of the nations, have cut him off, and have left him: upon the mountains and in all the valleys his branches are fallen, and his boughs are broken by all the rivers of the land; and all the people of the earth are gone down from his shadow, and have left him. Upon his ruin shall all the fowls of the heaven remain, and all the beasts of the field shall be upon his branches: *to the end that none of all the trees by the waters exalt themselves* for their height. . . .

"Thus saith the Lord God; In the day when he went down to the grave I caused a mourning: . . . and all the trees of the field fainted for him. I made the nations to shake at the sound of his fall." Ezekiel 31:10-16.

The pride of Assyria and its fall are to serve as an object lesson to the end of time. Of the nations of earth today who in arrogance and pride array themselves against Him, God inquires, "To whom art thou thus like in glory and in greatness among the trees of Eden? yet shalt thou be brought down with the trees of Eden unto the nether parts of the earth." Verse 18.

"The Lord is good, a stronghold in the day of trouble; and He knoweth them that trust in Him. But with an overrunning flood He will make an utter end" of all who endeavor to exalt themselves above the Most High. Nahum 1:7, 8.

"The pride of Assyria shall be brought down, and the scepter of Egypt shall depart away." Zechariah 10:11. This is true not only of the nations that arrayed themselves against

God in ancient times, but also of nations today who fail of fulfilling the divine purpose. In the day of final awards, when the righteous Judge of all the earth shall "sift the nations" (Isaiah 30:28), and those that have kept the truth shall be permitted to enter the City of God, heaven's arches will ring with the triumphant songs of the redeemed. "Ye shall have a song," the prophet declares, "as in the night when a holy solemnity is kept; and gladness of heart, as when one goeth with a pipe to come into the mountain of the Lord, to the Mighty One of Israel. And the Lord shall cause His glorious voice to be heard. . . . Through the voice of the Lord shall the Assyrian be beaten down, which smote with a rod. And in every place where the grounded staff shall pass, which the Lord shall lay upon him, it shall be with tabrets and harps." Verses 29-32.

chapter 31

Hope for the Heathen

THROUGHOUT his ministry Isaiah bore a plain testimony concerning God's purpose for the heathen. Other prophets had made mention of the divine plan, but their language was not always understood. To Isaiah it was given to make very plain to Judah the truth that among the Israel of God were to be numbered many who were not descendants of Abraham after the flesh. This teaching was not in harmony with the theology of his age, yet he fearlessly proclaimed the messages given him of God and brought hope to many a longing heart reaching out after the spiritual blessings promised to the seed of Abraham.

The apostle to the Gentiles, in his letter to the believers in Rome, calls attention to this characteristic of Isaiah's teaching. "Isaiah is very bold," Paul declares, "and saith, I was found of them that sought Me not; I was made manifest unto them that asked not after Me." Romans 10:20.

Often the Israelites seemed unable or unwilling to un-

The hope of the Messiah burned in the hearts of such men as Abel, Enoch, Moses, Abraham, David, Isaiah, and Daniel.

derstand God's purpose for the heathen. Yet it was this very purpose that had made them a separate people and had established them as an independent nation among the nations of the earth. Abraham, their father, to whom the covenant promise was first given, had been called to go forth from his kindred, to the regions beyond, that he might be a light bearer to the heathen. Although the promise to him included a posterity as numerous as the sand by the sea, yet it was for no selfish purpose that he was to become the founder of a great nation in the land of Canaan. God's covenant with him embraced all the nations of earth. "I will bless thee," Jehovah declared, "and make thy name great; and thou shalt be a blessing: and I will bless them that bless thee, and curse him that curseth thee: and in thee shall all families of the earth be blessed." Genesis 12:2, 3.

In the renewal of the covenant shortly before the birth of Isaac, God's purpose for mankind was again made plain. "All the nations of the earth shall be blessed in him," was the assurance of the Lord concerning the child of promise. Genesis 18:18. And later the heavenly visitant once more declared, "In thy seed shall all the nations of the earth be blessed." Genesis 22:18.

The all-embracing terms of this covenant were familiar to Abraham's children and to his children's children. It was in order that the Israelites might be a blessing to the nations, and that God's name might be made known "throughout all the earth" (Exodus 9:16), that they were delivered from Egyptian bondage. If obedient to His requirements, they were to be placed far in advance of other peoples in wisdom and understanding; but this supremacy was to be reached and maintained only in order that through them the purpose of God for "all nations of the earth" might be fulfilled.

The marvelous providences connected with Israel's deliverance from Egyptian bondage and with their occupancy of the Promised Land led many of the heathen to recognize the God of Israel as the Supreme Ruler. "The Egyptians shall know," had been the promise, "that I am the Lord, when I stretch forth Mine hand upon Egypt, and bring out the children of Israel from among them." Exodus 7:5. Even proud Pharaoh was constrained to acknowledge Jehovah's power. "Go, serve the Lord," he urged Moses and Aaron, "and bless me also." Exodus 12:31, 32.

The advancing hosts of Israel found that knowledge of the mighty workings of the God of the Hebrews had gone before them, and that some among the heathen were learning that He alone was the true God. In wicked Jericho the testimony of a heathen woman was, "The Lord your God, He is God in heaven above, and in earth beneath." Joshua 2:11. The knowledge of Jehovah that had thus come to her, proved her salvation. By faith "Rahab perished not with them that believed not." Hebrews 11:31. And her conversion was not an isolated case of God's mercy toward idolaters who acknowledged His divine authority. In the midst of the land a numerous people—the Gibeonites—renounced their heathenism and united with Israel, sharing in the blessings of the covenant.

No distinction on account of nationality, race, or caste, is recognized by God. He is the Maker of all mankind. All men are of one family by creation, and all are one through redemption. Christ came to demolish every wall of partition, to throw open every compartment of the temple courts, that every soul may have free access to God. His love is so broad, so deep, so full, that it penetrates everywhere. It lifts out of Satan's influence those who have been deluded by his deceptions, and places them within reach of the throne of God, the throne encircled by the rainbow of promise. In Christ there is neither Jew nor Greek, bond nor free.

In the years that followed the occupation of the Promised Land, the beneficent designs of Jehovah for the salvation of the heathen were almost wholly lost sight of, and it became necessary for Him to set forth His plan anew. "All the ends of the world," the psalmist was inspired to sing, "shall remember and turn unto the Lord: and all the kindreds of the nations shall worship before Thee." "Princes shall come out of Egypt; Ethiopia shall soon stretch out her hands unto God." "The heathen shall fear the name of the Lord, and all the kings of the earth Thy glory." "This shall be written for the generation to come: and the people which shall be created shall praise the Lord. For He hath looked down from the height of His sanctuary; from heaven did the Lord behold the earth; to hear the groaning of the prisoner; to loose those that are appointed to death; to declare the name of the Lord in Zion, and His praise in Jerusalem; when the people are gathered together, and the kingdoms, to serve the Lord." Psalms 22:27; 68:31; 102:15, 18-22.

Had Israel been true to her trust, all the nations of earth would have shared in her blessings. But the hearts of those to whom had been entrusted a knowledge of saving truth, were untouched by the needs of those around them. As God's purpose was lost sight of, the heathen came to be looked upon as beyond the pale of His mercy. The light of truth was withheld, and darkness prevailed. The nations were over-spread with a veil of ignorance; the love of God was little known; error and superstition flourished.

Such was the prospect that greeted Isaiah when he was called to the prophetic mission; yet he was not discouraged, for ringing in his ears was the triumphal chorus of the angels surrounding the throne of God, "The whole earth is full of His glory." Isaiah 6:3. And his faith was strengthened by visions of glorious conquests by the church of God, when "the earth shall be full of the knowledge of the Lord, as the waters cover the sea." Isaiah 11:9. "The face of the covering cast over all people, and the veil that is spread over all na-tions," was finally to be destroyed. Isaiah 25:7. The Spirit of God was to be poured out upon all flesh. Those who hunger and thirst after righteousness were to be numbered among the Israel of God. "They shall spring up as among the grass, as willows by the watercourses," said the prophet. "One shall say, I am the Lord's; and another shall call himself by the name of Jacob; and another shall subscribe with his hand unto the Lord, and surname himself by the name of Israel." Isaiah 44:4, 5.

To the prophet was given a revelation of the beneficent design of God in scattering impenitent Judah among the nations of earth. "My people shall know My name," the Lord declared; "they shall know in that day that I am He that doth speak." Isaiah 52:6. And not only were they themselves to learn the lesson of obedience and trust; in their places of exile they were also to impart to others a knowledge of the living God. Many from among the sons of the strangers were to learn to love Him as their Creator and their Redeemer; they were to begin the observance of His holy Sabbath day as a memorial of His creative power; and when He should make "bare His holy arm in the eyes of all the nations," to deliver His people from captivity, "all the ends of the earth" should see of the salvation of God. Verse 10. Many of these converts from heathenism would wish to unite themselves fully with the Israelites and accompany them on the return journey to Judea. None of these were to say, "The Lord hath utterly separated me from His people" (Isaiah 56:3), for the word of God through His prophet to those who should yield themselves to Him and observe His law was that they should thenceforth be numbered among spiritual Israel—His church on earth.

"The sons of the stranger, that join themselves to the Lord, to serve Him, and to love the name of the Lord, to be His servants, everyone that keepeth the Sabbath from polluting it, and taketh hold of My covenant; even them will I bring to My holy mountain, and make them joyful in My house of prayer: their burnt offerings and their sacrifices shall be accepted upon Mine altar; for Mine house shall be called an house of prayer for all people. The Lord God which gathereth the outcasts of Israel saith, Yet will I gather others to Him, beside those that are gathered unto Him." Verses 6-8.

The prophet was permitted to look down the centuries to the time of the advent of the promised Messiah. At first he beheld only "trouble and darkness, dimness of anguish." Isaiah 8:22. Many who were longing for the light of truth were being led astray by false teachers into the bewildering mazes of philosophy and spiritism; others were placing their trust in a form of godliness, but were not bringing true holiness into the life practice. The outlook seemed hopeless; but soon the scene changed, and before the eyes of the prophet was spread a wondrous vision. He saw the Sun of Righteousness arise with healing in His wings; and, lost in admiration, he exclaimed: "The dimness shall not be such as was in her vexation, when at the first He lightly afflicted the land of Zebulun and the land of Naphtali, and afterward did more grievously afflict her by the way of the sea, beyond Jordan, in Galilee of the nations. The people that walked in darkness have seen a great light: they that dwell in the land of the shadow of death, upon them hath the light shined." Isaiah 9:1, 2.

This glorious Light of the world was to bring salvation to every nation, kindred, tongue, and people. Of the work before Him, the prophet heard the eternal Father declare: "It is a light thing that Thou shouldest be My servant to raise up the tribes of Jacob, and to restore the preserved of Israel: I will also give Thee for a light to the Gentiles, that Thou mayest be My salvation unto the end of the earth." "In an acceptable time have I heard Thee, and in a day of salvation have I helped Thee: and I will preserve Thee, and give Thee for a covenant of the people, to establish the earth, to cause to inherit the desolate heritages; that Thou mayest say to the prisoners, Go forth; to them that are in darkness, Show yourselves." "Behold, these shall come from far: and, lo, these from the north and from the west; and these from the land of Sinim." Isaiah 49:6, 8, 9, 12.

Looking on still farther through the ages, the prophet beheld the literal fulfillment of these glorious promises. He saw the bearers of the glad tidings of salvation going to the ends of the earth, to every kindred and people. He heard the Lord saying of the gospel church, "Behold, I will extend peace to her like a river, and the glory of the Gentiles like a flowing stream;" and he heard the commission, "Enlarge the place of thy tent, and let them stretch forth the curtains of thine habitations: spare not, lengthen thy cords, and strengthen thy stakes; for thou shalt break forth on the right hand and on the left; and thy seed shall inherit the Gentiles." Isaiah 66:12; 54:2, 3.

Jehovah declared to the prophet that He would send His witnesses "unto the nations, to Tarshish, Pul, and Lud, . . . to Tubal, and Javan, to the isles afar off." Isaiah 66:19.

> "How beautiful upon the mountains
> Are the feet of him that bringeth good tidings,
> That publisheth peace;
> That bringeth good tidings of good,
> That publisheth salvation;
> That saith unto Zion, Thy God reigneth!"
> Isaiah 52:7.

The prophet heard the voice of God calling His church to her appointed work, that the way might be prepared for the ushering in of His everlasting kingdom. The message was unmistakably plain:

> "Arise, shine; for thy light is come,
> And the glory of the Lord is risen upon thee.

> "For, behold, the darkness shall cover the earth,
> And gross darkness the people:
> But the Lord shall arise upon thee,
> And His glory shall be seen upon thee.
> And the Gentiles shall come to thy light,
> And kings to the brightness of thy rising.

"Lift up thine eyes round about, and see:
All they gather themselves together, they come to thee:
Thy sons shall come from far,
And thy daughters shall be nursed at thy side."

"And the sons of strangers shall build up thy walls,
And their kings shall minister unto thee:
For in My wrath I smote thee,
But in My favor have I had mercy on thee.
Therefore thy gates shall be open continually;
They shall not be shut day nor night;
That men may bring unto thee the forces of the Gentiles,
And that their kings may be brought."

"Look unto Me, and be ye saved, all the ends of the earth:
For I am God, and there is none else."
                    Isaiah 60:1-4, 10, 11; 45:22.

These prophecies of a great spiritual awakening in a time of gross darkness are today meeting fulfillment in the advancing lines of mission stations that are reaching out into the benighted regions of earth. The groups of missionaries in heathen lands have been likened by the prophet to ensigns set up for the guidance of those who are looking for the light of truth.

"In that day," says Isaiah, "there shall be a root of Jesse, which shall stand for an ensign of the people; to it shall the Gentiles seek: and his rest shall be glorious. And it shall come to pass in that day, that the Lord shall set His hand again the second time to recover the remnant of His people. . . . And He shall set up an ensign for the nations, and shall assemble the outcasts of Israel, and gather together the dispersed of Judah from the four corners of the earth." Isaiah 11:10-12.

The day of deliverance is at hand. "The eyes of the Lord run to and fro throughout the whole earth, to show Himself strong in the behalf of them whose heart is perfect toward Him." 2 Chronicles 16:9. Among all nations, kindreds, and tongues, He sees men and women who are praying for light and knowledge. Their souls are unsatisfied; long have they fed on ashes. See Isaiah 44:20. The enemy of all righteousness has turned them aside, and they grope as blind men. But they are honest in heart and desire to learn a better way. Although in the depths of heathenism, with no knowledge of the written law of God nor of His Son Jesus, they have revealed in manifold ways the working of a divine power on mind and character.

At times those who have no knowledge of God aside from that which they have received under the operations of divine grace have been kind to His servants, protecting them at the risk of their own lives. The Holy Spirit is implanting the grace of Christ in the heart of many a noble seeker after truth, quickening his sympathies contrary to his nature, contrary to his former education. The "Light, which lighteth every man that cometh into the world" (John 1:9), is shining in his soul; and this Light, if heeded, will guide his feet to the kingdom of God. The prophet Micah said: "When I sit in darkness, the Lord shall be a light unto me. . . . He will bring me forth to the light, and I shall behold His righteousness." Micah 7:8, 9.

Heaven's plan of salvation is broad enough to embrace the whole world. God longs to breathe into prostrate humanity the breath of life. And He will not permit any soul to be disappointed who is sincere in his longing for something higher and nobler than anything the world can offer. Constantly He is sending His angels to those who, while surrounded by circumstances the most discouraging, pray in faith for some power higher than themselves to take possession of them and bring deliverance and peace. In various ways God will reveal Himself to them and will place them in touch with providences that will establish their confidence in the One who has given Himself a ransom for all, "that they might set their hope in God, and not forget the works of God, but keep His commandments." Psalm 78:7.

"Shall the prey be taken from the mighty, or the lawful captive delivered?" "Thus saith the Lord, Even the captives of the mighty shall be taken away, and the prey of the terrible shall be delivered." Isaiah 49:24, 25. "They shall be greatly ashamed, that trust in graven images, that say to the molten images, Ye are our gods." Isaiah 42:17.

"Happy is he that hath the God of Jacob for his help, whose hope is in the Lord his God!" Psalm 146:5. "Turn you to the stronghold, ye prisoners of hope!" Zechariah 9:12. Unto all the honest in heart in heathen lands—"the upright" in the sight of Heaven—"there ariseth light in the darkness." Psalm 112:4. God hath spoken: "I will bring the blind by a way that they knew not; I will lead them in paths that they have not known: I will make darkness light before them, and crooked things straight. These things will I do unto them, and not forsake them." Isaiah 42:16.

chapter 32

Manasseh and Josiah

THE kingdom of Judah, prosperous throughout the times of Hezekiah, was once more brought low during the long years of Manasseh's wicked reign, when paganism was revived, and many of the people were led into idolatry. "Manasseh made Judah and the inhabitants of Jerusalem to err, and to do worse than the heathen." 2 Chronicles 33:9. The glorious light of former generations was followed by the darkness of superstition and error. Gross evils sprang up and flourished—tyranny, oppression, hatred of all that is good. Justice was perverted; violence prevailed.

Yet those evil times were not without witnesses for God and the right. The trying experiences through which Judah had safely passed during Hezekiah's reign had developed, in the hearts of many, a sturdiness of character that now served as a bulwark against the prevailing iniquity. Their

During the long and wicked reign of King Manasseh tyranny and oppression almost silenced the witness of the true God.

[*381*] 371

testimony in behalf of truth and righteousness aroused the anger of Manasseh and his associates in authority, who endeavored to establish themselves in evil-doing by silencing every voice of disapproval. "Manasseh shed innocent blood very much, till he had filled Jerusalem from one end to another." 2 Kings 21:16.

One of the first to fall was Isaiah, who for over half a century had stood before Judah as the appointed messenger of Jehovah. "Others had trial of cruel mockings and scourgings, yea, moreover of bonds and imprisonment: they were stoned, they were sawn asunder, were tempted, were slain with the sword: they wandered about in sheepskins and goatskins; being destitute, afflicted, tormented; (of whom the world was not worthy:) they wandered in deserts, and in mountains, and in dens and caves of the earth." Hebrews 11:36-38.

Some of those who suffered persecution during Manasseh's reign were commissioned to bear special messages of reproof and of judgment. The king of Judah, the prophets declared, "hath done wickedly above all . . . which were before him." Because of this wickedness, his kingdom was nearing a crisis; soon the inhabitants of the land were to be carried captive to Babyon, there to become "a prey and a spoil to all their enemies." 2 Kings 21:11, 14. But the Lord would not utterly forsake those who in a strange land should acknowledge Him as their Ruler; they might suffer great tribulation, yet He would bring deliverance to them in His appointed time and way. Those who should put their trust wholly in Him would find a sure refuge.

Faithfully the prophets continued their warnings and their

exhortations; fearlessly they spoke to Manasseh and to his people; but the messages were scorned; backsliding Judah would not heed. As an earnest of what would befall the people should they continue impenitent, the Lord permitted their king to be captured by a band of Assyrian soldiers, who "bound him with fetters, and carried him to Babylon," their temporary capital. This affliction brought the king to his senses; "he besought the Lord his God, and humbled himself greatly before the God of his fathers, and prayed unto Him: and He was entreated of him, and heard his supplication, and brought him again to Jerusalem into his kingdom. Then Manasseh knew that the Lord He was God." 2 Chronicles 33:11-13. But this repentance, remarkable though it was, came too late to save the kingdom from the corrupting influence of years of idolatrous practices. Many had stumbled and fallen, never again to rise.

Among those whose life experience had been shaped beyond recall by the fatal apostasy of Manasseh, was his own son, who came to the throne at the age of twenty-two. Of King Amon it is written: "He walked in all the way that his father walked in, and served the idols that his father served, and worshiped them: and he forsook the Lord God of his fathers" (2 Kings 21:21, 22); he "humbled not himself before the Lord, as Manasseh his father had humbled himself; but Amon trespassed more and more." The wicked king was not permitted to reign long. In the midst of his daring impiety, only two years from the time he ascended the throne, he was slain in the palace by his own servants; and "the people of the land made Josiah his son king in his stead." 2 Chronicles 33:23, 25.

With the accession of Josiah to the throne, where he was

to rule for thirty-one years, those who had maintained the purity of their faith began to hope that the downward course of the kingdom was checked; for the new king, though only eight years old, feared God, and from the very beginning "he did that which was right in the sight of the Lord, and walked in all the way of David his father, and turned not aside to the right hand or to the left." 2 Kings 22:2. Born of a wicked king, beset with temptations to follow in his father's steps, and with few counselors to encourage him in the right way, Josiah nevertheless was true to the God of Israel. Warned by the errors of past generations, he chose to do right, instead of descending to the low level of sin and degradation to which his father and his grandfather had fallen. He "turned not aside to the right hand or to the left." As one who was to occupy a position of trust, he resolved to obey the instruction that had been given for the guidance of Israel's rulers, and his obedience made it possible for God to use him as a vessel unto honor.

At the time Josiah began to rule, and for many years before, the truehearted in Judah were questioning whether God's promises to ancient Israel could ever be fulfilled. From a human point of view the divine purpose for the chosen nation seemed almost impossible of accomplishment. The apostasy of former centuries had gathered strength with the passing years; ten of the tribes had been scattered among the heathen; only the tribes of Judah and Benjamin remained, and even these now seemed on the verge of moral and national ruin. The prophets had begun to foretell the utter destruction of their fair city, where stood the temple built by Solomon, and where all their earthly hopes of national greatness had centered. Could it be that God was about to turn aside from His avowed purpose of bringing deliverance to those who should put their trust in Him? In the face of the long-continued persecution of the righteous, and of the apparent prosperity of the wicked, could those who had remained true to God hope for better days?

These anxious questionings were voiced by the prophet Habakkuk. Viewing the situation of the faithful in his day, he expressed the burden of his heart in the inquiry: "O Lord, how long shall I cry, and Thou wilt not hear! even cry out unto Thee of violence, and Thou wilt not save! Why dost Thou show me iniquity, and cause me to behold grievance? for spoiling and violence are before me: and there are that raise up strife and contention. Therefore the law is slacked, and judgment doth never go forth: for the wicked doth compass about the righteous; therefore wrong judgment proceedeth." Habakkuk 1:2-4.

God answered the cry of His loyal children. Through His chosen mouthpiece He revealed His determination to bring chastisement upon the nation that had turned from Him to serve the gods of the heathen. Within the lifetime of some who were even then making inquiry regarding the future, He would miraculously shape the affairs of the ruling nations of earth and bring the Babylonians into the ascendancy. These Chaldeans, "terrible and dreadful," were to fall suddenly upon the land of Judah as a divinely appointed scourge. Verse 7. The princes of Judah and the fairest of the people were to be carried captive to Babylon; the Judean cities and villages and the cultivated fields were to be laid waste; nothing was to be spared.

Confident that even in this terrible judgment the purpose of God for His people would in some way be fulfilled, Habakkuk bowed in submission to the revealed will of Jehovah. "Art Thou not from everlasting, O Lord my God, mine Holy One?" he exclaimed. And then, his faith reaching out beyond the forbidding prospect of the immediate future, and laying fast hold on the precious promises that reveal God's love for His trusting children, the prophet added, "We shall not die." Verse 12. With this declaration of faith he rested his case, and that of every believing Israelite, in the hands of a compassionate God.

This was not Habakkuk's only experience in the exercise of strong faith. On one occasion, when meditating concerning the future, he said, "I will stand upon my watch, and set me upon the tower, and will watch to see what He will say unto me." Graciously the Lord answered him: "Write the vision, and make it plain upon tables, that he may run that readeth it. For the vision is yet for an appointed time, but at the end it shall speak, and not lie: though it tarry, wait for it; because it will surely come, it will not tarry. Behold, his soul which is lifted up is not upright in him: but *the just shall live by his faith.*" Habakkuk 2:1-4.

The faith that strengthened Habakkuk and all the holy and the just in those days of deep trial was the same faith that sustains God's people today. In the darkest hours, under circumstances the most forbidding, the Christian believer may keep his soul stayed upon the source of all light and power. Day by day, through faith in God, his hope and courage may be renewed. "The just shall live by his faith." In the service of God there need be no despondency, no wavering, no fear.

The Lord will more than fulfill the highest expectations of those who put their trust in Him. He will give them the wisdom their varied necessities demand.

Of the abundant provision made for every tempted soul, the apostle Paul bears eloquent testimony. To him was given the divine assurance, "My grace is sufficient for thee: for My strength is made perfect in weakness." In gratitude and confidence the tried servant of God responded: "Most gladly therefore will I rather glory in my infirmities, that the power of Christ may rest upon me. Therefore I take pleasure in infirmities, in reproaches, in necessities, in persecutions, in distresses for Christ's sake: for when I am weak, then am I strong." 2 Corinthians 12:9, 10.

We must cherish and cultivate the faith of which prophets and apostles have testified—the faith that lays hold on the promises of God and waits for deliverance in His appointed time and way. The sure word of prophecy will meet its final fulfillment in the glorious advent of our Lord and Saviour Jesus Christ, as King of kings and Lord of lords. The time of waiting may seem long, the soul may be oppressed by discouraging circumstances, many in whom confidence has been placed may fall by the way; but with the prophet who endeavored to encourage Judah in a time of unparalleled apostasy, let us confidently declare, "The Lord is in His holy temple: let all the earth keep silence before Him." Habakkuk 2:20. Let us ever hold in remembrance the cheering message, "The vision is yet for an appointed time, but at the end it shall speak, and not lie: though it tarry, wait for it; because it will surely come, it will not tarry. . . . The just shall live by his faith." Verses 3, 4.

"O Lord, revive Thy work in the midst of the years,
In the midst of the years make known;
In wrath remember mercy.

"God came from Teman,
And the Holy One from Mount Paran.
His glory covered the heavens,
And the earth was full of His praise.
And His brightness was as the light;
He had bright beams out of His side:
And there was the hiding of His power.
Before Him went the pestilence,
And burning coals went forth at His feet.
He stood, and measured the earth:
He beheld, and drove asunder the nations;
And the everlasting mountains were scattered,
The perpetual hills did bow:
His ways are everlasting."

"Thou wentest forth for the salvation of Thy people,
Even for salvation with Thine anointed."

"Although the fig tree shall not blossom,
Neither shall fruit be in the vines;
The labor of the olive shall fail,
And the fields shall yield no meat;
The flock shall be cut off from the fold,
And there shall be no herd in the stalls:
Yet I will rejoice in the Lord,
I will joy in the God of my salvation.
The Lord God is my strength."
Habakkuk 3:2-6, 13, 17-19, margin.

Habakkuk was not the only one through whom was given a message of bright hope and of future triumph as well as of present judgment. During the reign of Josiah the word of the Lord came to Zephaniah, specifying plainly the results of continued apostasy, and calling the attention of the true church to the glorious prospect beyond. His prophecies of impending judgment upon Judah apply with equal force to the judgments that are to fall upon an impenitent world at the time of the second advent of Christ:

"The great day of the Lord is near,
It is near, and hasteth greatly,
Even the voice of the day of the Lord:
The mighty man shall cry there bitterly.

"That day is a day of wrath,
A day of trouble and distress,
A day of wasteness and desolation,
A day of darkness and gloominess,

"A day of clouds and thick darkness,
A day of the trumpet and alarm
Against the fenced cities,
And against the high towers."
Zephaniah 1:14-16.

"I will bring distress upon men, that they shall walk like blind men, because they have sinned against the Lord: and their blood shall be poured out as dust. . . . Neither their silver nor their gold shall be able to deliver them in the day of the Lord's wrath; but the whole land shall be devoured by the fire of His jealousy: for He shall make even a speedy riddance of all them that dwell in the land." Verses 17, 18.

"Gather yourselves together, yea, gather together,
O nation not desired;
Before the decree bring forth,
Before the day pass as the chaff,
Before the fierce anger of the Lord come upon you,
Before the day of the Lord's anger come upon you.

"Seek ye the Lord, all ye meek of the earth,
Which have wrought His judgment;
   Seek righteousness,

Seek meekness:
It may be ye shall be hid
In the day of the Lord's anger."
              Zephaniah 2:1-3.

"Behold, at that time I will deal with all them that afflict thee: and I will save her that halteth, and gather her that was driven away; and I will make them a praise and a name, whose shame hath been in all the earth. At that time will I bring you in, and at that time will I gather you: for I will make you a name and a praise among all the peoples of the earth, when I bring again your captivity before your eyes, saith the Lord." Zephaniah 3:19, 20, R.V.

"Sing, O daughter of Zion; shout, O Israel;
Be glad and rejoice with all the heart,
   O daughter of Jerusalem.
The Lord hath taken away thy judgments,
He hath cast out thine enemy:
The King of Israel, even the Lord,
   Is in the midst of thee:
Thou shalt not see evil any more.

"In that day it shall be said to Jerusalem, Fear thou not:
And to Zion, Let not thine hands be slack.
   The Lord thy God in the midst of thee
Is mighty; He will save,
He will rejoice over thee with joy;
   He will rest in His love,
He will joy over thee with singing."
             Verses 14-17.

Zephaniah denounced the apostasy of the age and called for repentance, warning that "the great day of the Lord is near."